Study Guide

for

Andersen and Taylor's

Sociology

The Essentials

Second Edition

Margie L. Kiter
University of Delaware

THOMSON
™
WADSWORTH

Australia • Canada • Mexico • Singapore • Spain • United Kingdom • United States

ISBN 0-534-58827-1

For more information about our products, contact us at:
Thomson Learning Academic Resource Center
1-800-423-0563

For permission to use material from this text, contact us by:
Phone: 1-800-730-2214
Fax: 1-800-731-2215
Web: www.thomsonrights.com

Asia
Thomson Learning
5 Shenton Way, #01-01
UIC Building
Singapore 06880

Australia
Nelson Thomson Learning
102 Dodds Street
South Street
South Melbourne, Victoria 3205
Australia

Canada
Nelson Thomson Learning
1120 Birchmount Road
Toronto, Ontario M1K 5G4
Canada

Europe/Middle East/South Africa
Thomson Learning
High Holborn House
50/51 Bedford Row
London WC1R 4LR
United Kingdom

Latin America
Thomson Learning
Seneca, 53
Colonia Polanco
11560 Mexico D.F.
Mexico

Spain
Paraninfo Thomson Learning
Calle/Magallanes, 25
28015 Madrid, Spain

PREFACE

This study guide accompanies the second edition of *Sociology: The Essentials* by Margaret Andersen and Howard Taylor. Used as a supplement to the textbook, this guide can assist students in learning course material by highlighting core concepts, key people, principal theories, and relevant research on a variety of interesting topics in sociology.

Each chapter in the study guide begins with a summary statement and a set of questions to guide your reading. These questions direct your attention to some of the most important issues covered in the corresponding chapter of the textbook. For each chapter, you should be able to: define and give an example of the key terms presented; identify the main contributions of key people, where listed; and apply each theoretical perspective to the topics discussed in the textbook. You can evaluate your comprehension of the material by completing the practice tests located at the end of each chapter in the study guide. Each practice test includes multiple choice, true-false, fill in the blank, and essay questions, followed by page number references and a detailed answer key. To examine specific issues further, go to the recommended web sites and consider the questions posed.

Enjoy the journey.

TABLE OF CONTENTS

Page

CHAPTER 1
SOCIOLOGICAL PERSPECTIVES AND SOCIOLOGICAL RESEARCH

BRIEF CHAPTER OUTLINE

What is Sociology?
    The Sociological Perspective
    Debunking in Sociology
    Discovering Unsettling Facts
The Significance of Diversity
    Defining Diversity
    Society in Global Perspective
The Development of Sociological Theory
    The Influence of the Enlightenment
    Classical Sociological Theory
    The Development of Sociology in America
    Theoretical Frameworks in Sociology: Functionalism, Conflict Theory, and Symbolic Interaction
Doing Sociological Research
    Sociology and the Scientific Method
    The Research Process
The Tools of Sociological Research
    The Survey: Polls, Questionnaires, and Interviews
    Participant Observation
    Controlled Experiments
    Content Analysis
    Historical Research
    Evaluation Research
Prediction and Sampling
Research and Ethics: Is Sociology Value-Free?

CHAPTER FOCUS: This chapter provides a comprehensive overview of sociology – its historical development, utility as both an academic discipline and a personal way of understanding the world, and methodological approach to conducting research.

QUESTIONS TO GUIDE YOUR READING
1.   What is the primary difference between sociology and other social sciences as frameworks for understanding human behavior?
2.   What are the three major theoretical perspectives in sociology, and what core assumptions do theorists associated with each perspective make about society?
3.   How does the American tradition of sociology differ from classical European sociology?
4.   Why is sociology considered an empirical discipline?
5.   What is a research design, and what components must be included in it to make it useful for conducting research?
6.   What are the main advantages and disadvantages of each research method discussed in the text?
7.   What are the most common types of statistical mistakes made by researchers?
8.   What are some common ethical dilemmas that sociologists might encounter when doing research?

SOCIOLOGY IN ACTION: AN INTERNET EXERCISE

Go to www.norc.uchicago.edu to learn more about the National Opinion Research Center, an organization devoted to collecting and analyzing data on the attitudes and behaviors of the American public. What issues does NORC investigate? Which research method does the center use to gather data? How are the results of this research used?

KEY TERMS (defined at page number shown and in glossary)

anthropology 3	applied sociology 16
conflict theory 19	content analysis 28
controlled experiment 27	data 21
data analysis 25	debunking 9
dependent variable 25	diversity
economics 3	empirical 5
Enlightenment 17	evaluation research 30
functionalism 18	generalization 26
hypothesis 24	independent variable 25
issues 7	organic metaphor 16
participant observation 27	political science 3
population 30	positivism 13
postmodernism 20	probability 30
psychology 3	qualitative research 24
quantitative research 24	random sample 30
reliability 25	replication study 24
sample 30	scientific method 22
social action 16	social change 9
Social Darwinism 16	social facts 15
social institution 9	social interaction 9
social sciences 3	social speedup 5
social structure 5	social work 3
sociological imagination 5	sociological perspective 3
sociology 2	symbolic interaction theory 20
troubles 5	validity 25
variable 25	verstehen 16

KEY PEOPLE (identified at page number shown)

Jane Addams 16	Peter Berger 6
Charles Horton Cooley 17	Auguste Comte 13
Charles Darwin 16	Alexis de Tocqueville 13
W.E.B. Du Bois 18	Emile Durkheim 14
Michael Foucalt 20	Harriet Martineau 14
Karl Marx 15	George Herbert Mead 17
Robert Merton 19	C. Wright Mills 13
Robert Park 16	Talcott Parsons 19
W.I. Thomas 16	Lester Frank Ward 16
Max Weber 15	Florian Znaniecki 16

CHAPTER OUTLINE

I.   WHAT IS SOCIOLOGY?

Sociology is the scientific study of human behavior and the social context in which it occurs. Academic disciplines concerned with social behavior make up the **social sciences**. For sociologists, the unit of analysis is groups or whole societies, whereas **psychology** analyzes individual behavior. **Anthropology** is the study of human culture as the basis for society. **Political science** is the study of politics and the organization of government. **Economics** is the study of the production, distribution, and consumption of goods and services. Sociologists view culture and specific social institutions as interrelated parts of a complex set of systems that comprise society. **Social work** is an applied field that draws on the lessons of all the social sciences to serve people in need.

A.   The Sociological Perspective

     The **sociological perspective** allows you to see the societal patterns that influence individual and group life.

     1.   C. Wright Mills (1916-1962) explored the concept of the **sociological imagination**, the ability to identify the societal patterns that influence individual and group life. He emphasized the importance of understanding the social and historical context in which people live.

          a.   **Social speedup**, which results from managing the multiple demands of work and family in today's economy, increases stress. People respond with individual solutions, such as exercising or using alcohol to relieve the stress, but the basic problem lies in the structure of the society.

          b.   Mills distinguished between **troubles** – privately felt problems that develop from events or emotions in an individual's life, and **issues** – problems that affect large numbers of people and are based in the history and institutional arrangements of society. This distinction is the crux of the difference between individual experience and **social structure**.

     2.   Sociology is an **empirical** discipline where rigorous methods of research are used to investigate everyday life, and conclusions must be based on careful, systematic observations, rather than personal opinion.

B.   Debunking in Sociology

     1.   Peter Berger used the term **debunking** to refer to sociology's "unmasking tendency," or its role in looking beyond the facades of everyday life. For example, sociology helps reveal situations in schools whereby the opportunities of some children are stifled, in contrast to the common belief that all children are given the opportunity to learn and succeed.

     2.   Debunking is sometimes easier to do when examining cultures other than one's own because one's thinking is less restricted by the common assumptions within the culture. For example, Westerners may view the traditional Chinese custom of footbinding as bizarre, but the practice of enhancing women's breasts by implanting silicone may seem normal.

     3.   Elaine Bell Kaplan's investigation of the social structural context of Black teen mothers' lives reveals that stereotypes about this group are inaccurate but persistent.

C.   Discovering Unsettling Facts

     Sociological research provides evidence that persistent problems, such as the high rate of infant mortality in the United States, are embedded in society, not just individual behavior. Sociology often reveals troubling facts about society; for example, the United States has the highest rate of imprisonment in the world.

D.   Key Sociological Concepts

     1.   **Social structure** is the organized pattern of social relationships and social institutions that together constitute society. Social forces guide human behavior.

     2.   **Social institutions** are established, organized systems of social behavior with particular, recognized purposes. Institutions include the family and religion.

     3.   Sociologists do not view society as fixed or immutable; thus, they are interested in the process of **social change**, or the alteration of society over time.

4. **Social interaction**, which is behavior between two or more people, is given meaning by the participants, illustrating that people are active agents in society.

II. THE SIGNIFICANCE OF DIVERSITY

A. Defining Diversity

Diversity is a broad concept that refers to the variety of group experiences that result from the social structure of society. Although race, class, and gender are critical components of diversity in the United States, factors such as age, nationality, sexual orientation, and region also influence people's identities, experiences, and opportunities.

B. Society in Global Perspective

Nations are increasingly connected to each other in complex ways, making it necessary to use a global perspective to understand topics such as employment and immigration. For example, a Latina woman may leave her child in her homeland to go to the United States to work as a domestic for an American woman who is pursuing her career.

III. THE DEVELOPMENT OF SOCIOLOGICAL THEORY

Sociology first emerged in the eighteenth and nineteenth centuries, when rapid political and economic changes were occurring in Western Europe.

A. The Influence of the Enlightenment

1. The **Enlightenment**, known as the Age of Reason, strongly influenced the development of sociology. The Enlightenment's faith in the ability of human reason to solve society's problems by identifying natural social laws and processes was strongly linked to the development of modern science.

2. Auguste Comte (1798-1857), who first used the term *sociology*, believed that the discipline was the most evolved of all sciences because it studied the complex and changing systems of society

3. **Positivism**, a system of thought in which accurate observation and description is considered the highest form of knowledge, also emerged at this time.

4. Alexis de Tocqueville (1805-1859), author of *Democracy in America*, explored democratic and egalitarian values in the United States, which he argued influenced social institutions and personal relationships. He believed that individualism made people self-centered and anxious about their position.

5. Harriet Martineau (1802-1876) was a British feminist and abolitionist who analyzed social customs in the United States in her book. She wrote the first sociological research methods book, *How to Observe Manners and Morals*, which examined the technique of participant observation.

B. Classical Sociological Theory

1. Emile Durkheim (1858-1917) explored *social solidarity*, or the bonds that link members of a group. For example, he believed that religious rituals reinforce the sense of belonging of group members, and members express social solidarity by condemning deviant behavior.

   a. Durkheim discussed society *sui generis*, referring to his belief that society is a subject that should be studied separately from the total of individuals who comprise it.

   b. Durkheim's work was the basis for *functionalism*, one of the major theories of sociology. He viewed society as an integrated whole, with each part contributing to the stability of the system.

   c. Durkheim noted that **social facts**, or the social patterns that are *external* to individuals (such as values) were the proper subject of sociology.

2. Karl Marx (1818-1883) investigated the effects of capitalism on individuals and societies, arguing that all other social institutions (family, law, education) are shaped by economic forces.

a. Capitalism is an economic system based on profit and private property, where the capitalist class owns the means of production.

b. Capitalists gain profit through the exploitation of the proletariat, or working class, who sell their labor in exchange for wages.

c. It is an error to dismiss Marx's work on the basis of the political orientation of some of his followers. He produced an important body of work that identified class as a fundamental dimension of society.

3. Max Weber (1864-1920) developed a multidimensional analysis of society that recognized the interplay between three basic institutions -- political, economic, and cultural.

   a. Weber theorized that there could not be a value-free sociology. Rather, he thought sociologists should acknowledge the influence of their values and beliefs so they would not interfere with their objectivity.

   b. Weber advocated that sociologists use the concept of **verstehen** in their work. This would facilitate a more subjective understanding of social behavior from the point of view of those engaged in it.

   c. Weber defined **social action** as behavior to which people give meaning. It is the responsibility of sociologists to identify those meanings and the context in which behavior occurs.

C. Sociology in America

Although sociology in the United States developed from the foundations of the discipline begun in Europe, American sociology had some unique characteristics. Pragmatism, or a belief in practicality, led sociologists to value social planning. There was an emphasis on identifying the causes of social problems and developing strategies to improve them.

1. Early sociologists viewed society as an organism, a system of interrelated parts that work together. This is referred to as the **organic metaphor.**

2. **Social Darwinism** adapted Charles Darwin's theory of biological evolution to analyze social change, asserting that societies evolve along a natural course; thus, this group supported a *laissez-faire* (hands-off) approach to society.

3. Lester Frank Ward (1831-1914) advocated *social telesis*, or human intervention in the evolution of society for the improvement of society. Ward and other activist sociologists of this period believed that sociology could address the social problems that developed from industrialization and urbanization.

4. **Applied sociology**, or the use of sociological research and theory in solving human problems, is based on the work of early activists who identified urbanization and industrialization as the cause of many social problems.

5. Two key aspects of the *Chicago School* of sociology were an interest in how society shaped the mind and identity of individuals, and the use of social settings as human laboratories for research.

   a. Charles Horton Cooley (1864-1929) believed that an individual's identity is based on his/her understanding of how others perceive them.

   b. George Herbert Mead (1863-1931) extended Cooley's idea by investigating how individuals develop through the relationships they establish with others.

   c. Sociologists W. I. Thomas (1863-1947) and Florian Znaniecki (1882-1958) used Polish immigrants' personal documents to examine their social relationships and feelings about their new lives. Thomas also identified the principle known as the *definition of the situation*: "If men define situations as real, they are real in their consequences." This concept indicates that social influences are so great that people behave according to what they think is true, even with evidence to the contrary.

d. Robert Park (1864-1944) investigated interaction between people of different races as well as the sociological design of cities. He developed the concentric circle model of urbanization.

e. Although sexism prevented most female sociologists from securing academic positions, many women, including Jane Addams (1860-1935), entered the applied field of social work. Addams won the Nobel Peace Prize in 1931 for her work in the settlement house movement.

3. African American sociologists have a long tradition of investigating Black communities, despite their historical exclusion from White universities. W.E.B. Du Bois (1868-1963) was the first Black person to receive a doctorate from Harvard in any field. Du Bois viewed sociology as a scientific, community-based, activist profession committed to social justice. DuBois co-wrote *The Philadelphia Negro*, one of the first empirical community studies published.

D. Theoretical Frameworks in Sociology: Functionalism, Conflict Theory, and Symbolic Interaction

Sociologists use theories to organize observations, produce logically related statements about observed behavior, and relate their observations to other data. Sociological theories use one of two basic approaches. *Macrosociological* theories, such as those developed by Durkheim, Marx, and Weber, seek to understand society as a whole. *Microsociological* theories, including those developed in the Chicago School, focus on face-to-face interaction. The three major sociological perspectives are functionalism, conflict theory, and symbolic interaction [Table 1.1].

1. **Functionalism** investigates how each part of society contributes to the stability of the whole system. Functionalist theorists emphasize order in society, noting that *disorganization* in the system leads to change. Because all parts of a society are related, a change in one part leads to changes throughout the society.

    1. Talcott Parsons (1902-1979) identified the four principal functions of society as adaptation to the environment, goal attainment, integration of members into harmonious units, and maintenance of basic cultural patterns.

    2. Robert Merton (born 1910) realized that social practices can have unintended consequences that are neither immediately apparent nor necessarily the same as their stated purposes, called **latent functions**. He distinguished these from **manifest functions**, or the stated, intended goals of social behavior.

    3. Critics of functionalism argue that this theory offers a conservative view of society and understates power differences.

2. Conflict theory emphasizes the role of coercion in producing social order, noting that **power** is the ability to influence and control others.

    a. This theory, based on Karl Marx's view of society as fragmented into groups that compete for social and economic resources, asserts that groups with the most resources utilize their power to defend and maintain their advantages in society.

    b. Conflict theorists view inequality as inherently unfair and believe social change is the result of struggles between competing groups

    c. Critics argue that this theory neglects shared values and understates the degree of cohesion and stability in society.

3. **Symbolic interaction theory** views social interaction as the basis of society. It is used to investigate face-to-face interactions as a way of identifying the subjective meanings that people give to objects, events, and behavior.

      a.   People behave based on what they *believe,* not just what is objectively true; thus, society is highly subjective.

      b.   Society is *socially constructed* through human interpretation and constantly modified through social interaction.

      c.   Critics of social interaction theory argue that has a weak analysis of inequality and overstates the objective basis of society.

  E.   Diverse Theoretical Perspectives

Sociological thought is diverse and includes other frameworks in addition to those discussed. **Postmodernism** argues that society is reflected in the words and images, or *discourses,* that people use to represent behavior and ideas. Theorists such as Foucault typically engage in detailed analyses of film, music, literature, and other cultural forms.

IV. DOING SOCIOLOGICAL RESEARCH

Sociologists use a variety of methods to conduct research, each of which involves careful observation and rigorous analysis. The kind of question being asked will determine which technique will be used and which type of **data** will be collected.

  A.   Sociology and the Scientific Method

Sociological research derives from the scientific method, which was originally defined by Sir Francis Bacon. The scientific method involves several steps in a research process: observation, hypothesis testing, data analysis, and generalization.

  B.   The Research Process

    1.   The first step in sociological research is to develop a research question, which typically involves reviewing the existing literature on the subject. Some researchers conduct **replications studies**, which repeat a prior investigation exactly, but on a different group of people in a different time or place.

    2.   A research design is the overall logic and strategy underlying a study. The design is created after the research question is developed because the technique to be used and other details of the design flow from the questions of the study.

      a.   **Quantitative research** uses statistical procedures to analyze numerical data.

      b.   **Qualitative research**, which is somewhat less structured and more interpretive than quantitative research, does not make extensive use of statistical methods, but tends to have greater depth.

      c.   Some research designs involve the testing of a **hypothesis**, which is a prediction or tentative assumption that one plans to investigate. Hypotheses are formulated as "if-then" statements.

      d.   *Exploratory research*, which is more open-ended, does not follow this model of hypothesis testing.

      e.   Sociological research often investigates the influence of one **variable** on another. Variables are conditions or characteristics that can have more than one value, such as income.

          1)   The **independent variable** is the one that the researcher wants to test as the presumed cause of something else.

          2)   The **dependent variable** is the one upon which there is a presumed effect.

      f.   The **validity** of a measurement is the degree to which it accurately measures or reflects a concept. To ensure validity, researchers usually measure more than one indicator for a particular concept.

      g.   A measure is **reliable** if a repeat of the measurement gives the same result. Researchers often rely on measures that have proven sound in past studies to ensure reliability.

3.   After the research design is created, data are collected. Sociologists may gather their own original material, known as *primary data*; or use information that was previously collected and organized by another party (such as the Bureau of the Census), known as *secondary data*.

4.   **Data analysis** is the process by which sociologists organize and examine the data collected to search for patterns. Depending on the question asked and the type of data collected, statistical procedures may or may not be used to analyze the data.

5.   The final stage in the research process involves reaching conclusions and reporting the results. Sociologists attempt to draw conclusions from specific data and apply them to a broader population, a process called **generalization**.

V. THE TOOLS OF SOCIOLOGICAL RESEARCH

A.   The Survey: Polls, Questionnaires, and Interviews

1.   Surveys, which may be conducted by mail, in person, or over the telephone, are among the most commonly used tools of sociological research.

       a.   In a *closed-ended* questionnaire, people choose a reply from the list of possible answers, similar to a multiple choice test.

       b.   In an *open-ended* survey, respondents can provide their own responses, similar to an essay test.

2.   Questionnaires are typically distributed to large numbers of people. The *return rate* refers to the percentage of questionnaires returned out of the total number distributed. A low return rate introduces possible bias in the results.

3.   Surveys can include questions about a wide variety of topics and results can be efficiently analyzed to identify relationships among many different variables. However, respondents may disguise their true opinions if their answers are not considered socially acceptable [Table 1.2].

B.   Participant Observation

1.   When using **participant observation**, the research becomes a member of the group they are studying, acting as both subjective participant and objective observer. This method is also known as *field research.*

2.   Judith Rollins' study of maids and their employers is an example of a participant observation study that reveals how social class, race, and gender shape the experiences of Black domestic workers.

3.   Participant observation is time-consuming and involves extensive note taking that generates a massive quantity of data that must be organized and examined. Because it involves investigating small groups, it may be difficult for the researcher to generalize the results of a participant observation study.

C.   Controlled Experiments

1.   **Controlled experiments** are highly focused ways of collecting data that are especially useful for determining a pattern of cause and effect.

2.   To conduct a controlled experiment, two groups with similar subjects are created: the experimental group, which is exposed to the factor being investigated, and the control group, which is not exposed to the factor in question.

3.   Although experiments can clearly establish causation, they often occur in artificial environments that eliminate some elements of real life, making it difficult to determine how much the laboratory setting affected the results.

D.   Content Analysis

1.   **Content analysis**, a method of investigating society and social behavior by examining cultural artifacts (including magazines, television commercials, novels, movies, and songs), is often used to indirectly determine how social groups are perceived over time.

2. This method has the advantage of being unobtrusive, yet it is limited to topics that are found in forms of mass communication. It only reveals how groups are depicted, not what people think about the images or how the images affect them.

E. Historical Research

Historical research, a type of qualitative research, is commonly used to investigate people's life experiences. This type of research relies on data contained in historical archives, such as government and church records as well as private diaries and letters.

F. Evaluation Research

Evaluation research assesses the effects of policies and programs on people in society. When the research is intended to produce policy recommendations, it is called *policy research*. *Market research* is another form of evaluation research where the sales potential of a product or service is determined by assessing customers' preferences.

VI. PREDICTION, SAMPLING, AND STATISTICAL ANALYSIS

The essence of science is prediction and explanation. Social, behavioral, and attitudinal characteristics can be measured and predicted within a reasonable margin of error. A **probability** is the likelihood that a specific behavior or event will occur. For example, age is a good predictor of the chances of dying. Probability statements reflect general patterns, but cannot predict with certainty that any specific person will adhere to the pattern. A **population** is a relatively large collection of people or other units that a researcher studies and about which generalizations can be made. When it is impossible to include every member of the population in the study, the researcher selects a **sample**, or subset of the population, for the study. Researchers attempt to select samples that are *representative* and large enough to overcome statistical abnormalities to avoid selecting a *biased* sample. The best way to ensure a representative sample is to use a **random sample**, which gives everyone in the population an equal chance of being selected. The statistical tools researchers use to analyze quantitative data, and the common statistical mistakes researchers make, are identified in the "Doing Sociological Research" box in this chapter.

VII. RESEARCH AND ETHICS: IS SOCIOLOGY VALUE-FREE?

Sociologists, who often study controversial topics, do not usually claim to be value-free, but they try to produce objective research. Doing research raises ethical questions, such as the issue of deception in controlled experiments, where the actual purpose of the study is usually concealed. In participant observation studies, where the researcher may conceal his or her identity and not reveal that s/he is doing research, informed consent is not obtained from the people being studied. The professional code of ethics is clear that if a research subject is at risk of physical, mental, or legal harm, the subject must be informed of his or her rights and the researcher's responsibilities.

PRACTICE TEST

Multiple Choice Questions

1. Which of the following is **not** one of the main goals of sociology as a discipline?
   a. increase awareness about the ways that social institutions shape people's lives
   b. highlight the accomplishments of famous individuals to society and history
   c. examine the common assumptions and beliefs underlying public opinion
   d. analyze the influence of social change on people's experiences

2. Mills referred to the ability to identify the societal patterns that influence individual and group life as the:
   a. sociological imagination.
   b. sociological structure.
   c. debunking dynamic.
   d. naturalizing attitude.

3. Which of the following is **not** one of the primary professional activities engaged in by most sociologists?
   a. teaching information about society to students
   b. providing expert testimony on public policy issues
   c. consulting with community groups working toward change
   d. providing therapeutic counseling to individuals under stress

4. Sociology is an empirical discipline, which means that:
   a. conclusions about behavior must be based on careful, systematic observations.
   b. common sense is a reliable source of information for understanding behavior.
   c. research on human behavior must occur in its natural setting.
   d. All of the above statements are true.

5. Elaine Kaplan Bell's study of teenage pregnancy in Black communities indicates that:
   a. most adolescent girls intentionally become pregnant and have a baby to become eligible for welfare benefits that make them economically self-sufficient.
   b. most adolescent girls who have a baby do not feel any stigma or shame about receiving welfare benefits because they believe the government owes them some assistance.
   c. most mothers of adolescent girls who have babies are disappointed by their daughters' pregnancies because they think it will limit their opportunities.
   d. most mothers of adolescent girls who have babies condone their daughters' early sexual behavior because they are happy that their daughters have boyfriends.

6. Shirley Hill's study of African-American women revealed that many of them became mothers even though doctors told them that they carried the gene that can cause sickle-cell anemia. Many of the women believed the medical warnings were unreliable and had children anyway because personal beliefs, rather than objective facts, motivate human behavior. This case illustrates the principles of which sociological theory?
   a. conflict
   b. functionalist
   c. social exchange
   d. symbolic interaction

7. Which of the following "unsettling facts" about the United States is true?
   a. The rate of imprisonment is lower than in all other industrialized nations.
   b. Women and men with college degrees now earn the same average incomes.
   c. The poverty rate among White citizens is higher than that of Asian immigrants.
   d. The gap between Black's and White's median income is the same as it was in 1970.

8. The idea that sociology can be used to intervene in the natural evolution of society for the improvement of society is social:
   a. posivitism.
   b. darwinism.
   c. organicism.
   d. telesis.

9. Emile Durkheim's research on social solidarity illustrates the principles of which social theory?
   a. conflict
   b. functionalist
   c. social exchange
   d. symbolic interactionist

10. Max Weber stated that sociologists should try to understand human behavior from the perspective of the people engaged in it. He referred to this concept as:
    a.   wohnen.
    b.   verstehen.
    c.   application.
    d.   debunking.

11. The concept of debunking refers to:
    a.   questioning the taken-for-granted assumptions of social life.
    b.   treating the people being studied as objects to avoid being biased.
    c.   studying only people who are similar to you to avoid misunderstandings.
    d.   making moral judgements about the beliefs and practices of the people being studied.

12. Social Darwinism suggested that:
    a.   sociologists should use research to improve the quality of life for all citizens.
    b.   social inequality is the result of the unequal distribution of economic resources.
    c.   sociology is not a real science because it does not use objective research methods.
    d.   social inequality is rooted in biological processes such as adaptation and evolution.

13. Joe was fired from his job because he repeatedly overslept and came to work late. This example illustrates the type of problem C. Wright Mills referred to as:
    a.   deficiencies.
    b.   troubles.
    c.   issues.
    d.   faults.

14. Two hundred men were laid off from their auto assembly jobs because the company closed the factory to cut costs. This example illustrates the type of problem C. Wright Mills referred to as:
    a.   deficiencies.
    b.   troubles.
    c.   issues.
    d.   faults.

15. Sociologists affiliated with the Chicago School of American sociology were:
    a.   involved in using social settings as laboratories for human research.
    b.   interested in how society shaped the mind and identities of individuals.
    c.   committed to the application of sociological ideas to real social problems.
    d.   All of the above are true.

16. Because of sex discrimination in academic settings, early female sociologists often worked as:
    a.   nurses.
    b.   secretaries.
    c.   book editors.
    d.   social workers.

17. Robert Merton realized that some social practices have consequences that are neither apparent nor consistent with their stated purpose. These unintended consequences of behavior are called:
    a.   manifest functions.
    b.   latent functions.
    c.   social issues.
    d.   social facts.

18. Dr. Smith is conducting a participant observation study in a college dormitory. She observes how the residents interact with each other and asks them how they feel about their living situation. The type of data she is collecting is:
   a. quantitative.
   b. qualitative.
   c. secondary.
   d. predictive.

19. The theoretical perspective that suggests society is reflected in the words and images that people use to represent behavior and ideas is called:
   a. feminism.
   b. functionalism.
   c. neodarwinism.
   d. postmodernism.

20. A teacher thinks that gender may cause differences in her students' performance on math tests. In this example, gender is which kind of variable?
   a. hypothetical
   b. independent
   c. secondary
   d. dependent

21. Which of the following potential ethical violations did Judith Rollins commit in her participant observation study of Black domestic workers?
   a. Rollins took a job as a maid and organized the other domestic workers to demand higher wages, eventually leading a strike against their White employers.
   b. Rollins took the role of an employer, hired several Black women as maids, and paid them without reporting their wages to the Internal Revenue Service.
   c. Rollins took the role of an employer and interviewed Black women for the job of maid but never intended to hire anyone.
   d. Rollins took a job as a maid without telling her employer that she was conducting research.

22. The disadvantage(s) of using surveys to investigate people's opinions on social issues is (are):
   a. this method of collecting and analyzing data is especially time-consuming.
   b. researchers can only study the views of a small number of people at one time.
   c. respondents may use deception to conceal opinions that they believe are unacceptable.
   d. All of the above are disadvantages of using surveys to collect data.

23. Dr. Lee wants to know how the portrayal of women in magazines has changed over the last two decades. The most useful technique for her to use in this investigation is:
   a. controlled experiment.
   b. program evaluation.
   c. content analysis.
   d. field research.

24. The statistical tool used by researchers that is not skewed or distorted by extreme scores at either end of the distribution is the:
   a. mean.
   b. mode.
   c. median.
   d. percentage.

25. The statement "If a man drops out of high school, then he will be more likely to be unemployed than a man who graduates from high school" is an example of a:
   a. sample.
   b. concept.
   c. variable
   d. hypothesis.

True-False Questions

1. The majority of professional sociologists work in applied settings, such as providing relief services to homeless people.

2. In *How to Observe Manners and Morals*, sociologist Harriet Martineau argued activists' efforts to grant women the vote in the United States threatened the stability of the American family.

3. W.I. Thomas' famous saying, "If men define situations as real, they are real in their consequences," is referred to as the *irrational condition*.

4. Social Darwinists supported *social telesis*, the idea that society was best left alone to follow its natural evolutionary course toward perfection.

5. There are larger concentrations of African American people in California and Texas than in any place in the United States.

6. Auguste Comte, who first coined the term *sociology*, believed that sociology was the most highly evolved of all the sciences because it involved the study of the entire society.

7. Robert Merton's primary contribution to sociology was the idea that social institutions may serve two kinds of functions – latent and manifest.

8. The overall logic and strategy underlying a research project is called the hypothetical map.

9. Numerical data, such as those collected by the United States Bureau of the Census, are useful for doing quantitative research.

10. In all cases, sociologists are ethically and legally prohibited from conducting research without the informed consent of the subjects being studied.

Fill in the Blank Questions

1. Emile Durkheim conceptualized social _____ as those values, customs, and other patterns of behavior that are external to individuals and therefore, the proper subject of sociology.

2. Dr. Brown wants to know if the particular measure she is using accurately reflects the concept she is studying; thus, she is interested in the _____ of the measure.

3. Dr. Wood selected his sample in such a way that everyone in the population he was studying had an equal chance of being included, resulting in a _____ sample.

4. When a sociologist repeats a prior investigation with a different group of subjects in a different time or place, it is referred to as a(n) _____ study.

5. A researcher has a hunch that family income influences a person's likelihood of going to college. In this example, attending college would be a _____ variable.

Essay Questions

1. Distinguish between *troubles* and *issues* using C. Wright Mills' definitions of these concepts. Give an example of a social problem that appears to have an individual cause, but can be explained in a different way using the sociological imagination.
2. Define *diversity* and identify the three most influential aspects of diversity in the United States today. Explain why sociologists think examining diversity is crucial for understanding society.
3. Describe and give an example of four common statistical mistakes that researchers make when analyzing or interpreting data.
4. You are a sociologist who wants to investigate the topic of alcohol consumption on college campuses. Describe what steps you will take to develop the research design for this study.
5. Discuss the utility, appropriateness, advantages, and disadvantages of using a survey, participant observation, and a controlled experiment to conduct a sociological study of drinking behavior among college students.

ANSWERS TO PRACTICE TEST

Answers to Multiple Choice Questions

1.	B	9	Sociologists study social institutions, socially patterned attitudes and behaviors, and patterns of social interaction, but the focus of sociology is not on the unique contributions of famous people.
2.	A	5	The sociological imagination is a way of looking at society that reveals social patterns. Social structure is the organized pattern of social relationships and social institutions that constitute society
3.	D	6	A majority of sociologists work in academic settings as teachers and researchers, and some work as consultants, but few provide individual counseling.
4.	A	5	Sociology is an empirical science because it is based on careful, systematic observations. Common sense is an unreliable source of information. Most researchers do not claim to be value-free, but they strive to be objective.
5.	C	8	Kaplan's research indicates that the common assumptions made about Black teenage mothers are myths. Her study showed that most of the mothers are disappointed and most of the girls feel shame about being pregnant and receiving welfare assistance.
6.	D	20	Hill's study illustrates the principles of symbolic interaction theory, which focuses on how people interpret information and attribute meanings to situations.
7.	D	9	The gap between White's and Black's median family income has not changed since 1970. Women's average earnings are less than men's at all education levels. Asian immigrants have higher rates of poverty than do Whites. The rate of imprisonment in the United States is higher than in other industrialized nations.
8.	D	16	Lester Frank Ward supported social telesis, the idea that sociology can be used to intervene in the natural evolution of society for the improvement of society. Postmodernism is an approach to understanding society that focuses on cultural images. Positivism is a system of thought in which scientific observation is considered the highest form of knowledge.
9.	B	14	Durkheim's research on solidarity reflects the principles of functionalist theory, which emphasizes the importance of integration, cohesion, and social order.

10.	B	16	Weber advocated that sociologists develop *verstehen*, or the ability to understand human behavior from the perspective of the people engaged in it. Debunking refers to questioning taken-for-granted assumptions about social life.
11.	A	6	Berger referred to debunking as the process of questioning the taken-for-granted assumptions of social life. Sociological research may debunk commonly held, but inaccurate, ideas about human behavior and social life.
12.	D	16	Social Darwinism supported a "hands-off" approach to society, which would allow it to follow its "natural" evolutionary course. This perspective adopts ideas from Charles Darwin's work on biological adaptation in animal species.
13.	B	5	According to Mills, troubles result from problems originating in individual emotions or conditions, such as being fired for oversleeping. Issues arise from social conditions.
14.	C	5	Issues such as mass layoffs and widespread unemployment affect large numbers of people and are rooted in the economic structure of society.
15.	D	17	Sociologists affiliated with the Chicago School, including W.I. Thomas, Florian Znaniecki, Robert Park, and Jane Addams, were interested in how society shaped the mind and identities of individuals. They used social settings as laboratories for human research to develop ways to solve social problems related to urbanization and industrialization.
16.	D	17	Jane Addams was a leader in the settlement house movement, which provided community services to the urban poor, immigrants, and others in need.
17.	B	19	Merton identified the unintended consequences of behavior or social institutions as latent functions. The stated or intended goals are manifest functions.
18.	B	24	This participant observation study is an example of qualitative research, which is somewhat less structured and more interpretive than quantitative research, which relies more heavily on statistical analysis.
19.	D	20	Postmodernism is a theoretical perspective that suggests society is reflected in the words and images that people use to represent behavior and ideas.
20.	B	25	The independent variable in a hypothesis is the one that the researcher wants to test as the presumed cause of something else. The dependent variable is the one on which there is a presumed effect. In this example, gender is presumed to effect test performance.
21.	D	31	Rollins posed as a maid to conduct research on the experiences of Black domestic workers without revealing her identity to her employer or the other maids; thus, she did not get informed consent from the people being studied. Her behavior did not constitute an ethical violation because her subjects were not at risk of being harmed as a result of the research.
22.	C	26	Surveys allow researchers to ask large numbers of people specific questions about many topics. Computers allow researchers to conduct sophisticated analyses in a relatively short amount of time. People may disguise their true opinions if they are concerned that their answers are not socially acceptable.
23.	C	28	Content analysis is a useful technique for examining the portrayal of groups in magazines and other media [Table 1.2].
24.	C	28	Several statistical tools are defined in the "Doing Sociological Research" box. The mean is the average of all scores, the mode is the most frequently appearing score, and the median is the midpoint in a series of values. Unlike the mean, the median is not skewed by extreme values at either end.
25.	D	24	A hypothesis indicates the expected relationship between two variables that can be scientifically tested. It is usually formulated as an if-then statement.

Answers to True-False Questions

1.	T	15	Karl Marx believed that the economy was the central social institution around which other features of society were organized.
2.	F	14	Harriet Martineau was an outspoken feminist and abolitionist who supported equal rights for women.
3.	F	17	W.I. Thomas' saying is referred to as the *defintion of the situation.*
4.	F	16	Social Darwinism supported a "hands off" approach to society. Ward advocated social telesis, or the use of sociology for the improvement of society.
5.	F	11	The group of maps depicted in Map 1.1 indicate that the largest concentrations of Black Americans are in southern states such as Georgia and Alabama. Texas and California contain the largest concentrations of Hispanic people in the nation.
6.	T	13	Auguste Comte, who coined the term *sociology*, believed that sociology could discover the laws of social behavior just as science had discovered the laws of nature. Comte viewed sociology as the most highly evolved of the sciences.
7.	T	19	Merton elaborated on functionalist theory by identifying latent functions, or the unintended consequences of social behavior.
8.	F	24	The overall logic and strategy of a research project is called the research design.
9.	T	24	Quantitative data refers to numerical data that lends itself to statistical analysis.
10.	F	32	Sociologists may conduct research without gaining informed consent in cases where the research poses no risk of harm to the people being studied.

Answers to Fill in the Blank Questions

1.	facts	15
2.	validity	25
3.	random	30
4.	replication	24
5.	dependent	25

BRIEF CHAPTER OUTLINE

Defining Culture
 Characteristics of Culture
 Biology and Human Culture
The Elements of Culture
 Language
 Norms
 Beliefs
 Values
Cultural Diversity
 Dominant Culture
 Subcultures
 Countercultures
 Ethnocentrism
The Globalization of Culture
Popular Culture
 The Influence of the Mass Media
 Racism and Sexism in the Media
Theoretical Perspectives on Culture
 Culture and Group Solidarity
 Culture, Power, and Social Conflict
 New Cultural Studies
Cultural Change
 Culture Lag
 Sources of Cultural Change

CHAPTER FOCUS: This chapter identifies the elements of culture, discusses the influence of culture on diverse groups' experiences, and introduces the sources of cultural change.

QUESTIONS TO GUIDE YOUR READING
1. What are the five common features of culture?
2. Why is language an essential feature of culture?
3. How can cultural diversity contribute to both group solidarity and social conflict?
4. What is the difference between cultural relativism and ethnocentrism? Which approach do sociologists recommend using in our attempts to study and understand culture?
5. What are the main causes of cultural change?

SOCIOLOGY IN ACTION: AN INTERNET EXERCISE
Go to www.ASLinfo.com to learn more about deaf culture and American Sign Language. Do you think that deaf people constitute a *subculture* according to the definition provided in the text? Why or why not? What norms have been established for engaging in social interaction with members of this group? How can sharing a language contribute to a stronger sense of identity and belonging for people who are deaf?

KEY TERMS (defined at page number shown and in glossary)

CHAPTER OUTLINE
I.   **DEFINING CULTURE**

It is difficult to understand the perception of our culture as "strange" by outsiders because we learn to accept the practices and beliefs of our culture as normal. Sociologists try to both know the culture as insiders and understand it as outsiders. **Culture**, the complex system of meaning and behavior that defines the way of life for a given group of people, includes both patterns of behavior (customs, habits, fashion) and ways of thinking (beliefs, values, knowledge, morals, language, laws). Material culture consists of the objects created in a society, such as buildings, art, tools, toys, and print and broadcast media. Non-material culture includes the norms, laws, ideas, and beliefs of a group of people.

A.   Characteristics of Culture

1.   **Culture is shared**. Culture is collectively experienced and agreed upon. The shared nature of culture makes society possible. Despite variations within the United States, certain symbols, language patterns, belief systems, and ways of thinking form a common American culture.

2.   **Culture is learned**. Even though the cultural beliefs and practices may seem perfectly natural to the members of the culture, they are learned through the formal and informal transmission of culture.

3.   **Culture is taken for granted**. Members of a culture seldom question their own culture; however, if a person becomes an outsider or establishes critical distance from typical cultural expectations, s/he may be able to examine the culture from a unique perspective. Although culture binds us together, lack of communication across cultures often has negative consequences.

4.   **Culture is symbolic. Symbols** are things or behaviors to which people give meaning, such as a flag or wedding band. Symbolic meanings guide behavior. The meaning attached to symbols depends on the cultural context in which they appear. For example, displaying a cross on a church has a different meaning than burning a cross on a front yard.

5.   **Culture varies across time and place.** People develop cultural solutions to adapt to the challenges posed by their particular physical and social environments. Culture links the past and the present as it gives shape to human experience. **Cultural relativism** is the idea that something can be understood and judged only in relationship to the cultural context in which it appears. Practices accepted within certain cultures, such as burying or cremating the dead, may be viewed negatively by members of other cultures.

B.   Biology and Human Culture

In addition to humans, some animal species, such as chimpanzees, develop culture. Although biological and environmental conditions place limitations on human development, cultural factors have an enormous influence on human life.

II. THE ELEMENTS OF CULTURE
A. Language
   1. **Language** is a set of interrelated symbols and rules that provides a complex communication system. Language is fluid and dynamic, and makes the formation of human culture possible.
   2. The **Sapir-Whorf hypothesis** stated that language determines other aspects of culture because language provides the categories through which social reality is defined and constructed, forcing people to perceive the world in certain terms. Although critics do not agree that language is this deterministic, sociologists agree that culture and language influence each other. For example, concepts of time in the United States are strongly linked to the Protestant work ethic.
   3. Patterns of race, class, gender, and other forms of social inequality are reflected in language. The labels given to various groups are used to convey certain attitudes and beliefs about those groups, and debates about those names have led to changes in the formal rules of language. For example, the term "handicapped" has been replaced by "people with disabilities" in social and political discourse.
B. Norms
   1. **Norms** are the specific cultural expectations for how to behave in certain situations. Norms exist to govern every situation, contributing to consistency and predictability in social interaction.
      a. Implicit norms, such as waiting in line rather than barging in front of people, need not be spelled out for people to understand them.
      b. Norms are explicit when the rules governing behaviors are written down or formally communicated.
   2. William Graham Sumner identified two types of norms.
      a. **Folkways** are the general standards of behavior adhered to by a group, or the ordinary customs of different groups, such as fashion and etiquette.
      b. **Mores,** the strict norms that control moral and ethical behavior, are often upheld by **laws**, which are the written set of guidelines that define right and wrong in a society.
   3. **Social sanctions**, which are mechanisms of social control that enforce norms, may be imposed on people who violate norms.
      a. Negative sanctions may be mild or severe, ranging from ridicule to imprisonment and physical coercion.
      b. Sanctions also include rewards, such as praise and encouragement, which reinforce socially acceptable behavior.
   4. **Ethnomethodology** is a technique for studying human interaction that involves deliberately disrupting social norms and observing how individuals respond.
C. Beliefs
   Beliefs are shared ideas held collectively by people within a given culture that form the basis for many norms and values. Beliefs provide a meaning system around which culture is organized, such as the belief in democracy in the United States.
D. Values
   1. **Values** are the abstract standards in a society or group that define ideal principles and provide a general outline for behavior by identifying what is desirable and morally correct.
   2. Values can be both a basis for cultural cohesion and a source of conflict. For example, conflict has developed over the competing values of protecting life and the right to privacy that are at the core of the controversy over abortion in the United States.

3.   Values guide the behavior of people in society, and norms reflect those underlying values. For example, the American Indian society, Kwakiutl, participates in a practice called *potlatch* that reflects its value of reciprocity, while *conspicuous consumption* characterizes dominant American culture.

III.   CULTURAL DIVERSITY

The United States hosts enormous cultural diversity, where more than 8 percent of the population is foreign born. The traditions and practices of many groups have influenced American culture. For example, the Native American Iroquois culture, with its emphasis on the principles of self-rule, federation, and representation, had a strong influence on the United States government.

A.   <u>Dominant Culture</u>

As the culture of the most powerful group in society, the **dominant culture** receives the most support from social institutions and constitutes the major belief system in that society. A dominant culture need not be the culture of the majority of people.

B.   <u>Subcultures</u>

Subcultures are the cultures of groups whose values, norms, and behavior are somewhat different from those of the dominant culture, but that share some elements of the dominant culture and coexist within it. An example is the distinctive Puerto Rican subculture in the United States, which created the Salsa music that represents the barrio experience of Puerto Ricans who migrated to the mainland.

C.   <u>Countercultures</u>

Countercultures are subcultures that reject the dominant cultural values, often for political or moral reasons. For example, "women's communities" have developed that are based on woman-centered, feminist social networks, relationships, and cultural activities. Another example of a counterculture is the militia movement in the United States, whose members share a unique mode of dress, a common worldview, and a distinct style of life.

D.   <u>Ethnocentrism</u>

Ethnocentrism is the habit of seeing things only from the perspective of one's own group. An ethnocentric view prevents people from understanding the world as it is experienced by others and can lead to negative conclusions about other cultures. Although ethnocentrism may build group solidarity, it discourages understanding between groups and may lead to terrorism, war, or genocide.

IV.   THE GLOBALIZATION OF CULTURE

From Disney films to McDonald's fast food items, the commercialized culture of the United States is marketed worldwide. The diffusion of a single culture throughout the world is known as **global culture**, which is increasingly marked by capitalist interests.

V.   POPULAR CULTURE

Popular culture includes the beliefs, practices, and objects that are part of daily traditions, including mass-produced, mass-marketed media that are shared by large audiences. Popular culture is distinct from elite culture or "high culture," which is shared by only a select group who can afford to participate in it. Thus, cultural tastes and participation in the arts are socially structured, because familiarity with different cultural forms stems from patterns of historical exclusion, as well as integration into networks that provide information about certain cultural products.

A.   <u>The Influence of the Mass Media</u>

1.   **Mass media** are those channels of communication that are available to wide segments of the population, including radio and television, which strongly shape public information and attitudes.

2.   Television is such a powerful force for transmitting cultural values in the United States that George Gerbner, a communications analyst, suggests television is the country's "national religion."

3.   Commercial interests and producer's perceptions of what matters to the public determine what and how news is presented. For example, the media now spend more time reporting about crime, even though violent crime has decreased.

B.   <u>Racism and Sexism in the Media</u>

The mass media promote narrow definitions of who people are and what they can be. For example, the media communicate that only certain forms of beauty are culturally valued by portraying characters differently according to their age, gender, race, and class. Television shows, films, and music play a significant part in molding public consciousness, including upholding stereotypes about women as sexual objects.

VI. THEORETICAL PERSPECTIVES ON CULTURE

The **reflection hypothesis** contends that the mass media reflect the values of the general population by trying to appeal to the most broad-based audience; however, media portrayals can also influence the values of those people who see them.

A.   <u>Culture and Group Solidarity</u>

1.   Sociologists such as Max Weber have studied the relationship of culture to other social institutions. Weber argued that the Protestant faith rested on cultural beliefs, such as the work ethic and a need to display material success as a sign of religious salvation, that were compatible with modern capitalism.

2.   Functionalist theorists believe that norms and values create social bonds that attach people to society, which provides coherence and stability. Putnam argues that a decline in civic participation in the U.S. has contributed to social disorder.

B   <u>Culture, Power and Social Conflict</u>

1.   Conflict theorists have analyzed culture as a source of power in society that is dominated by economic interests. A few powerful groups are viewed as the major producers and distributors of culture, a trend that is supported by corporate mergers in the media industry.

2.   Conflict theorists view culture as increasingly connected by economic monopolies, resulting in **cultural hegemony**, or an excessive concentration of cultural power that leads to the pervasive influence of one culture throughout society. This process creates a homogeneous mass culture that reduces political resistance to the dominant culture.

3.   Culture can also be a source of political resistance, as illustrated by the American Indian Movement (AIM), which organized to reassert the independence of Native American cultures in the United States.

4.   **Cultural capital** refers to those cultural resources that are socially designated as being worthy, such as knowledge of elite culture. Pierre Bourdieu argues that groups maintain their social status by appropriating culture.

C.   <u>New Cultural Studies</u>

Symbolic interaction theory analyzes behavior in terms of the meaning people give to it, noting that culture is produced through social relationships and in social groups. An interdisciplinary field known as *cultural studies* has emerged that builds on the insights of this theory, directing researchers to view culture as a series of images that can be interpreted in multiple ways, depending on the viewpoint of the observer.

VII. CULTURAL CHANGE

Culture is dynamic and develops as people respond to changes in their physical and social environments, despite economic forces that support the status quo.

A.   <u>Cultural Lag</u>

Culture lag refers to the delay in making cultural adjustments to changing social conditions. For example, culture lag is created when people's transportation habits do not change even though more efficient, lower-pollution forms of transit are available.

B. Sources of Cultural Change
The main causes of cultural change are changes in societal conditions, cultural diffusion, innovation, and the imposition of cultural change by an outside group.

1. *Cultures change in response to changed conditions in society.*
For example, cultural changes emerged as the Baby Boomers, the large cohort of children born after World War II, reached adulthood and became more affluent.

2. *Cultures change through cultural diffusion*
Cultural diffusion is the transmission of cultural elements from one society or culture to another, such as the diffusion of rap music from inner city African American neighborhoods into White youth culture.

3. *Cultures change as the result of innovation.*
The discovery and application of new knowledge, including technological innovations such as the microwave and the personal computer, have led to dramatic changes in lifestyles.

4. *Cultural change can be imposed*, as when a powerful group imposes a new culture on a society or manipulates the culture of a group as a way of exerting social control. Cultural expression can also be a form of political protest in which suppressed groups increase solidarity among members and attempt to establish a more powerful identity in the society.

PRACTICE TEST

Multiple Choice Questions

1. Certain elements of Black urban street culture, such as rap music, have been fully integrated into the dominant American culture. This is an example of cultural:
    a. lag.
    b. diffusion.
    c. innovation.
    d. oppression.

2. The norms, laws, customs, ideas, and beliefs of a group of people constitute its _____ culture.
    a. global
    b. counter
    c. material
    d. nonmaterial

3. Which of the following statements about culture is **false**?
    a. Culture is learned by direct instruction and observation.
    b. Culture is innate, or part of the basic instinctive patterns of human beings.
    c. Cultural values are represented by symbols to which people attribute meaning.
    d. Culture is fluid, so it changes in response to new environmental and social conditions.

4. The idea that something can be understood and judged only in relationship to the cultural context in which it appears is cultural:
    a. hegemony.
    b. relativism.
    c. shock.
    d. lag.

5. Which theory argues that culture serves the interests of powerful groups in society and is increasingly connected by economic monopolies?
    a. symbolic interaction
    b. functionalist theory
    c. solidarity theory
    d. conflict theory

6. From 1951 to 1960, the majority of immigrants to the U.S. came from _____, whereas the majority of immigrants to the U.S. in the 1990's came from _____.

    a. Asia; Europe
    b. Europe; South America
    c. North America; Asia
    d. Europe; North America

7. The Sapir-Whorf hypothesis argues that language:
    a. determines other aspects of culture because it provides the categories through which social reality is constructed.
    b. constantly changes because people actively construct words and phrases that reflect emerging social conditions.
    c. is not necessary for acquiring the other social skills needed to participate in social life.
    d. None of the above statements are consistent with the Sapir-Whorf hypothesis.

8. Which of the following terms reflects social inequality in language?
    a. Chairman
    b. President
    c. Director
    d. Leader

9. At the grocery store, people are expected to wait in line, rather than barge in front of other people, to pay for the items they are purchasing. This is an example of a:
    a. core value.
    b. sacred more.
    c. implicit norm.
    d. explicit norm.

10. William Graham Sumner referred to food preparation techniques and standards of etiquette as:
    a. laws.
    b. mores.
    c. folkways.
    d. sanctions.

11. There is a strict norm against murder in the United States, and this morally offensive behavior may be severely punished. Thus, norms against killing are:
    a. mores.
    b. beliefs.
    c. folkways.
    d. sanctions.

12. Which of the following statements about sanctions is (are) true?
    a.   Violations of mores carry stricter sentences than violations of folkways.
    b.   Sanctions are mechanisms of social control that enforce norms.
    c.   Sanctions involve both punishments and rewards.
    d.   All of the above statements about sanctions are true.

13. The technique for studying human interaction by deliberately disrupting social norms and observing how individuals respond is known as:
    a.   postmodernism.
    b.   cultural studies.
    c.   etiquette analysis.
    d.   ethnomethodology.

14. A shared idea held collectively by people within a given culture, such as cherishing democracy in the United States, is a:
    a.   more.
    b.   norm.
    c.   value
    d.   belief.

15. An abstract standard that defines ideal principles within a given society, such as the primacy individual freedom in the United States, is a:
    a.   more.
    b.   norm.
    c.   value.
    d.   belief.

16. When asked to identify famous Japanese people, respondents to Professor Akuto's survey named Yoko Ono (an American citizen), Bruce Lee (a Chinese film star) and Godzilla (a fictional character). This reflects:
    a.   androcentrism.
    b.   ethnocentrism.
    c.   cultural relativism.
    d.   cultural resistance.

17. The greatest concentration of people speaking a language other than English at home is located in which region of the United States?
    a.   Midwest
    b.   Northeast
    c.   Southwest
    d.   Northwest

18. Which perspective views culture as a changing system that is socially constructed through the activities of social groups?
    a.   conflict theory
    b.   functionalist theory
    c.   globalization theory
    d.   symbolic interaction theory

19. The principle that suggests the mass media reflect the values of the general population is known as the:
    a. looking glass principle.
    b. globalization process.
    c. reflection hypothesis.
    d. hegemonic hypothesis.

20. Although we have the technology to develop more efficient, less polluting public transit systems, people's personal transportation habits have been difficult to change. This situation reflects the problem of cultural:
    a. lag.
    b. diffusion.
    c. ignorance.
    d. oppression.

True-False Questions

1. Sociologists agree that using ethnocentrism is the best way to fully understand and appreciate a culture other than their own.

2. Material culture consists of the objects created by a given society, such as buildings, art, tools, and toys.

3. Because culture is so critical to human survival, it is a stable, permanent system that rarely changes.

4. According to the Sapir-Whorf hypothesis, social inequality in language is justified because women are naturally inferior to men, and language reflects that fact.

5. Because participation in *elite culture* is so expensive, it is usually restricted to high status groups.

6. *Nationalist movements* focus on celebrating the indigenous culture of an oppressed group as a mechanism for building group solidarity and resisting the oppression.

7. Subcultures may be based on a variety of shared understandings and experiences, including racial or ethnic heritage, religion, and musical preferences.

Fill in the Blank Questions

1. Cultural _____ refers to the pervasive, excessive influence of one homogeneous culture throughout a society.

2. Things to which people attribute meaning, such as a cross or a flag, are _____.

3. According to _____ theory, culture provides coherence and stability in society and integrates , people into groups.

4. Members of the modern militia movement, who reject dominant cultural values, physically isolate themselves from other Americans, and share a distinct style of life, represent a _____.

5. Mass-produced, mass-marketed media that are shared by large audiences are a form of _____ culture, whereas expensive activities that are restricted to people of higher status are forms of _____ culture.

Essay Questions

1. Identify the four main sources of cultural change and provide an example of how each one has influenced behaviors or conditions in the United States.
2. Explain the statement, "Culture is symbolic." Give several examples of specific symbols and discuss how their meanings vary according to the social context in which they appear.
3. Discuss the issue of social inequality in language, noting how language reinforces the current power structure in the United States. Provide specific examples to support your answer.

ANSWERS TO PRACTICE TEST

Answers to Multiple Choice Questions

1.	B	59	Diffusion and innovation are both sources of cultural change. Diffusion refers to the transmission of cultural elements from one group to another. Innovation refers to the discovery of new knowledge, such as technological advances. Cultural lag refers to the delay in making cultural adjustments to new social conditions.
2.	D	37	Non-material culture includes the norms, customs, laws, and beliefs of a group. Material culture includes the objects produced by the group, such as art.
3.	B	38	Culture is learned through socialization, which includes direct instruction and observation. Culture is fluid and dynamic, but not innate.
4.	B	39	Cultural relativism is the idea that something can be understood and judged only in relationship to its cultural context. Cultural hegemony refers to an excessive concentration of power that leads to the pervasive influence of one culture throughout society. Culture shock is a feeling of disorientation and alienation that can occur when a person encounters a new or changing situation.
5.	D	56	Conflict theory views culture as increasingly connected by economic monopolies. Functionalist theory views culture as a cohesive force in society. Symbolic interaction theory analyzes behavior in terms of the meaning people give to it [Table 2.1].
6.	D	47	Figure 2.1 indicates that the majority of immigrants to the United States during the 1950's came from Europe, whereas the majority of recent immigrants have come from Northern America.
7.	A	41	The Sapir-Whorf hypothesis argues that language determines other aspects of culture because it provides the categories through which social reality is defined and constructed. Acquisition of language is necessary to full participation in society. Changes in language may alter the way people think about certain groups, because what someone is called imposes a social identity on them.
8.	A	43	Social inequality in language is reflected in the term "chairman," which suggests only a man may hold that position.
9.	C	43	Norms are the specific cultural expectations for how to behave in a given situation. Mores are explicit norms governing moral behavior. Implicit norms are understood without being spelled out for people. Values are abstract ideals.
10.	C	43	Folkways are norms governing customary practices, such as table manners.
11.	A	43	Mores are strict norms governing moral behavior, such as murder.

12.	D	44	Social sanctions are mechanisms of social control that enforce norms. Sanctions include both rewards and punishments. The most severe sanctions are encoded in law and used for violations of mores.
13.	D	44	Ethnomethodology helps reveal the normal social order by deliberately disrupting patterns of human interaction. The field of cultural studies examines how different people interpret the images that comprise culture.
14.	D	44	Beliefs are shared ideas held collectively by people within a given culture.
15.	C	45	Values are the abstract standards in a society or group that define ideal principles and provide a general outline for behavior.
16.	B	51	Ethnocentrism is the habit of seeing things only from the point of view of one's own group, which includes ignorance about other cultures.
17.	C	47	Map 2.1 indicates that the Southwest region of the United States contains the highest percentage of people who speak a language other than English at home.
18.	D	58	Table 2.1 indicates that symbolic interaction theory focuses on the meanings people attribute to cultural symbols.
19.	C	56	The reflection hypothesis contends that the mass media reflect the values of the general population.
20.	A	36	Cultural lag occurs when there is a delay in adjustments to changes in society.

Answers to True-False Questions

1.	F	39	Sociologists advocate using cultural relativism to avoid judging cultural practices in different groups and societies.
2.	T	37	Material culture includes tangible objects such as art, while non-material culture refers to the beliefs and norms of a society.
3.	F	39	Not only does culture vary from place to place, it also changes over time as people adapt to changes in the physical and social environment.
4.	F	41	According to the Sapir-Whorf hypothesis, language provides the categories through which social reality is defined and constructed by people. The hypothesis does not suggest that inequality among social groups is innate or natural.
5.	T	52	Popular culture is mass-produced and distributed, whereas elite culture is expensive. Thus, popular culture is available to the largest number of people, while elite culture is restricted to those of higher status.
6.	T	60	Nationalist movements, which identify a common culture as the basis for group solidarity, encourage members to celebrate their cultural heritage and challenge dominant cultural forms. Examples in the United States are Black Nationalism, (also known as Afrocentrism) and the Latino movement, *La Raza Unida*.
7.	T	49	Sociologist Rebecca Adams conducted extensive research on Deadheads, the group of people who followed the band, the Grateful Dead, on national tours. Although members of this group participated in the dominant culture, they also questioned, challenged, and attempted to change it by drawing on the band's music to develop a language and habits that reflected an alternative worldview.

Answers to Fill in the Blank Questions

1.	hegemony	57
2.	symbols	39
3.	functionalist	56
4.	counterculture	49
5.	popular; elite	52

CHAPTER 3
SOCIALIZATION

BRIEF CHAPTER OUTLINE

The Socialization Process
> Socialization as Social Control
> Conformity and Individuality
> The Consequences of Socialization

Theories of Socialization
> Psychoanalytic Theory
> Object Relations Theory
> Social Learning Theory
> Symbolic Interaction Theory

Agents of Socialization
> The Family
> The Media
> Peers
> Religion
> Sports
> Schools

Growing Up in a Diverse Society

Socialization Across the Life Cycle
> Childhood
> Adolescence
> Adulthood and Old Age
> Rites of Passage

Resocialization
> The Process of Conversion
> The Brainwashing Debate

CHAPTER FOCUS: This chapter compares psychological and sociological explanations of the process of identity development, defines the stages of the life course, and identifies the primary agents of socialization in the United States.

QUESTIONS TO GUIDE YOUR READING
1. Why do sociologists consider socialization a form of social control?
2. What are the four main consequences of the life-long socialization process?
3. How does the socialization process vary by gender, race, ethnicity, and social class?
4. What are the primary agents of socialization in most societies?
5. What characteristics and expectations are associated with each of the main stages of the life course in the contemporary United States?

SOCIOLOGY IN ACTION: AN INTERNET EXERCISE
Go to www.secularceremonies.com and read about the types of ceremonies offered by this organization. Why do you think organizations offering such services have developed in the contemporary United States? How are these rituals similar to, and different from, traditional rites of passage, such as those organized by formal religious organizations?

KEY TERMS (defined at page number shown and in glossary)
adult socialization 84   anticipatory socialization 84

ego 69
game stage 73
id 69
imitation stage 100
looking-glass self 72
play stage 73
psychoanalytic theory 69
rites of passage 85
significant others 73
socialization 64
social learning theory 70
taking the role of the other 72

feral children 64
generalized other 73
identity 67
life course 80
object relations theory 70
peers 76
resocialization 86
roles 64
social control 65
socialization agents 73
superego 69

KEY PEOPLE (identified at page shown)
Peter Berger 65
Charles Horton Cooley 72
Sigmund Freud 68
Lawrence Kohlberg 71
Michael Messner 77
Jean Piaget 70

Nancy Chodorow 70
Erik Erikson 83
Carol Gilligan 71
George Herbert Mead 72
C. Wright Mills 81
Barrie Thorne 79

CHAPTER OUTLINE

Many people are fascinated by the notion of individuals raised with little to no human contact, called **feral children**. In 1970, Genie, a thirteen year old girl who had been kept in nearly complete isolation in her California home, was discovered. After intense language instruction and psychological treatment, she developed some verbal ability and showed progress in her mental and physical development, but she eventually moved to a home for mentally retarded adults.

I.   **THE SOCIALIZATION PROCESS**

Socialization is the process through which people learn the expectations of society, including social **roles**, the expected behavior associated with a given status in society. The socialization process varies by race, ethnicity, gender, and social class. Socialization contributes to *internalization*, which occurs when behaviors and assumptions are learned so thoroughly that people no longer question them, but simply accept them as correct. People's lives are socially constructed; that is, the organization of society and the life outcomes of people within it are the result of social definitions and processes. For sociologists, what a person becomes is more a result of their social experiences than their innate, or inborn, traits.

A.   Socialization as Social Control

Socialization works as a subtle mechanism of **social control** because the socialization process brings individuals into conformity with dominant social expectations. When people successfully internalize their culture, they are likely to conform to social expectations. Deviating from cultural expectations can lead to ridicule as well as more coercive means of social control, including violence.

B.   Conformity and Individuality

Despite the importance of social influences, human beings are individuals who interact with their environments in creative ways. Men and women who try to balance feminine and masculine characteristics enjoy greater mental health, while those who rigidly conform to their gender role may experience stress and other negative consequences.

C.   The Consequences of Socialization

Socialization is a life-long process that affects how we think of ourselves and how we behave toward other people.

1. *Socialization establishes self-concepts:* **identity** is established through social experiences.
2. *Socialization creates the capacity for role-taking*: we are able to see ourselves as others see us through this reflective process.
3. *Socialization creates the tendency for people to act in acceptable ways:* we learn social expectations and this creates some predictability in human behavior.
4. *Socialization makes people bearers of culture*: we learn and internalize attitudes, beliefs, and behaviors and pass these cultural expectations on to others.

II. **THEORIES OF SOCIALIZATION**
    Several different theoretical perspectives have been used to explain the process of development, including psychoanalytic theory, object relations theory, social learning theory, and symbolic interaction. Each theory relies on unique assumptions about the effects of socialization on individual identity.
    A. Psychoanalytic Theory
       1. **Psychoanalytic theory**, rooted in the work of **Sigmund Freud**, argues that the unconscious mind shapes human behavior. Psychoanalysis is used to discover the causes of psychological problems that exist deep within a patient's mind.
       2. This theory suggests the human psyche is comprised of three parts.
          a. The **id** consists of deep drives and impulses, such as sexuality.
          b. The **superego** is the dimension of the self that represents the standards of society. Because social standards (superego) will always be in conflict with impulses (id), individuals develop defense mechanisms such as repression, avoidance, and denial.
          c. As the psychological component of common sense and reason, the **ego** balances the id and the superego.
       3. Freud's work is controversial and questions have been raised about the ability to generalize his findings beyond his small, unrepresentative group of clients.
       4. Psychoanalytic theory is a popular way to think about human behavior that views identity as relatively fixed at an early age and motivations for behavior as internal and mostly unconscious.
    B. Object Relations Theory
       1. **Object relations theory**, an adaptation of psychoanalytic theory that places less emphasis on biological drives, argues that the social relationships children experience determine the development of their adult personalities.
       2. Two developmental processes are believed to be key in development: *attachment* to the primary caregiver and *individuation* (physical and emotional separation) from the caregivers.
       3. Nancy Chodorow uses object relations theory to explain how gender shapes men's and women's personalities, asserting that the modern family has an *asymmetrical division of labor*, in which women "mother" and men do not.
       4. Because children identify with the same-sex parent, they individuate from mothers and fathers differently, creating gendered personalities in adulthood.
       5. Chodorow's work has interesting practical implications; namely, if men acquired more mothering skills and participated more in daily care giving, the result would be a society where men and women have less gender-stereotyped personalities.
    C. Social Learning Theory
       1. **Social learning theory** considers the formation of identity to be a learned response to social stimuli. Identity is viewed as the result of modeling oneself in response to reinforcement.

2. **Jean Piaget** believed that socialization and imagination have critical roles in learning, and noted that the human mind organizes experiences into mental categories called *schema*.

3. Piaget proposed that children go through four distinct stages of cognitive development.
    a. In the s*ensorimotor stage*, children experience the world directly through the senses-- touch, taste, sight, and sound.
    b. In the *preoperational stage*, children begin to use language and other symbols and to see things as others might see them, but cannot yet think abstractly.
    c. In the *concrete operational stage*, children learn logical principles about the concrete world.
    d. In the *formal operational stage*, children are able to think abstractly and imagine alternatives to their reality.

4. Piaget conceptualized humans as actively creating their mental and social worlds, noting that people's behavior can be changed by altering their environments.

5. Lawrence Kohlberg elaborated on Piaget's work by developing a three stage theory of moral development.
    a. *Preconventional stage*: young children judge right and wrong in simple terms of obedience and punishment, based on their own needs and feelings.
    b. *Conventional stage*: adolescents develop moral judgement in terms of cultural norms, especially social acceptance and following authority.
    c. *Postconventional stage*: people are able to consider abstract ethical questions, demonstrating maturity in moral reasoning.

6. Kohlberg argued that men, who are more concerned with authority, reach a higher level of moral development than women, because women remain more concerned with feelings and social opinions.

7. Carol Gilligan challenged Kohlberg's theory, arguing that men's moral development is not more mature than women's development; rather, women conceptualize morality differently than do men.

D. Symbolic Interaction Theory

1. According to symbolic interaction theory, people's actions are based on the meanings they attribute to things, and these meanings emerge through social interaction.

2. For symbolic interactionists, the *self* is what we imagine we are, rather than an internal set of drives, instincts, and motives, and that people make conscious, meaningful adaptations to their social environment.

3. Symbolic interactionists view socialization as a dynamic, ongoing process and the self as evolving over the life span. **Charles Horton Cooley** and **George Herbert Mead** viewed the self as developing in response to the expectations and judgements of other people in their social environments.
    a. Cooley developed the **looking-glass self** to explain how a person's conception of self develops through reflection about his/her relationships to others. This is a three-step process.
        1) We carefully note the reactions of others toward us.
        2) We develop an understanding of how others judge us.
        3) We develop feelings about ourselves based on the way we understand other people's perceptions of us.
    b. Mead believed that the basis of all social interaction is social **roles**, or sets of expectations that govern a person's relationships with other group

members and society. He stated that the self has two dimensions: the active, creative, self-defining, unique part of the personality ("I") and the passive, conforming self that reacts to others ("me"). He also suggested that there are three stages of childhood socialization, based on the child's developing ability to engage in the process of **taking the role of the other**, or imagining oneself from someone else's point of view.

1) **Imitation stage**: children only copy the behavior of those around them, without the ability to take on the role of the other.

2) **Play stage**: children begin to take on the roles of significant people in their environments. Of particular importance is taking on the role of **significant others**, or those with whom they have close relationships, such as their parents.

3) **Game stage**: the child becomes capable of taking on multiple roles at the same time; understands how people are related to each other and him or her; gains a more general, comprehensive view of the self; and acquires the **generalized other**, or the abstract composite of social roles and social expectations.

III. **AGENTS OF SOCIALIZATION**

Socialization agents are those who pass on social expectations. Socialization occurs in the context of social institutions, including the family, peers, the media, religion, sports, and schools.

A. The Family

Although the family is the first source of socialization for most people, families are quite diverse within and across cultures. For example, researchers found that Japanese mothers speak in ways that use objects as part of a ritual of social exchange in their interactions with their children, thereby emphasizing polite routines. American mothers, on the other hand, focus on labeling things for their children. These different styles of interaction are interpreted as reflecting the beliefs and practices of each culture.

B. The Media

In the U.S., the media (including television, films, music, video games, radio, and print messages) are an especially important agent of socialization that expose us to images that shape our definitions of ourselves and the world. For example, research on violence in the media has yielded conflicting results about the effects of television on children. Both the images themselves and the broader social context in which children live must be considered when explaining children's behavior and attitudes.

C. Peers

Peers are those people with whom you interact on equal terms, such as friends, fellow students, and coworkers. For children, peer culture is an important source of identity, where they learn concepts of self, gain social skills, and form values and attitudes. Members of minority groups often experience isolation and stress when they are "token" members of a dominant group, which may result in the formation of same-sex or same-race peer groups for support, social activities, and information sharing.

D. Religion

Religious instruction greatly contributes to the identities children construct for themselves and shapes the beliefs that guide adults in organizing their lives.

E. Sports

1. Through sports, men and women learn concepts of self and form ideas about gender differences. In interviews with male athletes, Messner identified sports as very important to male identity. He reported that playing or watching sports is often the context in which men develop relationships with their fathers.

2. Although sports were less significant in the formation of women's identity in the past, women's participation in sports has increased. Traditionally, negative

stereotypes of female athletes were a form of social control that reinforced traditional gender roles. Current research indicates that women who play sports develop a strong sense of bodily competence and self-confidence.

    F.   Schools
1. Research shows that teachers have different expectations for boys and girls and for students from different racial, ethnic, and social class backgrounds.
2. Negative appraisals are often *self-fulfilling prophecies*, because the expectations they create may become the basis for actual behavior, thereby affecting children's likelihood of success.
3. Schools have a *hidden curriculum* that is composed of informal and often subtle messages about social roles that are conveyed through classroom interaction and materials.
4. Gender is especially relevant in the interactions of boys and girls when they are placed together in working groups. The results of Barrie Thorne's research on school-aged children suggests that gender has a "fluid" character, so relationships between boys and girls can be improved by consciously discouraging gender separation in schools.
5. Schools emphasize conformity to societal needs, such as respect for authority and punctuality; however, students internalize these lessons differently.

IV.   GROWING UP IN A DIVERSE SOCIETY
Socialization instills in us the values of the culture. It brings society into our self-definitions, our perceptions of others, and our understanding of the world. In a heterogeneous cultural system such as the United States, variation in social contexts creates vastly different social experiences. The socialization process is structured by social factors such as race, ethnicity, class, gender, religion, regional background, sexual preference, and age.

V.   SOCIALIZATION ACROSS THE LIFE CYCLE
Socialization begins at birth and continues throughout the lifespan. The term **life course** describes the connection between individuals, their roles, their experiences, and the social and historical context of life events. Mills noted that personal biographies are linked to specific socio-historical periods.

    A.   Childhood
1. During childhood, socialization establishes one's initial identity and values, and the family is an especially influential agent of socialization.
2. Cultural experiences for children typically vary according to the sex and race of the child. For example, childhood play seems to encourage more rule-based, aggressive play for boys and more conversation in play for girls.
3. Ausdale and Feagin's research indicates that even preschool children use race and ethnicity to define themselves and others, often revealing awareness of negative racial attitudes.
4. Although American culture defines children as "priceless," the image of childhood as a carefree time is inconsistent with the harsh realities of life for children who experience violence and poverty.

    B.   Adolescence
1. Adolescence developed as a distinct stage of the life course when formal education was extended to people of all social classes.
2. **Erik Erikson** stated that the central task of adolescence is the formation of a consistent identity. Conflict and confusion may arise as the adolescent moves between childhood and adulthood because adolescence lacks clear boundaries.
3. Patterns of adolescent socialization vary significantly by race, gender, and social class. Among the upper- and middle- classes, friendships tend to be based on

shared activities and interests, while working class youth tend to base friendship on loyalty and stability, with friendships determining activities.

   C.   Adulthood and Old Age

   1.   **Adult socialization** involves learning behavior and attitudes appropriate to specific situations and roles, such as being a college student.

   2.   Events such as marrying, divorcing, beginning a career, and entering the military all transform an individual's identity and require the adult to adopt new roles.

   3.   Another part of learning new roles is **anticipatory socialization**, a process in which an individual learns, and perhaps rehearses, the expectations associated with a role that she or he expects to enter in the future.

   4.   In the transition from an old role to a new one, individuals may vacillate between their old and new identities For example, coming out, or openly identifying oneself as gay or lesbian, is an example of a process that typically occurs in stages and creates a new sense of self.

   5.   The transition to adulthood now takes longer than in the past, and social conditions make it difficult for many people to transition into adulthood by following the traditional path of finishing school, getting a job, marrying, and starting a family.

   6.   The transition to old age is one of the most difficult for adults to make, partly due to the devaluing of the elderly in the United States.

   D.   Rites of Passage

   1.   A **rite of passage** is a ceremony or ritual that marks the passage of an individual from one role to another. Rites of passage, including graduation ceremonies and religious affirmations, define and legitimize abrupt role changes that begin or end each stage of life. These events publicly announce the individual's new status.

   2.   Sociologists note that contemporary American society does not have a standardized, formal rite of passage marking the transition from childhood to adulthood, which contributes to the ambivalence and uncertainty of adolescence.

VI.   RESOCIALIZATION

Resocialization is the process by which existing social roles are radically altered or replaced. It is especially likely when people enter institutional settings where the institution gains almost complete control over the individual, such as prisons and the military. When people enter hierarchical organizations such as the military, they must respond to authority on principle, not loyalty, and act as soldiers, not individuals. Resocialization may involve degrading new members physically and psychologically with the aim of breaking down and redefining their old identity.

   A.   The Process of Conversion

   A *conversion* is a far-reaching transformation of identity, often related to a significant change in religious or political beliefs. *The Autobiography of Malcolm X*, for example, describes a personal conversion that spanned religious, political, and social convictions. Through his encounter with the Nation of Islam while in prison, Malcolm X transformed his identity from a prisoner to that of a Black leader who analyzed racial oppression in the context of international capitalism.

   B.   The Brainwashing Debate

   1.   Highly suggestible people, such as young adults who are socially isolated and drifting, are the most susceptible to cult influence. Despite the belief that people have to be deprogrammed to get them out of cults, many leave on their own.

   2.   Forcible confinement and physical torture can be used as instruments of extreme resocialization. The *Stockholm Syndrome* refers to a captive who is dependent on the captor and may come to identify with him or her under conditions of severe deprivation. Prisoners of war, hostages, and battered women may all experience this phenomenon.

PRACTICE TEST

Multiple Choice Questions

1. The few rare individuals who were raised in extreme isolation from other human beings and later found, sometimes referred to as feral children, are:
   a. usually able to reach a similar level of development as their peers after several years of intense language instruction.
   b. never able to learn to speak the language of their culture because the capacity for learning language is only present during early childhood.
   c. always able to emotionally recover from such severe neglect after they undergo intensive psychological treatment.
   d. sometimes able to develop limited verbal ability and progress slightly in their physical and mental development after comprehensive training and treatment.

2. Most people accept the norms of their society as correct because:
   a. norms are derived from the Bible and it would be blasphemous to question a sacred text.
   b. people are innately motivated to desire similarity and seek conformity.
   c. people internalize social expectations so well that they no longer question them.
   d. most social norms are established by the government and people trust the government to act in their best interest.

3. According to the U.S. Bureau of the Census, the largest population of people age five years and younger is located in which region of the country?
   a. Northwest (including Washington and Oregon)
   b. Southwest (including California and New Mexico)
   c. Southeast (including Florida and Georgia)
   d. Northeast (including New York and Pennsylvania)

4. The stage of the life course characterized by tension, contradiction, and the task of establishing one's identity is:
   a. childhood.
   b. adolescence.
   c. middle adulthood.
   d. old age.

5. Which of the following statements about socialization is (are) true?
   a. Socialization creates the tendency for people to act in deviant ways.
   b. Socialization makes it difficult for individuals to see themselves as others see them.
   c. Socialization takes place during childhood and adolescence but is complete by adulthood.
   d. None of the above statements about socialization are true.

6. Carol Gilligan's research on moral development indicates that:
   a. men reach a higher standard of moral reasoning than women because men are more concerned with authority.
   b. women reach a higher standard of moral reasoning than men because women are more concerned with relationships and other people's feelings.
   c. even though women and men define morality differently, neither women's nor men's moral reasoning is more mature.
   d. there are no differences between women and men in the ways that they define morality and respond to moral dilemmas.

7. According to Freud, the part of the personality that represents common sense and reason and helps balance the conflict between the other two components is the:
   a. superego.
   b. ego.
   c. me.
   d. id.

8. Which of the following statements about Freud's work on identity development is true?
   a. Freud's work has been criticized for being unrepresentative because he only wrote about women's development.
   b. Freud's work suggests that people make conscious, meaningful adaptations to their environments.
   c. Freud's work has been widely accepted because it was based on a representative sample that can be accurately generalized to a large population.
   d. Freud's work views identity as deeply rooted in the unconscious processes of the mind.

9. Symbolic interaction theory views identity as developing:
   a. through interaction and conscious, meaningful adaptation to one's environment.
   b. from tensions between strong instinctual impulses and social standards.
   c. from a passive, learned response to social stimuli such as reinforcement.
   d. through the largely unconscious processes of attachment to, and separation from, one's caregivers.

10. Object relations theory views identity as developing:
   a. from tensions between strong instinctual impulses and social standards.
   b. from a passive, learned response to social stimuli such as reinforcement.
   c. through interaction and conscious, meaningful adaptation to one's environment.
   d. through the largely unconscious processes of attachment to, and separation from, one's caregivers.

11. Which theory considers the formation of identity to be a learned response to social stimuli such as encouragement from others and rewards for desired behavior?
   a. Mead's game theory
   b. Piaget's social learning theory
   c. Freud's psychoanalytic theory
   d. Chodorow's identification theory

12. According to Piaget, the preoperational stage of development is characterized by:
   a. experiencing the world directly through the senses of taste, touch, and sound.
   b. beginning to use language and other symbols but not thinking abstractly.
   c. thinking abstractly and imaging alternatives to one's own reality.
   d. learning logical principles about the concrete world.

13. According to Piaget, children are able to think abstractly and imagine alternatives to the reality in which they live in which of the following stages of development?
   a. formal operational
   b. concrete operational
   c. preoperational
   d. sensorimotor

14. Which of the following is **not** a component of the looking-glass self concept?
    a.   your perception of how you appear to other people
    b.   your beliefs about how other people perceive you
    c.   your feelings about how you are perceived by others
    d.   your beliefs about how you should treat other people

15. George Herbert Mead identified three stages of childhood. In which of the following stages do children typically begin to take on the roles of their significant others?
    a.   game
    b.   play
    c.   imitation
    d.   reflection

16. According to Mead, the abstract composite of social roles and social expectations that children acquire in the game stage is known as the:
    a.   attachment process.
    b.   significant other.
    c.   resocialization effect.
    d.   generalized other.

17. Through which source of socialization are boys and men best able to form both an appropriate masculine identity and socially acceptable bonds with other men?
    a.   religion
    b.   sports
    c.   media
    d.   family

18. Tara, a graduate student, interacts regularly and on equal terms with the other graduate students in her program. The other students are Tara's:
    a.   significant others.
    b.   generalized others.
    c.   models.
    d.   peers.

19. The informal and often subtle messages about social roles that are conveyed through classroom interaction and materials is called the:
    a.   hidden curriculum.
    b.   official curriculum.
    c.   teacher effect.
    d.   student bias.

20. Barrie Thorne's study of school-aged children indicates that gender:
    a.   becomes less relevant in the interactions of boys and girls when they are grouped together in common working groups.
    b.   is so central to the formation of identity that children should be grouped into boys-only and girls-only working groups to facilitate their development.
    c.   has a "rigid" character that cannot be changed to improved gender relationships between boys and girls, who both benefit from gender separation.
    d.   None of the above statements are true.

21. Research on adolescent socialization indicates that:
    a. working-class youth are more likely to base their friendships on shared activities and interests, so they change friends as their activities change.
    b. middle-class youth are likely to base their friendships on loyalty and stability.
    c. middle-class youth are more likely to base their friendships on shared activities and interests, so they change friends as their activities change.
    d. None of the above statements are true, because social class does not influence the development of friendship groups.

22. Elizabeth is a high school senior who wants to attend college, so she visits several college campuses, observes how college students dress, and begins to imitate their actions. Elizabeth is engaged in:
    a. resocialization.
    b. unsocialization.
    c. optimistic socialization.
    d. anticipatory socialization.

23. What metaphor did Cooley use to describe how individuals form their identities?
    a. undressing
    b. playing games
    c. looking in a mirror
    d. constructing a building

24. When military recruits enter boot camp, their heads are shaved, they are given identical uniforms, and they must subordinate their identities to the group. This process is:
    a. resocialization.
    b. unsocialization.
    c. optimistic socialization.
    d. anticipatory socialization.

25. The phenomenon whereby a hostage identifies with his or her captor is known as the:
    a. Victimization Hypothesis.
    b. Stockholm Syndrome.
    c. Looking-Glass Self.
    d. Imitation Stage.

True-False Questions

1. According to Mead, the "I" is the component of self that is active, creative, and unique.

2. During initiation into a hierarchical organization, the resocialization process promotes individuality through the personalized treatment of new members.

3. Women who participate in organized sports tend to develop poor self-esteem because they are aware that they violate important cultural standards for femininity.

4. Most people who join cults must be deprogrammed to be freed from the cult's influence, because they are rarely able to leave on their own.

5. According to research conducted by Van Ausdale and Feagin, young children (ages three to five years old) do not understand the concepts of race and ethnicity well enough to use them as a basis for their concepts of themselves and other children.

6. According to Chodorow, it is not possible for men to acquire genuine mothering skills, even if they participate more in the daily care of their families, because mothering is an innate, unconscious process located deep in the mind, rather than a learned behavior.

7. Research indicates that women who strictly conform to the traditional feminine gender role tend to have higher rates of depression than women who adopt traits associated with both femininity and masculinity.

Fill in the Blank Questions

1. In the _____ stage of Mead's theory or socialization, children only copy the behavior of people around them and role taking is nonexistent.

2. According to Mead, the _____ other is the abstract composite of social roles and social expectations that children acquire in the game stage.

3. According to Erikson, the central task of _____ is the formation of a consistent identity.

4. A _____ is a far-reaching transformation of identity, often related to a change in political or religious beliefs.

5. According to Freud, the _____ is the dimension of self that represents the standards of society.

Essay Questions

1. Using Cooley's concept of the looking-glass self, explain why gay and lesbian people might develop low self-esteem.
2. Discuss the practical implications of Chodorow's application of object relations theory to gender identity development.
3. Explain how teachers' perceptions of gender and social class differently affect the school experiences of boys and girls and working-class and middle-class children.
4. Identify the four stages of the life course in the United States and describe the main activities and social expectations associated with each stage.
5. Explain what purpose rites of passage serve for both individuals and society, and discuss how adolescents in the United States could benefit from participating in a formal rite of passage.

ANSWERS TO PRACTICE TEST

Answers to Multiple Choice Questions

1.	D	44	The few cases of feral children that have been scientifically documented have suffered severe intellectual and physical developmental problems and were unable to achieve a "normal" level of functioning.
2.	C.	65	Socialization is the process through which people learn and internalize the expectations of society; thus, most people accept them as correct..
3.	B	81	As shown in Map 3.1, California and Texas, which are in the southwest, have the largest populations of children ages five years old and younger.

4. B 83 According to Erikson, adolescence is a period characterized by conflict and confusion in which individuals have the task of establishing their identities.

5. A 68 Socialization is a life-long process that creates the tendency for people to act in socially acceptable ways. It makes people bearers of culture and creates the capacity for role-taking, or seeing ourselves as others see us.

6. C 71 Gilligan argues that women's moral reasoning should not be judged according to theories of men's moral development because men and women define morality differently.

7. B 69 According to Freud, the ego is the part of the personality that represents common sense and reason. It balances the conflict between the other two dimensions of self, the id and the superego.

8. D 69 Freud's work has been criticized for relying on a small, unrepresentative sample of patients undergoing psychoanalysis. He argued that personality is relatively fixed at an early age and identity development is mainly the result of unconscious processes deeply rooted in the mind.

9. A 71 As indicated in Table 3.1, symbolic interaction theory views individuals as active participants in the ongoing development process. Psychoanalytic theory views personality as the result of tensions between unconscious processes and social standards. Social learning theory views development as a response to social stimuli. Object relations theory argues that young children's relationships with their caregivers determine adult development.

10. D 70 As indicated in Table 3.1, object relations theory emphasizes the importance of the largely unconscious processes of attachment and individuation in explaining adult personality development.

11. B 70 Social learning theory, associated with Piaget, considers identity formation to be a learned response to social stimuli. Chodorow's analysis of the role of gender in personality development is based on object relations theory. Freud's psychoanalytic theory focused on unconscious mental processes. Mead's theory of role taking is based on symbolic interaction theory.

12. B 71 According to Piaget, children experience the world through the senses during the sensorimotor stage. They use language but cannot think abstractly at the preoperational stage. At the concrete operational state, children learn logical principles about the concrete world.

13. A 71 According to Piaget, children are able to think abstractly and imagine alternatives to the reality in which they live in the formal operational stage of development.

14. D 72 In Cooley's model of the looking-glass self, individuals note the reactions of of others toward them, understand how others view them, and develop feelings about themselves based on their perceived evaluations from others. Cooley's concept does not address how people feel about how they treat others.

15. B 73 Mead identified three stages of childhood. In the imitation stage, children mimic the behavior of people around them. In the play stage, children take on the roles of significant people in their environment. In the game stage, children develop an awareness of community values and general social expectations.

16. D 73 According to Mead, the abstract composite of social roles and social expectations that children acquire in the game stage is called the generalized other.

17. B 73 Messner's research indicates that sports are very important in the development of masculine identity and the formation of male relationships.

18. D 76 Individuals with whom a person interacts on equal terms, such as friends, fellow students, and co-workers, are peers.

19. A 79 The informal, often subtle, messages about social roles that are conveyed through classroom interaction and materials is called the hidden curriculum.

20.	A	79	Thorne notes that gender becomes less relevant in boy-girl interactions when they are placed together in working groups. Because gender has a "fluid" character, relationships between boys and girls can be improved through conscious changes that discourage gender separation.
21.	C	84	Middle- and upper-class youth tend base their friendships on shared activities and interests, while working-class youth are more likely to base their friendships on loyalty and stability.
22.	D	84	Anticipatory socialization involves learning the expectations associated with a role one expects or hopes to enter in the future. Resocialization involves a dramatic transformation in one's identity.
23.	C	72	Cooley used the concept of the looking-glass self to compare the process of development to looking at one's reflection in a mirror.
24.	A	86	The process whereby existing social roles are radically altered or redefined is resocialization.
25.	B	87	Some hostages, prisoners of war, and battered women may identify with their captors, a phenomenon known as the Stockholm Syndrome.

Answers to True-False Questions

1.	T	73	According to Mead, the self has two dimensions. The "I" is the active, creative, self-defining part. The "me" is the passive, conforming part.
2.	F	87	Resocialization radically alters existing social roles and often involves breaking down members' individual identities to make them part of the group.
3.	F	78	Research indicates that women who participate in organized sports have high self-esteem and are confident and willing to take risks.
4.	F	89	Many people leave cults by themselves and do not require deprogramming.
5.	F	82	Preschool children use race and ethnicity to define themselves and others.
6.	F	70	According to Chodorow, if men were to acquire more mothering skills and participate more in daily care giving, the result would be a society where men and women have less gender-stereotyped personalities.
7.	F	67	Women who overconform to the feminine gender role tend to have higher rates of depression than women who combine masculine and feminine traits.

Answers to Fill in the Blank Questions

1.	imitation	73
2.	generalized	73
3.	adolescence	83
4.	conversion	87
5.	superego	69

CHAPTER 4
SOCIETY AND SOCIAL INTERACTION

BRIEF CHAPTER OUTLINE

What is Society?
      Microanalysis and Macroanalysis
      Groups
      Statuses
      Roles

Theories About Analyzing Social Interaction
      The Social Construction of Reality
      Ethnomethodology
      Impression Management and Dramaturgy
      Social Exchange
      Interaction in Cyberspace

A Study in Diversity: Forms of Nonverbal Communication
      Touch
      Paralinguistic Communication
      Kinesic Communication
      Use of Personal Space

Interpersonal Attraction and the Formation of Pairs
      Proximity
      Mere Exposure Effect
      Perceived Physical Attractiveness
      Similarity

Social Institutions and Social Structure
      Social Institutions
      Social Structure

What Holds Society Together?
      Mechanical and Organic Solidarity
      Gemeinschaft and Gesellschaft

Types of Societies: A Global View
      Preindustrial Societies
      Industrial Societies
      Postindustrial Societies

CHAPTER FOCUS: This chapter examines the various levels and components of society, from small group interaction to core social institutions and large-scale social forces.

QUESTIONS TO GUIDE YOUR READING
1.   For which topics would sociologists use macroanalysis? When would they use microanalysis?
2.   What are the four types of nonverbal communication and why are they such important components of social interaction?
3.   Which social factors are most important in determining to whom individuals will be attracted and with whom they will form relationships?
4.   What are the major institutions in society and what are their primary functions?
5.   What are the three main types of societies found in the world and how do sociologists distinguish among the types?

SOCIOLOGY IN ACTION: AN INTERNET EXERCISE

Go to www.epic.org/free to view the Electronic Privacy Information Center's statement concerning the application of the First Amendment to communications in cyberspace. Now go to www.CyberAngels.org to learn about this organization's attempts to restrict communication on the Internet. Do you think that Internet communications should be regulated? If so, who should be responsible for monitoring cyberspace interaction? Is electronic communication fundamentally different from other forms of communication?

KEY TERMS (defined at page number shown and in glossary)

achieved status 94	ascribed status 94
collective consciousness 110	cyberspace interaction 100
division of labor 110	ethnomethodology 97
gemeinschaft 111	gesellschaft 111
group 93	impression management 98
master status 94	mechanical solidarity 110
organic solidarity 110	preindustrial society 112
proxemic communication 104	role 95
role conflict 95	role strain 95
social institution 98	social interaction 92
social organization 93	social structure 109
society 92	status 93
status inconsistency 94	status set 94

KEY PEOPLE (identified at page number shown)

Elijah Anderson 102	Emile Durkheim 92
Marilyn Frye 109	William Gamson 97
Harold Garfinkle 97	Debra Gimlin 104
Erving Goffman 98	E.T. Hall 104
Arlie Hochschild 95	W.I. Thomas 97

CHAPTER OUTLINE

I.   WHAT IS SOCIETY?

Social forces guide human interaction and humans shape the social institutions that exist in society. **Society** is a system of social interaction that includes both culture and social organization. Culture refers to people's general way of life, including norms, customs, beliefs, and language. Members of a society view themselves as distinct from other societies, maintain social ties through interaction, and have a high degree of interdependence. **Social interaction** refers to meaningful behavior between two or more people. Interaction involves communication, or the conveyance of information to other people. Durkheim viewed society as an organism, or something composed of different parts that work together to create a unique whole, such as the human body. Sociologists use the sociological imagination to picture society as a whole, while also investigating its various parts and the complex relationships among the components.

A.   Microanalysis and Macroanalysis

1.   *Microanalysis* refers to the technique sociologists use to investigate the microlevel of society, or the patterns of social interaction that are relatively small, less complex, and less differentiated. For example, this approach could be used to study interpersonal attraction and the formation of friendships.

2.   *Macroanalysis* refers to the technique sociologists use to comprehend society as a whole, including how it is organized and how it changes. Macrolevel sociology investigates patterns of social interaction that are vast, complex, and highly

differentiated. For example, this approach is useful for studying social problems such as poverty.

      3.   **Social organization** describes the order established in social groups. This order brings regularity and predictability to human behavior.

B.   Groups

      1.   Sociologists define a **group** as a collection of individuals who interact and communicate with each other, share goals and norms, and have a subjective awareness of themselves as a distinct social unit.

      2.   In sociological terms, not all social units are groups.

         a.   *Social categories* are people who are categorized together based on one or more shared characteristic, such as teenagers or teachers.

         b.   *Audience*s are comprised of all of the people who are simultaneously watching the same program or performance.

         c.   *Formal organizations* are highly structured social groupings that form to pursue a set of shared goals, including formal associations, such as the PTA, and bureaucracies, such as business corporations.

C.   Statuses

      1.   **Status** is an established position or rank in a social structure that carries with it a degree of *prestige*, or social value, such as a person's occupation.

      2.   A **status set** is the complete set of statuses occupied by a person at a given time. Each status is associated with a different level of prestige.

      3.   **Status inconsistency** occurs when a person's several statuses are associated with significantly different amounts of prestige. For example, recent immigrants who were professionals in their home countries but are forced into jobs with little status in the United States experience status inconsistency.

      4.   There are two ways by which a person receives a particular status.

         a.   **Achieved statuses** are those attained by independent effort, such as occupational and educational statuses.

         b.   **Ascribed statuses** are those automatically assigned to a person at birth, such as race. These statuses are sometimes ambiguous, as in the case of biracial individuals. Although biological sex is ascribed, gender is a social construct, because regardless of genetic characteristics, gender appropriate behavior is learned, not innate.

         c.   Class status includes both ascribed and achieved components. For example, upper-class membership is more likely if one's parents are wealthy (ascribed status) *and* if one works in a high-paying occupation (achieved status).

      5.   A **master status** is a dominant status for an individual that overrides all other features of a person's identity. It may be imposed by others (e.g. criminal) or voluntarily chosen by the individual (e.g. mother). Because master statuses override other identities, they may be the basis for stereotypes, as in the case of someone who has a disability.

D.   Roles

      1.   A **role** is the expected behavior or collection of expectations associated with a particular status. A *role set* includes all of the roles occupied by a person at a given time.

      2.   **Role conflict** occurs when two or more roles have contradictory expectations. For example, Arlie Hochschild identified the problem of the "second shift," which refers to women who are employed outside of the household but still expected to fulfill traditional expectations at home.

3. **Role strain** is a condition in which a single role brings conflicting expectations. For example, first-generation college students may experience role strain if their parents expect them to live at home and continue a traditional family role, while choosing the best college may require leaving home and thinking independently.

4. Although role conflict and role strain are experienced at the individual level, they originate in the social expectations rooted in specific roles.

II. THEORIES ABOUT ANALYZING SOCIAL INTERACTION

Sociologists analyze social interaction through different theoretical frameworks and perspectives, including social exchange theory and symbolic interaction theory, from which the social construction of reality, ethnomethodology, and impression management perspectives are derived.

A. The Social Construction of Reality

1. The principle of *the social construction of reality*, central to symbolic interaction theory, argues that our perception of what is real is determined by the subjective meaning that we attribute to an experience. Things do not have their own intrinsic meaning; rather, people subjectively impose meaning on things.

2. As a result of the social construction of reality, we see what we want to see. In fact, people sometimes attribute certain meanings to things when it benefits them to perceive it that way, even if the perception seems to be contrary to fact.

3. W.I. Thomas coined the phrase *definition of the situation* to refer to the idea that *situations defined as real are real in their consequences*. Through the process of defining the situation, people adjust their attitudes and perceptions based on the context in which they find themselves. For example, researchers found that the way physicians define emergency room patients has important consequences for how the patients are treated. In one study, older patients were examined less thoroughly before being pronounced dead than were younger patients.

4. Understanding the social construction of reality allows us to gain insight into the social significance of race and gender. Race and gender have meaning because we choose to give them meaning, which may change our behavior toward others.

B. Ethnomethodology

Ethnomethodology is a technique for studying human interaction by deliberately disrupting social norms and observing how individuals try to restore normalcy. Because many norms that influence social behavior are not conscious, it is impossible to identify all of them simply by asking people to list them. For example, an ethnomethodologist might demand to pay more for a product than its listed price to reveal shopping norms.

C. Impression Management and Dramaturgy

1. **Impression management**, labeled by Erving Goffman, is a process by which people control how others perceive them by willfully attempting to manipulate other peoples' impressions of him or her.

2. Goffman's theory is sometimes referred to as the *dramaturgy model* of interaction because we present different "selves" to other people in different settings. This approach analyzes interaction by assuming that all participants are actors on a stage in the drama of everyday life.

3. Even when we define ourselves as individuals, our behavior is shaped by social forces. For example, a teacher's behavior when s/he returns graded papers is influenced by his/her relationship with the students and by the students' performance on the papers.

D. Social Exchange

1. The *social exchange model* argues that social interactions are determined by the rewards or punishments that we receive from other people. If the reward for an interaction exceeds the punishments for it, a potential for *social profit* exists and the interaction is likely to continue. If the rewards are less than punishments,

however, the interaction produces a social loss or negative profit and will be less likely to continue.

      a.   Rewards include tangible gains, such as gifts, recognition, and money, as well as subtle rewards, such as smiles and hugs.

      b.   Punishments include both subtle gestures, such as a frown, and extreme behaviors, such as public humiliation, beating, and banishment.

    2.   Because social exchange tends to encourage conformity and discourage deviance, it is a force for stability in society. For example, exchange theory posits that racist and sexist stereotypes that are rewarded by one's group tend to persist, while those that are punished tend to change.

  E.   Interaction in Cyberspace

    1.   *Cyberspace interaction* occurs when people interact and communicate with each other using a personal computer to access "chat rooms," computer bulletin boards, and e-mail.

    2.   Through virtual reality, what the individual perceives to be real is created by and on the computer. When two or more people share a virtual reality experience, they are engaged in **cyberspace interaction.**

    3.   Cyberspace interaction differs from face-to-face interaction because of its anonymity, so a person is free to become a different self by interacting via a virtual self that may have a different gender, for example, than one's real self.

    4.   Goffman's principle of impression management and dramaturgy can be applied to cyberspace interaction because a person can present him- or herself as having any set of characteristics, thereby controlling the impression the other person receives and producing a particular reality.

    5.   A *cyberculture* is evolving that has its own norms, language, set of beliefs, and practices, including: encouraging a new identity while engaging in cyberspace interaction; permitting or encouraging certain negative forms of interaction, such as aggression, intolerance, and exclusion; and maintaining a "frontier mentality," or sense that virtual interaction is a new frontier in our society.

III.   A STUDY IN DIVERSITY: FORMS OF NONVERBAL COMMUNICATION

Social interaction includes both verbal and nonverbal communication. *Verbal interaction* consists of spoken and written language, whereas n*onverbal interaction* is conveyed by touch, tone of voice, gestures, body postures, eye contact, and facial expressions. The meanings of nonverbal communication are strongly dependent upon race, ethnicity, social class, and gender.

  A.   Touch

      Tactile communication involves any conveyance of meaning through touch, whether positive (embracing) or negative (hitting). The meanings associated with tactile communication vary by cultural context and social factors such as gender. For example, as children, girls tend to be touched tenderly and protectively while boys are touched more roughly. As adults, women are more likely to touch as an expression of emotional support, whereas men touch more often to assert power or to express sexual interest.

  B.   Paralinguistic Communication

    1.   *Paralinguistic communication* is the component of communication that is conveyed by the pitch and loudness of the speaker's voice, its rhythm, emphasis, and frequency, and the frequency and lengths of hesitations.

    2.   The meaning of paralanguage varies by cultural context and ethnicity. For example, Japanese people regard silent periods during conversations as opportunities to collect their thoughts, while Americans avoid such periods with small talk. Americans often consider paralinguistics to be a small part of communication, while the Japanese consider them much more important.

3.   *Nonverbal leakage* refers to an individual's emotions and feeling being revealed by paralinguistic slips despite the person's attempts to conceal them. For example, when a person is lying, the pitch of his or her voice is slightly higher than when that same person is telling the truth.

C.   Kinesic Communication

1.   *Kinesic communication* involves gestures, facial expressions, and body language, which form a crucial part of nonverbal communication. Meanings conveyed by kinesis usually vary by cultural context, ethnicity, and gender. For example, avoiding eye contact is a sign of respect in some cultures, but making eye contact can be evaluated as a sign of sexual interest or hostility in other cultures.

2.   Certain modes of kinesic communication, however, are identical across groups and different cultures. For example, the facial expressions for anger, happiness, sadness, and disgust are recognized in all cultures, as are many hand gestures, including "stop," "good-bye," and "OK."

D.   Use of Personal Space

1.   **Proxemic communication** refers to the amount of space present between interacting individuals. Generally, the more friendly a person feels toward someone, the closer he or she will stand.

2.   According to Hall, each individual has a *proxemic bubble* that represents our personal 3-dimensional space. We feel threatened and may take evasive action when people we do not know enter our proxemic bubble. This largely unconscious process is illustrated by a typical person's behavior in an elevator.

3.   Proxemic interaction varies by gender and ethnicity. The proxemic bubbles of different groups have different sizes, and people from different groups may experience difficulty when they interact if they are not aware of cultural differences in the use of personal space.

IV. **INTERPERSONAL ATTRACTION AND THE FORMATION OF PAIRS**
The formation of human pairings, including romantic couples and friendship groups, has a strong social structural component; that is, patterned by social forces. Humans have a strong need for *affiliation*, or a desire to be with other people, and women generally reveal this tendency more than men. The affiliation tendency is similar to *imprinting*, a phenomenon observed in newly hatched animals that attach themselves to the first living creature they encounter, regardless of species. In humans, infant attachment is a more complex and changeable process that is influenced more by social factors. Interpersonal attraction is a nonspecific, positive response toward another person that can be understood using sociological principles.

A.   Proximity
Because we are more likely to meet and become attracted to people that we live or work near, proximity strongly affects relationship formation. In one study of friendships among recruits at a police academy, proximity in seating had a stronger effect on friendship formation than did all other factors, including race, socioeconomic background, and age.

B.   Mere Exposure Effect
The *mere exposure effect* refers to the fact that the more you see someone, the more you like him or her. This effect even occurs when a person only sees someone in a photograph. The initial response of the viewer can determine how much liking will increase with exposure to additional photographs. Furthermore, "overexposure" can result when a photograph is seen too often and the viewer becomes "saturated."

C.   Perceived Physical Attractiveness

1.   The attractions we feel toward people of either gender are based on our perceptions of their physical attractiveness. Perceived physical attractiveness is an important dimension of human interaction. For example, adults react more leniently to the bad behavior of an attractive child than to the same behavior of

an unattractive child, and teachers evaluate cute children of either gender as "smarter" than physically unattractive children with identical academic records.

    2.   Standards of attractiveness vary across cultures and among subcultures within a society, yet there is surprising agreement within a culture about who is attractive.

    3.   Studies of dating patterns among college students show that the more attractive one is, the more likely one will be asked to go on a date; however, attractiveness predicts only the early stages of a relationship.

  D.   <u>Similarity</u>

    1.   With few exceptions, people are attracted to others who are similar in socioeconomic status, race, ethnicity, religion, perceived personality traits, and general attitudes and opinions.

    2.   The less similar a heterosexual relationship is with respect to race, social class, age, and educational aspirations (how far in school the person wants to go), the quicker the relationship is to end.

    3.   Although people tend to date within their own race, nationality, or ethnicity, many interracial couples enjoy long-lasting relationships. For interracial couples, similarities in other social characteristics tend to predict relationship duration.

V.   SOCIAL INSTITUTIONS AND SOCIAL STRUCTURE

  A.   <u>Social Institutions</u>

    1.   A **social institution** is an established and organized system of social behavior with a recognized purpose that develops to meet various needs in society.

    2.   Institutions cannot be directly observed, although their impact and structure can be studied. Specific schools are organizations where learning occurs, while at the broadest level, education is a social institution that includes all schools, as well as the norms, values, and beliefs that guide education at the societal level.

    3.   The major institutions in society include: family, education, work and the economy, politics (or state), religion, and health care. There are other institutions as well, such as the mass media and organized sports.

    4.   Functionalist theorists, who see societal needs as universal, have identified the purposes of institutions, although all societies do not fill these needs in the same way or through the same institution. In the United States:

        a.   the **socialization of new members of the society** is a primary function of the family and education, although religious organizations and the mass media contribute to this function;

        b.   the **production and distribution of goods and services** is the responsibility of the economic and political institutions;

        c.   **replacement of the membership** is achieved through the family and other heterosexual pairings, although the government establishes policies that influence membership replacement;

        d.   the **maintenance of stability and existence** is achieved through the government, law enforcement agencies, and the military; and

        e.   **providing the members with an ultimate sense of purpose** involves virtually all institutions because commonly held purposes, values, and assumptions are evident in diverse institutions.

    5.   Conflict theorists argue that social institutions do not provide for all social members equally. Institutions affect individuals differently because they grant more power to some social groups than to others. Generally, the lower one's social class, the less one's political power, wealth, influence, and prestige.

B.   Social Structure
1.   **Social structure** refers to the organized pattern of social relationships and social institutions that together comprise society. Sociologists analyze social structure by examining the patterns in social life that reflect and produce social behavior.
2.   Social class distinctions are an example of a social structure, because class shapes social interactions as well as the access that different groups have to social resources.
3.   Social structures form invisible patterns that can be identified by using the sociological imagination. Marilyn Frye uses the metaphor of a birdcage to describe the concept of social structure. Just as a birdcage is a network of wires, society is a network of micro and macro structures that holds society together, sometimes oppressing certain groups.

VI.   WHAT HOLDS SOCIETY TOGETHER?

Emile Durkheim argued that people in a society have a **collective consciousness**, or a body of common beliefs that that give people a sense of belonging and a feeling of moral obligation to its demands and values. Collective consciousness develops from participation in the common activities of social institutions. Durkheim, identified two different kinds of social solidarity.

A.   Mechanical and Organic Solidarity
1.   **Mechanical solidarity** occurs when individuals play similar roles within the society. This form of solidarity characterized Native American groups prior to European conquest. Durkheim argued that collective consciousness was strongest in such societies; however, they are rare today due to the global trend of increasing interrelatedness.
2.   In societies with **organic solidarity** (or contractual solidarity), individuals play a great variety of different roles and social unity is based on role differentiation and shared interdependence, as in the United States and other industrialized societies. Such societies have a complex **division of labor**, or the systematic interrelatedness of different tasks. Within any division of labor, tasks become distinct from each other, yet they are woven together as a whole.
3.   Unlike societies characterized by organic solidarity, societies characterized by mechanical solidarity manifest tensions among competing groups, often due to divisions based on gender, race, and class.

B.   Gemeinschaft and Gesellschaft
1.   *Gemeinschaft*, a German word meaning "community," refers to a society in which there is a sense of "we" feeling among members, a moderate division of labor, strong personal ties and family relationships, and a sense of personal loyalty. Social control is largely achieved through the sense of belongingness that members share.
2.   *Gesellschaft*, a German word for "society," refers to a society in which there is increasing importance on less intimate, more instrumental, secondary relationships. There is a reduced sense of personal loyalty to the total society, an elaborate division of labor, and a somewhat diminished role of the nuclear family. Social control is partly achieved through mechanisms external to the individual, such as the police.
3.   Social solidarity is weaker in a gesellschaft society than in a gemeinschaft society because gesellschaft societies are more likely to experience class conflicts and racial-ethnic divisions that reduce internal cohesiveness.

VII.   TYPES OF SOCIETIES: A GLOBAL VIEW

Over time and across different cultures and continents, societies are distinguished by different forms of social organization that evolve from both the relationship of the society to its environment, and from the processes that the society develops to meet basic human needs.

Societies differ in many critical ways, including size, population, and resource base. Contemporary societies are increasingly global, with highly evolved systems of social differentiation and inequality, particularly along class, gender, racial, and ethnic lines. Sociologists distinguish six types of societies based on the complexity of their social structure, the amount of overall cultural accumulation, and the level of their technology [Table 4.1].

A.   Preindustrial Societies

A **preindustrial society** is one that directly uses the land as a means of survival for society's members. There are four types of preindustrial societies.

1.   Foraging societies depend on hunting animals and gathering vegetation. Most are nomadic, such as the Pygmies of Central Africa.

2.   Pastoral societies, which tend to be nomadic, depend on the domestication of animals in primarily desert areas, such as the Bedouins of Africa.

3.   Horticultural societies, such as the Incas of Peru, are non-nomadic and use elaborate tools to cultivate the land.

4.   Agricultural societies have large, complex economic systems and depend on technologically advanced, large-scale farming, as in the American south during the pre-Civil War period.

B.   Industrial Societies

1.   An *industrial society* uses machines and other advanced technologies to produce and distribute goods and services. The "industrial revolution," accompanied by the growth of science, brought advances in farming techniques and medical developments, for example, that led to the development of industrial societies.

2.   Industrial societies rely upon a highly differentiated labor force and the intensive use of capital and technology. Large formal organizations (bureaucracies) and institutions with a high division of labor (economy and work, government and politics) are of critical importance in holding industrial societies together.

3.   Industrial societies use a cash-based economy that pays wages for labor performed in factories, while household labor remains unpaid. This situation introduced the *family-wage economy*, in which families become dependent on wages to support themselves, but work within the family becomes increasingly devalued, and an increasing wage gap between men and women develops.

4.   Industrial societies tend to be highly productive and have a large working class of industrial laborers. With industrialization, the population becomes increasingly urbanized, immigration is common, economic activities move outside of the family, and other institutions, such as schools, become increasingly important.

5.   Although industrialization brought many benefits to the United States, it also produced some of the nation's most serious social problems, including pollution, widespread wage inequality and job dislocation, and urban crime and crowding.

C.   Postindustrial Societies

1.   *Postindustrial society* depends economically on the production and distribution of services, information, and knowledge.

2.   The transition to a postindustrial society strongly influences the character of social institutions. For example, education and science become critically important, and workers without technical skills often find themselves in low-pay, unskilled work or permanent joblessness.

3.   The United States is suspended between an industrial and a postindustrial society. Manufacturing jobs are still a segment of the labor force, but they are in decline. Most American workers are employed in the service sector of the economy, where they participate in the delivery of services and information rather than the production of material goods.

4. Postindustrial societies are increasingly dependent on the global economy as more goods are produced in economically dependent areas of the world for consumption in wealthier nations, resulting in greater global inequality.

PRACTICE TEST

Multiple Choice Questions

1. Which model of social interaction suggests that racist and sexist behavior tends to persist when individuals are rewarded for such practices, yet those stereotypes are diminished when stereotypical attitudes result in punishment?
   a. social exchange model
   b. norm disruption model
   c. social conformity model
   d. construction of reality model

2. Sociologists refer to behavior involving communication between two or more people as social:
   a. interaction.
   b. impression.
   c. institution.
   d. linguistics.

3. A(n) _____ society uses machines and other technologies to produce and distribute goods, relies on a highly differentiated labor force, and uses a cash-based economy.
   a. horticultural
   b. agricultural
   c. industrial
   d. foraging

4. Which type of status do individuals gain through personal effort, such as educational attainment?
   a. achieved
   b. ascribed
   c. shared
   d. master

5. Which of the following statements about groups is (are) true?
   a. A group is a collection of individuals who interact and communicate with each other.
   b. Group members possess a subjective awareness of themselves as a distinct social unit.
   c. Group members share a common set of goals and norms.
   d. All of the above statements are true.

6. A highly structured social grouping that forms to pursue a set of shared goals is a(n):
   a. social category.
   b. social institution.
   c. dispersed audience.
   d. formal organization.

7. Natasha is a recent immigrant who holds a college degree. She was a well-respected nurse in Russia, but she speaks limited English and is not licensed to practice nursing in the United States. She currently works as a maid, a job that carries little prestige. She is experiencing:
   a. status inconsistency.
   b. status dysfunction.
   c. role conflict.
   d. role strain.

8. Sociologists refer to those statuses that are automatically assigned to a person at birth, such as race, as:
   a. created.
   b. ascribed.
   c. achieved.
   d. secondary.

9. Mark was born with Cerebral Palsy, a physical disability that impedes his speech and mobility. Other people perceive Mark's disability as a dominant status that overrides all other features of his identity. Sociologists refer to Mark's disability as a(n):
   a. status dysfunction.
   b. achieved status.
   c. master status.
   d. organic role.

10. Your boss asked you to work this weekend, you need to study for a test, and your mother expects you to come home from college for a family celebration. You are experiencing role:
    a. strain.
    b. conflict.
    c. disruption.
    d. dysfunction.

11. According to research on interpersonal attraction and couple formation,
    a. there is considerable evidence that opposites attract.
    b. the more you see someone, the more you like them.
    c. characteristics such as race and class have relatively little influence on your selection of dating and marriage partners.
    d. All of the above statements are true.

12. Which phrase did W.I. Thomas coin to refer to the idea that if people define things as real, then they are real in their consequences?
    a. normative disruption
    b. impression management
    c. definition of the situation
    d. false construction of reality

13. According to ethnomethodologists,
    a.   social interaction is determined primarily by the rewards and punishments we receive from other people.
    b.   interpersonal attraction is determined primarily by biological and chemical processes located within the human nervous system.
    c.   the most effective technique for identifying social norms is directly asking people to identify them.
    d.   the most effective technique for identifying social norms is disrupting social settings.

14. Which of the following observations about cyberspace interaction is false?
    a.   It has resulted in the formation of a new subculture in society.
    b.   It eliminates the opportunity to develop intimate, long-term relationships.
    c.   It provides greater anonymity than do most other forms of social interaction.
    d.   It is supported by a set of beliefs and practices that encourage creating alternative identities.

15. The social positions, networks of relationships, and institutions that hold a society together and shape people's experiences make up:
    a.   a status set.
    b.   an organization.
    c.   the social structure.
    d.   the division of labor.

16. When Emily's mother asked her how she performed on her sociology test, she told her that she received a C even though she failed the test. Her mother knew that Emily was lying because the pitch and loudness of her voice betrayed her, reflecting the importance of _____ communication.
    a.   paralinguistic
    b.   proxemic
    c.   kinesic
    d.   tactile

17. Because Harry is sexually attracted to Joanne, he stands very close to her when they talk, which reflects his use of _____ communication to convey his feelings.
    a.   paralinguistic
    b.   proxemic
    c.   kinesic
    d.   tactile

18. Tactile communication refers to the:
    a.   pitch and volume of our voices when we speak.
    b.   touching we do while we interact with other people.
    c.   distance we maintain between ourselves and other people.
    d.   facial expressions and gestures we exhibit while talking to other people.

19. According to functionalist theorists, the purpose of the economic institution in the U.S. is to:
    a.   replace members of society.
    b.   maintain stability and existence.
    c.   socialize new members of society.
    d.   produce and distribute goods and services.

20. Joe notices that some boys he would like to be friends with frequently play basketball after school. Although he is not that interested in sports, Joe talks excitedly about the upcoming championship playoffs when he is with the boys so that they will invite him to join their group. According to Goffman, Joe is practicing:
   a. social deception.
   b. normative disruption.
   c. impression management.
   d. interpersonal manipulation.

True-False Questions

1. Microanalysis refers to the technique sociologists use to investigate patterns of social interaction that are relatively small, less complex, and less differentiated.

2. Like individuals, social institutions can be directly observed by people who want to study them.

3. Marilyn Frye compares the concept of social structure to a birdcage because she views both birdcages and society as havens that protect vulnerable groups from harm.

4. A gesellschaft society is held together by organic solidarity.

5. Research indicates that perceptions of physical attractiveness influence how people are evaluated and treated, with attractive children being viewed as "smarter" and more attractive adult defendants receiving lighter sentences for their crimes.

6. Most foraging and pastoral societies, such as the Pygmies and Bedouins of Africa, are nomadic.

7. Social solidarity is stronger in a gemeinschaft than in a gesselschaft society due to the greater homogeneity of the population in a gemeinshcaft.

Fill in the Blank Questions

1. Role _____ occurs when a single role consists of conflicting expectations.

2. When a person rolls his or her eyes to indicate disbelief or frowns to indicate disappointment, s/he is using _____ communication to convey information.

3. According to Durkheim, less complex, more homogeneous societies in which individuals play similar roles within the society are held together by _____ solidarity.

4. Erving Goffman's _____ model is based on the idea that members of society interact with each other in different settings as if they are actors on a stage.

5. In a(n) _____ society, a majority of workers are employed in the service sector, where they participate in producing distributing information and services, rather than tangible goods.

Essay Questions

1. Describe the basic principles of symbolic interaction theory and explain how Gilman used this theory to analyze status differences between hair stylists and their clients.

2. Compare and contrast gesellschaft and gemeinschaft societies in terms of their social organization, division of labor, degree of heterogeneity, and mechanisms of social control.
3. Identify four negative consequences of industrialization and the corresponding social problems that have developed in the United States since industrialization occurred.
4. Apply Goffman's principle of impression management to the phenomenon of cyberspace interaction and explain how the rituals of cyberculture contribute to the specific ways that individuals behave when engaged in cyberspace interaction.

ANSWERS TO PRACTICE TEST

Answers to Multiple Choice Questions

| 1. | A | 100 | The social exchange model of social interaction suggests that when an interaction elicits approval, it is more likely to be repeated than an interaction that incites disapproval. |

1. A   100   The social exchange model of social interaction suggests that when an interaction elicits approval, it is more likely to be repeated than an interaction that incites disapproval.

2. A   92   Social interaction is behavior involving communication between two or more people. Social institution is an abstract concept referring to an established, organized system of social behavior with a recognized purpose in society.

3. D   113   As indicated in Table 4.1, an industrial society uses machines and other complex technologies to produce and distribute goods, relies on a highly differentiated labor force, and uses a cash-based economy

4. A   94   Ascribed statuses, such as race and biological sex, are present at birth. Achieved statuses are gained through individual effort, such as educational attainment.

5. D   93   A group is a collection of individuals who interact and communicate with each other. Group members share goals and norms and possess a "we" feeling.

6. D   93   Social organization brings regularity and predictability to human behavior. A formal organization is a highly structured social grouping that forms to pursue a set of shared goals. A social category refers to people who are categorized together based on a shared characteristic. An audience includes all of the people watching a program or performance. A social institution is an established and organized system of behavior with a recognized purpose.

7. A   94   Status inconsistency occurs when several statuses held by one person are associated with significantly different amounts of prestige. Role conflict occurs when the expectations of multiple roles conflict, while role strain occurs when one role has conflicting expectations.

8. B   94   Statuses that are automatically assigned to a person at birth, such as race, are ascribed. Achieved statuses are gained through individual effort.

9. C   94   The dominant status for an individual, which overrides all other features of the person's identity, is a master status.

10. B   95   Role conflict occurs when multiple roles have contradictory expectations, while role strain occurs when a single role includes conflicting expectations.

11. B   106   Poximity and shared social characteristics such as race and class increase the likelihood of attraction and relationship formation.

12. C   97   W.I. Thomas argued that situations defined as real are real in their consequences This concept is known as the *definition of the situation.*

13. D   97   Because many norms are unconscious, asking people to identify them is not a useful strategy. Using the technique of ethnomethodology to disrupt social situations can reveal norms.

14. B   100   Cyberspace interaction occurs when people interact and communicate with each other electronically through the use of a personal computer. People can develop long-term, intimate relationships in cyberspace.

15.	C	109	Social structure consists of the social positions, networks of relationships, and social institutions that hold a society together. A status set is the complete set of statuses occupied by a person at a given time.
16.	A	103	Paralinguistic communication is conveyed by the pitch and loudness of the speaker's voice, as well as its rhythm, emphasis, and frequency.
17.	B	104	The amount of distance maintained between people engaged in social interaction Refers to proxemic communication. People who are sexually attracted to each other stand especially close.
18.	B	103	Tactile communication refers to physical touch, including positive (hugging) and negative (hitting) forms of touching.
19.	D	108	Functionalist theorists argue that all social institutions fulfill specific purposes in society. The economy produces and distributes goods and services, the political institution maintains stability and order, the family replaces membership and socializes members, and religion provides members with a sense of purpose.
20.	C	98	Impression management is a process by which a person consciously manipulates other people's perceptions of him or her. Goffman examined this process with his dramaturgy model of social interaction.

Answers to True-False Questions

1.	T	92	Microanalysis refers to the technique that sociologists use to investigate patterns of social interaction that are relatively small and immediately visible.
2.	F	108	Social institutions cannot be directly observed, but their impact and structure an still be studied.
3.	F	109	Frye uses the metaphor of a birdcage to describe social structure as an oppressive network that confines and exploits some social groups.
4.	T	110	A complex, diverse gesellschaft is held together by organic solidarity, whereas a more homogeneous gemeinschaft is held together by mechanical solidarity.
5.	T	107	Adults tend to treat attractive children more leniently than they do unattractive children when they misbehave.
6.	T	113	Foraging and pastoral societies have subsistence economies and are nomadic.
7.	T	110	Social solidarity is stronger in gemeinschaft societies, where the population is more homogeneous. Greater diversity in gesellschaft societies can cause conflict and social divisions that undermine solidarity.

Answers to Fill in the Blank Questions

1.	strain	95
2.	organization	93
3.	kinesic	103
4.	status	93
5.	post-industrial	114

CHAPTER 5
GROUPS AND ORGANIZATIONS

BRIEF CHAPTER OUTLINE

Types of Groups
> Dyads and Triads: Group Size Effects
> Primary and Secondary Groups
> Reference Groups
> In-Groups and Out-Groups
> Social Networks
> The Small World Problem

Social Influence
> The Bystander Intervention Problem
> The Asch Conformity Experiment
> The Milgram Obedience Studies
> Groupthink
> Risky Shift

Formal Organizations and Bureaucracies
> Types of Organizations
> Bureaucracy
> Bureaucracy's Other Face
> Problems of Bureaucracy
> The McDonaldization of Society
> New Global Organizational Forms: The Japanese Model

Diversity; Race, Gender, and Class in Organizations

Functionalist, Conflict, and Symbolic Interaction: Theoretical Perspectives

CHAPTER FOCUS: This chapter classifies types of groups and formal organizations, discusses group dynamics, and examines the emergence, characteristics, and problems of bureaucracies.

QUESTIONS TO GUIDE YOUR READING

1. What characteristics do sociologists consider necessary for a collection of individuals to be considered a group?
2. How does the size of a group influence the behavior of the people in it?
3. What are the three main types of organizations identified by sociologists, and on what basis are organizations classified?
4. What influence do race, class, and gender have on the development of social networks for individuals from diverse groups?
5. How does bureaucracy serve positive functions for organizations but also encourage the development of problems within the organization?

SOCIOLOGY IN ACTION: AN INTERNET EXERCISE

Go to www.un.org/depts/ to view the organizational structure of the United Nations, an international organization devoted to developing collaborative relationships among nations around the world. Why is this organization divided into so many different departments and offices? Why would this bureaucratic structure be useful for accomplishing numerous tasks? What kinds of problems might develop in such a large, complex organization?

attribution theory 123

bureaucracy 133

dyad 121

expressive needs 122

formal organization 131

group 121

group size effects 122

groupthink 129

instrumental needs 122

primary group 122

reference groups 122

risky shift 130

secondary groups 122

social network 125

status generalization 127

total institution 133

triad 121

triadic segregation 121

KEY PEOPLE (identified at page number shown)

Solomon Asch 127

Charles Horton Cooley 122

Erving Goffman 133

I.L. Janis 129

Stanley Milgram 127

Thomas F. Pettigrew 123

George Ritzer 136

Georg Simmel 121

James Stoner 130

Max Weber 133

Robert Wuthnow 124

Philip Zimbardo 126

CHAPTER OUTLINE

Juries are groups, and groups behave differently than individuals. Studies have shown that jury verdicts correlate not just with evidence, but also with jury composition. Because groups are influenced by social forces, sociological analyses of group decision-making processes can help predict trial outcomes.

I.   **TYPES OF GROUPS**

A **group** is two or more individuals who interact with one another, share goals and norms, and have a subjective awareness as "we." Certain gatherings are not groups, but may be *social categories*, such as truck drivers, or *audiences*, such as persons watching a movie. Sociologists are able to identify characteristics that reliably predict trends in the behavior of specific groups, as well as the behavior of particular individuals within groups.

A.   Dyads and Triads: Group Size Effects

1.   Georg Simmel investigated the effects of size on groups, noting that the difference between a **dyad** (two people) and a **triad** (three people) creates entirely different group dynamics.

2.   Simmel identified **group size effects**, noting that triads are *unstable* social groupings, whereas dyads are relatively stable, because triads tend to separate into a pair an isolate in the process of **triadic segregation**.

B.   Primary and Secondary Groups

1.   Charles Horton Cooley introduced the concept of a **primary group**, or a group consisting of intimate, face-to-face interaction and relatively long-lasting relationships, such as the family.

2.   **Secondary groups** are larger in membership, less intimate, and less permanent. Although they tend to be less significant in people's emotional lives, some secondary groups can take on the characteristics of primary groups, in times of crisis or high stress, as when a community experiences a natural disaster.

3.   Primary groups usually serve **expressive needs** and secondary groups generally serve **instrumental needs**. The difference between primary and secondary groups is less in why they form, however, than in how strongly the participants feel about each other and how dependent they are on the group for identity.

C.   Reference Groups

Reference groups are those to which you may or may not belong, but that you use as a standard for evaluating your values, attitudes, and behaviors. Imitation of reference groups can have both positive and negative effects. Identification with reference groups can strongly affect self-evaluation. For example, multicultural educational programs may help Black and Latino children develop higher self-esteem.

D.   In-Groups and Out-Groups

1.   W.I. Thomas noted that people like and trust *in-group* members, as with families and fraternities, whereas *out-group* members are often regarded with suspicion.

2.   **Attribution theory** asserts that all people make judgments about others, called *dispositional attributions.*

3.   Pettigrew's summary of research on attribution indicates that individuals commonly generate a significantly distorted perception of the motives and capabilities of other people's acts based on whether that person is an in-group or out-group member.

    a.   These misperceptions are *attribution errors*, or errors made in attributing causes for people's behavior to their membership in a particular group.

    b.   Attribution error has several dimensions, which tend to favor the in-group over the out-group.

        1)   When they observe improper behavior by an out-group member, onlookers are likely to attribute the deviance to the *disposition*, or perceived "true nature," of the wrong doer. This nature is viewed as genetically determined.

        2)   When an in-group member exhibits the same behavior, the act is commonly perceived as a result of the *situation* of the wrong doer, rather than his or her disposition.

        3)   If an out-group member performs in an exceptional way, it is often attributed to good luck, or the individual is viewed as "exceptional" for his or her group.

        4)   An in-group member who performs in the same positive way is credited for having a valued disposition.

E.   Social Networks

A **social network** is a set of links between individuals or between other social units, such as bureaucratic organizations or entire nations. Individual membership in several groups provides links between groups and groups overlap. Research indicates that people get jobs, especially high paying, prestigious jobs, via personal networks more often than through formal job listings, want ads, or placement agencies. Networks are influenced by race, class, and gender and include religious, fraternal, and occupational groups.

F.   The Small World Problem

Research into the *small world problem* indicates that networks make the world much smaller than commonly thought. Taylor's study of Black national leaders revealed that they form a closely-knit network that is considerably more dense than that of the longer-established White leadership. When considering only personal acquaintances, not including indirect links, one-fifth of the entire national Black leadership is included.

II.   **SOCIAL INFLUENCE**

The influences of our youth extend to adulthood through, for example, our choices of political party and religious affiliation, which correlate strongly with those of our parents. Research reveals gaps between what people think they will do and what they actually do in some situations.

A.   The Bystander Intervention Problem

Bystander intervention studies examine the dynamics of when and how people come to the aid of someone in trouble. One example of a **group size effect** is that the failure of bystanders to offer help to someone on the street who is in danger directly correlates with an increase in the group's size.

B. The Asch Conformity Experiment
1. Solomon Asch designed an experiment showing that even simple objective facts cannot withstand the distorting pressure of group influence. Rather mild social pressure was sufficient to cause an astonishing rise in the number of wrong answers participants gave during the study.
2. Individuals accorded higher status tend to have even more influence on small groups than those of lesser status. **Status generalization** occurs when the status hierarchy in a society has a measurable effect on behavior within a closed group.

C. The Milgram Obedience Studies
1. Stanley Milgram's research on obedience to authority reveals the personal dilemma caused by conflicts between conscience and authority. His interest in conformity developed when people were trying to understand why members of Hitler's army in Nazi Germany engaged in brutality toward Jews.
2. In Milgram's experiments, subjects believed that they were administering an increasingly powerful set of electric shocks to another subject under the direction of the researcher.
3. Sixty-five percent of the original volunteer subjects obeyed the researcher, believing that they had administered shocks of 450 volts to the test subjects. Surprisingly, gender, race, class, and ethnic differences had no detectable effect on subjects' compliance rates.

D. Groupthink
1. I.L. Janis described **groupthink** as the common tendency for group members to reach a consensus opinion, even if that decision is stupid.
2. In his investigation of presidential decisions, Janis found that the process of groupthink is more likely to occur under four conditions.
    a. Group members possess **an illusion of invulnerability**, believing that members are so talented that any group decision will succeed.
    b. Group members develop **a falsely negative impression of those who are antagonists to the group's plans**, which results in an underestimation of their strength and power.
    c. Groups **discourage dissenting opinions,** and view dissent as disloyalty, thereby prohibiting a full discussion of alternative strategies.
    d. Group members develop **an illusion of unanimity**, so that despite the personal reservations of some group members, there is a prevailing sense that the entire group is in complete agreement.

E. Risky Shift
Risky shift, also called *polarization shift*, is another group phenomenon that helps explain why the products of groupthink are frequently calamities. Risky shift is the tendency for groups to weigh risk differently than individuals. The risky shift is probably caused by *group-size effect* known as *deindividuation*, which is the sense that one's self has merged with the group.

III. **FORMAL ORGANIZATIONS AND BUREAUCRACIES**
A **formal organization** is a large, secondary group, highly organized to accomplish a complex task and achieve goals in an efficient manner. Although an organization is ultimately a collection of people, organizations develop their own routine practices and cultures that may be reflected in symbols, values, rituals, and norms.
A. Types of Organizations
1. People voluntarily join normative organizations to receive personal satisfaction and pursue goals they personally consider worthwhile.

        a.   Examples include service and charitable organizations such as the PTA, the National Organization for Women (NOW), and the NAACP (National Association for the Advancement of Colored People).

        b.   Gender, class, race, and ethnicity structure who joins which voluntary organizations. Lower-income people cannot afford membership in many organizations. Due to their historical exclusion from White voluntary organizations, many racial-ethnic minority groups formed their own.

    2.   Membership in coercive organizations, such as prisons and mental hospitals, is largely involuntary. Goffman described these organizations as **total institutions**, or organizations cut off from the rest of society where residents are subject to strict social control over all aspects of their lives.

    3.   Utilitarian organizations are large organizations, either for profit (e.g., Microsoft) or nonprofit (e.g., colleges), that individuals voluntary join for specific purposes, such as monetary reward.

B.   Bureaucracy

A **bureaucracy** is a type of formal organization characterized by an authority hierarchy, a clear division of labor, explicit rules, and impersonality. An example is the federal government. Max Weber identified the characteristics of the *ideal type* bureaucracy.

    1.   There is a *high degree of division of labor and specialization* with clearly defined responsibilities and privileges.

    2.   There is a *hierarchy of authority* that is often depicted in a complex organizational chart, which is a diagram identifying the position of each participant in the chain of command.

    3.   There are detailed *rules and regulations*, designed to handle virtually all situations and problems that govern the activities of a bureaucracy.

    4.   Establishing efficient *impersonal relationships* is important because social interaction in a bureaucracy is supposed to be guided by instrumental criteria, such as organizational rules, rather than by social or emotional criteria.

    5.   *Career ladders* are created within bureaucracies where job candidates are supposed to be hired and promoted on the basis of their qualifications.

    6.   *Efficiency* is important to coordinate the activities of a large number of people who are pursuing organizational goals.

C.   Bureaucracy's Other Face

    1.   In addition to the formal structure of a bureaucracy, an *informal structure* exists, which includes social interactions in bureaucracies that ignore, change, or otherwise bypass the formal structure and rules of the organization.

    2.   *Bureaucracy's other face*, or the informally evolved culture that evolves over time as a reaction to the formality and impersonality of the bureaucracy, can be seen in the workplace subcultures that develop.

    3.   The informal culture may become exclusionary, thereby increasing some workers' feelings of isolation, as when sexual harassment is allowed to occur.

    4.   The informal norms that develop within a bureaucracy may cause worker productivity to change, dependent upon the norms and how they are informally enforced. In the Hawthorne Studies, for example, researchers found that workers who produced too much or too little each day were labeled or ridiculed by others.

D.   Problems of Bureaucracies

    1.   Several problems, including the risky shift in work groups and the development of groupthink, develop from the nature of the complex bureaucracy.

    2.   Another problem in bureaucracies is *organizational ritualism*, which refers to workers' rigid adherence to the rules, regardless of whether their behavior accomplishes the purpose for which the rule was originally designed.

        a.   The 1986 explosion of the Space Shuttle *Challenger* was caused by a problem with the "O-ring" gasket on the solid fuel booster rockets, which NASA managers and engineers were aware of as a potential problem.

        b.   Such rigid group conformity within an organizational setting can lead to deviant behavior being redefined so that it is perceived as normal.

3.   Alienation also develops within bureaucracies. It is characterized by the individual becoming psychologically separated from the organization and its goals, which may result in increased turnover, tardiness, absenteeism, and overall dissatisfaction with the organization.

E.   The McDonaldization of Society

1.   George Ritzer used the term the *McDonaldization of society* to describe the phenomenon whereby the principles that characterize fast food organizations increasingly dominate more aspects of American society. The four features are:

        a.   **efficiency**: things move from start to completion in a standardized, streamlined way, often with machines or customers doing work once done by an employee;

        b.   **calculability**: emphasis is placed on the quantitative aspects of products sold, including size, cost, and time of production, rather than quality;

        c.   **predictability**: assurance that products will be exactly the same, regardless of where or when purchased, is offered; and

        d.   **control**: the primary organizational principle of McDonaldization, control refers to the reduction of people's behavior to a series of machine-like actions. Both customers and workers are carefully monitored in these organizations.

2.   McDonaldization brings benefits, such as greater availability of goods and services to a wider portion of the population and instantaneous service and convenience to a public with less free time. Additionally, there is predictability and familiarity in the goods bought and sold, and standardization of pricing and uniform quality of the goods.

3.   McDonaldization also has disadvantages, such as a danger of dehumanization of workers and the threat of loss of creativity as people accept increasingly standardized products and services.

4.   Ritzer's theory is based on Weber's prediction that human behavior would be increasingly guided by rational systems -- rules, regulations, and formal structures -- rather than by abstract values.

F.   New Global Organizational Forms: The Japanese Model

1.   At one time, managers in the United States used *Theory X* to guide their behavior. Theory X was based on a belief that workers do not care about the organization, but only about their personal needs, and will only work when they are rigidly monitored and controlled.

2.   An alternative view, *Theory Y*, suggests that people have a desire to work and be responsible, but become passive and irresponsible because of their experience within the organization. Management's task is to organize things so that people can accomplish both the personal and organizational goals.

3.   There has been increasing interest in *Theory Z*, which is the organizational form used by many Japanese corporations and recently adopted by some American companies. This approach is based on long-term employment, interpersonal trust, and close personal relationships at work, features that appear to decrease feelings of alienation while increasing solidarity among workers.

IV. DIVERSITY: RACE, GENDER, AND CLASS IN ORGANIZATIONS

The hierarchical structuring of positions within organizations, which concentrates power and influence in the hands of a few individuals at the top, reflects the inequality in race, gender, and class relations evident throughout society. Traditionally, White men of upper class status have held the most powerful positions in organizations. A "glass ceiling," or invisible barrier, has prevented women and racial minorities from gaining access to higher ranks of management; however, the greater the involvement of the federal government in a given industry, the more favorable jobs and earnings are for these groups. Kanter found that *token* employees, who comprise a small percent of the employees hired and are viewed as representing all women or racial minorities, have difficulty gaining credibility in the organization and experience stress as a result. Social class plays a similar role in determining people's place within organizations, because middle and upper class employees tend to make higher wages and salaries and receive more promotions than people of lower social class status. Thus, class stratification produces differences in the opportunities and life chances of individuals.

V. FUNCTIONALIST, CONFLICT, AND SYMBOLIC INTERACTION: THEORETICAL PERSPECTIVES

All three major sociological perspectives are exhibited in the analysis of formal organizations and bureaucracies [Table 5.1]. The functionalist perspective argues that certain positive functions, called *eufunctions*, characterize bureaucracies and contribute to the overall unity of the bureaucracy. The bureaucracy exists to accomplish these eufunctions, including efficiency, control, impersonal relations, and the chance for the individual to develop a career in the bureaucracy. The conflict perspective argues that the hierarchical nature of the bureaucracy encourages conflict among the individuals within it, which interferes with the smooth and efficient running of the bureaucracy. The symbolic interaction perspective, which underlies Theories Y and Z, stresses the role of the self in any group, especially how the self develops as a product of social interaction.

PRACTICE TEST

Multiple Choice Questions

1. Which of the following statements about juries is (are) true?
    a. As groups, juries behave differently than do the individual members who comprise each jury.
    b. Sociologists can make educated predictions about who will become the most influential member in a jury.
    c. Jury verdicts correlate not only with the evidence, but also with the racial-ethnic and gender composition of the jury.
    d. All of the above statements are true.

2. A group is a collection of individuals who:
    a. regularly interact with each other.
    b. share a subjective sense of "we."
    c. share norms and goals.
    d. All of the above are features of groups.

3. Simmel identified the tendency for triads to separate into a pair and an isolate as triadic:
    a. aggregation.
    b. segregation.
    c. alignment.
    d. isolation.

4. A group consisting of intimate, face-to-face interaction and relatively long-lasting relationships, such as a family, is a(n):
    a. secondary group.
    b. social category.
    c. primary group.
    d. audience.

5. Which of the following statement about secondary groups is true?
    a. They serve primarily instrumental or task-oriented needs.
    b. They generally have fewer members than do primary groups.
    c. They tend to have long-lasting, powerful influences on their members' self-concepts.
    d. None of the above statements are true.

6. Although James has never met or interacted with a professional athlete, he reveres major league baseball players and uses them as a standard for determining his own values about physical fitness and good sportsmanship. For James, professional athletes represent a _____ group.
    a. secondary
    b. reference
    c. primary
    d. ideal

7. Because of *attribution error*, when people observe an *in-group* member behaving in an exceptional manner, they attribute the behavior to the:
    a. person's good luck.
    b. influence of a supreme deity.
    c. situation in which the behavior occurs.
    d. person's good disposition or "true nature."

8. When a person is prejudiced toward a particular *out-group* and observes a member of that group behaving in a positive, non-stereotypical manner, the observer will probably:
    a. dismiss his/her prejudice about the out-group because s/he realizes that the stereotype is based on inaccurate information.
    b. retain his/her original prejudice because s/he will assume that the behavior was a special exception to the person's usual behavior.
    c. attempt to become a member of the out-group so that s/he can better understand the members' perspectives and experiences.
    d. consult members of his/her in-group about the observation to evaluate the new information more objectively.

9. The set of links between individuals or other social units, such as bureaucratic organizations or entire nations, is referred to as a:
    a. global form.
    b. social network.
    c. social organization.
    d. dispositional network.

10. The tendency for group members to reach a consensus opinion, even if the decision is stupid, is referred to as:
    a. generalization.
    b. polarization.
    c. groupthink.
    d. attribution.

11. Wuthnow's study of small group membership in the United States indicates that:
    a. membership in formal religious organizations has increased as the society has become more remote and alienating.
    b. very few people voluntarily participate in any type of small group today because these groups threaten American's strong sense of individuality and personal freedom.
    c. a growing number of people have joined recovery and reading groups in their communities to garner emotional support in an increasingly impersonal society.
    d. the common assumption that geographic mobility and modernization have eroded the family's role in providing a sense of belonging and integration for individuals is a myth.

12. The Marriot Corporation now provides the same food to students and staff at over 500 college campuses across the United States. George Ritzer suggests that the predictability and uniformity associated with these meals is due to the process known as the:
    a. Bureaucratization of society.
    b. McDonaldization of society.
    c. Monopolization of society.
    d. Ritualization of society.

13. According to Goffman, which of the following statements about people who enter total institutions is true?
    a. Most people who enter total institutions do so voluntarily.
    b. The main reason that people enter total institutions is to gain personal satisfaction.
    c. When people enter total institutions, they are subjected to practices designed to make them surrender their former identities.
    d. All of the above statements about participation in total institutions are true.

14. According to Max Weber's ideal type, which of the following is (are) typical of a bureaucracy?
    a. extensive, detailed lists of rules and procedures
    b. cooperative, non-hierarchical management styles
    c. low degree of division of labor and specialization
    d. All of the above are typical characteristics of a bureaucracy.

15. The informally evolved culture that develops over time as a reaction to the formality and impersonality of bureaucracy represents:
    a. the McDonaldization of society.
    b. bureaucracy's other face.
    c. the small world problem.
    d. groupthink.

16. That NASA proceeded with the *Challenger* launch despite signs of potential danger illustrates:
    a. ritualism.
    b. alienation.
    c. rate busting.
    d. rationalization.

17. Which common problem is developing when individuals become psychologically separated from a bureaucratic organization and its goals and there is an increase in tardiness and absenteeism?
   a. ritualism
   b. alienation
   c. rate busting
   d. rationalization

18. According to George Ritzer, the *McDonaldization* of society is characterized by an increasing emphasis on the:
   a. level of creativity encouraged by management.
   b. range of choice provided to the customers.
   c. quantity of the products created.
   d. quality of the products created.

19. According to Theory Y:
   a. people are passive and irresponsible by nature.
   b. people are responsible and have a desire to be creative.
   c. people will only work when they are rigidly monitored and controlled.
   d. management's sole task is to further the organization's goals at any cost.

20. The symbolic interaction perspective:
   a. assumes that people hate their jobs and try to avoid working and taking responsibility.
   b. stresses the role of the self in any group, especially how the self develops as a product of social interaction.
   c. argues that bureaucracies exist to accomplish positive functions such as efficiency, control, and impersonal relations.
   d. All of the above statements reflect the basic assumptions of symbolic interaction theory.

21. Which of the following characteristics increases the likelihood that groupthink will occur?
   a. a full discussion of all possible options
   b. an illusion of invulnerability
   c. an illusion of disunity
   d. All of the above contribute to the development of groupthink.

22. The Black sorority known as the Deltas is a(n) _____ organization whose members voluntary join the organization primarily for personal fulfillment.
   a. total
   b. coercive
   c. utilitarian
   d. normative

True-False Questions

1. The size of a group has relatively little effect on how members of the group behave.

2. In times of crisis or high stress, such as a natural disaster, some secondary groups can take on the characteristics of primary groups.

3. Simmel noted that a triad is inherently unstable, whereas dyads are relatively stable groups.

4. In his *risky shift* experiments, Stoner found that Americans are less likely to take greater risks as members of a group than as individuals.

5. A total institution is a charitable organization such as NOW or the NAACP, that people voluntary join because they support the organizations' goals.

6. In his conformity studies, Milgram found that the race and sex of the subjects had no significant effect on whether they would comply with the request to administer shocks during the experiment.

7. Choices of political party and religious affiliation in adulthood correlate strongly with those of one's parents.

8. Informal norms within a bureaucracy are almost always beneficial to management because they usually contribute to increased productivity.

9. Research indicates that people get high-paying, prestigious jobs through formal job listings, want ads, and placement agencies more often than through personal networks.

10. Theory X views workers as irresponsible, concerned only about their own needs, and in need of close monitoring.

Fill in the Blank Questions

1. Risky shift is caused partly by _____, a process in which a person perceives his or her own identity as merging with the group.

2. A _____ group is a group to which you may or may not belong, but that you use as a standard for evaluating your values, attitudes, and behaviors.

3. Status _____ occurs when the status hierarchy in society has a measurable effect on behavior within a closed group, as illustrated by the greater influence of men than women on the small groups in Asch's Conformity Experiment.

Essay Questions

1. Provide evidence to support George Ritzer's argument that American society resembles fast-food organizations such as McDonald's.
2. Use the principles of attribution theory to explain why racial prejudice persists.
3. Explain how group size contributes to the *bystander intervention problem.*
4. Identify the four specific conditions that tend to promote *groupthink* according to Janis, and give an example of a real situation in which groupthink produced a poor decision.
5. Identify the six characteristics of bureaucracy according to Weber and explain how each feature supports the goals of bureaucratic organizations.

ANSWERS TO PRACTICE TEST

Answers to Multiple Choice Questions

1. D   120   Juries are groups, and groups behave differently than individuals. Predictions can be made about who will become the most influential jury member, and jury composition is related to the verdict rendered.

2. D   121   A group is a collection of individuals who interact with each other and share goals and norms. A group also has a subjective awareness of "we." By contrast, an audience is an example of a social category, rather than a group.

3. B.   121   A triad is an unstable group with a tendency to segregate into a pair (a dyad) and an isolate, resulting in triadic segregation.

4. C   122   According to Cooley, a group consisting of intimate, face-to-face interaction and relatively long-lasting relationships is a primary group. It usually consists of fewer members than a secondary group, and is concerned primarily with meeting members' expressive needs.

5. A   122   Secondary groups are generally less permanent and larger than primary groups and primarily serve members' instrumental needs.

6. B   122   Reference groups are those to which you may or may not belong, but that you use as a standard for evaluating your values, attitudes, and behaviors. They may have both positive and negative influences on individual behavior.

7. D   123   Attribution errors include the following: If an in-group member performs in an exceptional way, they are given credit for a valued disposition. Also, when observing improper behavior by an out-group member, onlookers are likely to attribute the deviance to the disposition of the wrong doer. If an out-group member performs in an exceptional way, it is often attributed to good luck or the individual is viewed as "exceptional." When observing improper behavior by an in-group member, onlookers are likely to attribute the behavior to the situation of the wrong doer.

8. B   123   If an out-group member behaves in an exceptional way, the person is often perceived as an exception to the rule or as exceptionally lucky.

9. B   125   A set of links between individuals or between other social units, such as bureaucratic organizations or entire nations, is a social network. Social network membership varies by gender, race, and class.

10. C   129   Janis argues that groupthink results from an illusion of invulnerability, a falsely negative impression of those who are antagonistic toward the group's plans, discouragement of dissenting opinion, and an illusion of unanimity.

11. C   124   Wuthnow's research on small group participation indicates that an increasing number of people have joined small recovery, reading, and spiritual groups in their search for emotional support, commitment, and meaning. These groups provide a sense of belonging and integration in an otherwise impersonal society, and individuals are free to leave the group if it no longer meets their needs. The role of the family as a source of integration has been eroded by several fundamental changes in society, including geographic mobility.

12. B   136   George Ritzer identified four dimensions of the McDonalidization process: efficiency, calculability, predictability, and control.

13. C   133   Goffman referred to coercive organizations as *total institutions*, such as prisons and mental hospitals. Most people enter these organizations involuntarily and must surrender their former identities and rights to privacy, which is facilitated by subjecting them to "degradation ceremonies."

14.   A   133   A bureaucracy is an organizational form characterized by an authority hierarchy, clear division of labor, explicit rules, and impersonality.

15.   B   134   The informally evolved culture that develops over time as a reaction to the formality and impersonality of the bureaucracy is *bureaucracy's other face*. McDonaldization refers to the tendency for features of the fast-food business to be adopted in the larger society. The small world problem refers to the high density of social networks in the U.S., particularly among African Americans. Groupthink refers to the tendency of groups to urge consensus among the participants, even if a poor decision is the result.

16.   A   135   Problems that may develop from the nature of bureaucracy include alienation, ritualism, and groupthink. The Challenger accident reflects workers' and managers' rigid adherence to rules, or *organizational ritualism*.

17.   B   136   Alienation may be widespread in organizations where individuals have little control over their work and engage in repetitive tasks. It results from worker's psychological separation from the organization and its goals.

18.   D   136   McDonaldization stresses quantity over quality of products. It involves greater Control, resulting in less worker autonomy and fewer choices for customers.

19.   B   137   According to Theory Y and Theory Z, management should encourage workers' personal development while furthering the organization's goals. Theory Y states that people have a desire to work, but become passive and irresponsible because of their experiences with the organization. According to Theory X, workers need to be rigidly monitored and controlled.

20.   B   141   The symbolic interaction perspective stresses the role of the self in any group, Especially how the self develops as a product of social interaction. This perspective underlies two management theories, Theory Y and Theory Z.

21.   B   129   Groupthink, the tendency for group members to reach a consensus opinion, is likely to occur when there is an illusion of invulnerability, a falsely negative impression of those who are antagonists to the group's plans, discouragement of dissenting opinion, and an illusion of unanimity.

22.   D   131   People generally join normative, or voluntary, organizations to pursue personal fulfillment, and utilitarian organizations for rewards such as wages. Membership in coercive organizations is usually involuntary.

Answers to True-False Questions

1.   F   149   Simmel noted that group size influences group behavior. The group size effect is reflected in both the bystander intervention problem and triadic segregation.

2.   T   122   Secondary groups may take on the characteristics of primary groups in certain social situations.

3.   T   121   Simmel noted that a triad is an unstable grouping that tends to separate into a dyad (pair) and an isolate (individual).

4.   F   130   Americans are more likely to take risks, such as streaking, when they are in groups because they experience deindividuation, or the merging of the self with the group, coupled with a decreased sense of personal responsibility.

5.   F   133   Goffman referred to coercive organizations, such as prisons and mental hospitals, as total institutions. People do not usually join these organizations voluntarily. People voluntarily join charitable, or normative, organizations, such as NOW and the NAACP, for personal fulfillment.

6.   T   129   Milgram did not detect any significant effects of race, class, or gender on the research subjects' behavior in his studies of conformity.

7.	T	122	Primary groups such as the family have a powerful influence on people's values and behavior throughout their lives.
8.	F	134	The informal norms that develop as a result of bureaucracy's other face may lead to exclusionary practices and reduced worker productivity.
9.	F	125	Research indicates that people get jobs, especially high-paying, prestigious jobs, via personal networks rather than through formal job listings.
10.	T	136	Theory X views workers as irresponsible and in need of close monitoring.

Answers to Fill in the Blank Questions

1.	deindividuation	130
2.	reference	122
3.	generalization	127

CHAPTER 6
DEVIANCE AND CRIMINAL JUSTICE

BRIEF CHAPTER OUTLINE

Defining Deviance
  Sociological Perspectives on Deviance
  Psychological Explanations of Deviance
Sociological Theories of Deviance
  Functionalist Theories of Deviance
  Conflict Theories of Deviance
  Symbolic Interaction Theories of Deviance
Forms of Deviance
  Mental Illness
  Social Stigma
Crime and Criminal Justice
  Crime: How Much Is There?
  Race, Class, Gender, and Crime
  The Criminal Justice System
Deviance and Crime in Global Perspective: Terrorism and International Crime Networks

CHAPTER FOCUS: This chapter examines deviance from a sociological perspective, which emphasizes that deviant behavior has its origins in social conditions. This chapter also classifies various types of crime and discusses how deviant behavior is managed by the American criminal justice system.

QUESTIONS TO GUIDE YOUR READING
1.   What is the *medicalization of deviance* and why do sociologists find it problematic?
2.   How can social movements influence changes in the classification and management of certain behaviors as deviant?
3.   How do race, class, and gender shape perceptions of, reactions to, and participation in deviant and criminal behavior?
4.   What are the main sources of data that researchers use to assess the prevalence of crime in the United States, and what are the limitations of those data?
5.   What types of crimes are especially likely to cross national borders today, and what social conditions make the development of international crime networks possible?

SOCIOLOGY IN ACTION: AN INTERNET EXERCISE
Go to www.nami.org to learn more about social stigma from the National Alliance for the Mentally Ill (NAMI), a non-profit organization that provides advocacy and support for people with mental illness and their families. What suggestions does this organization make for reducing the stigma associated with having a mental illness? Which of NAMI's recommendations focus on changes at the individual level, and which focus on societal level changes?

KEY TERMS (defined at page number shown and in glossary)

altruistic suicide 152	anomic suicide 152
anomie 152	crime 161
deviance 147	deviant career 157
deviant community 157	deviant identity 157
differential association theory 156	egoistic suicide 152
elite deviance 154	hate crime 161
labeling theory 156	master status 160

KEY PEOPLE (identified at page number shown)

CHAPTER OUTLINE

From a sociological perspective, any deviance, including cannibalism, resides not in the act itself but in the social context in which it occurs. Social attitudes and beliefs contribute to the number of people who violate specific norms, as well as the way in which society's members respond to deviance.

I.   **DEFINING DEVIANCE**

    Sociologists define **deviance** as behavior that is recognized as violating expected rules and norms. Sociological understandings of deviance stress social context, not individual behavior, recognizing that established rules and norms are socially created, rather than just morally decreed or individually imposed. All groups do not judge all behaviors similarly, and some groups have more power than others to define behaviors as deviant.

    A.   Sociological Perspectives on Deviance

        1.   Sociologists distinguish between *formal deviance*, which is behavior that breaks laws or official rules and elicits formal sanctions (such as fines or imprisonment), and *informal deviance*, which is behavior that violates customary norms, such as body piercing or dyeing one's hair pink.

        2.   The meaning of deviant behavior is not just in the violation of norms, but also in how people react to the behavior.

        3.   Behavior that is deviant in one circumstance may be normal in another, or behaviors may be ruled deviant only when performed by certain people, reflecting the importance of social context in sociological analyses of deviance.

            a.   A heterosexual couple who kisses in public are viewed as romantic, while a homosexual couple who displays such affection is deviant.

            b.   The definition of deviance can vary over time, which is reflected in the relatively recent criminalization of date rape.

            c.   The student subculture on college campuses often encourages and praises excessive drinking.

        4.   Emile Durkheim argued that deviance is "functional" for society because the social order is threatened by deviance, so judging and punishing deviant acts confirms social standards and produces social solidarity by integrating people into society. This point was clearly illustrated by the public displays of patriotism after the September 11, 2001 terrorist actions against the United States.

        5.   *Social movements*, or networks of groups that organize to support or resist changes in society, may influence perceptions of deviance. For example, MADD (Mothers Against Drunk Driving) has changed public perceptions of drunk driving, resulting in increased legal penalties and social stigma for drunk drivers.

        6.   The public commonly understands deviance as the result of individualistic or personality factors and labels deviants "crazy" or "sick."

        7.   Rather than viewing gang membership, for example, as the irrational behavior of maladjusted youth, sociologists understand it as adaptive behavior that develops in the context of particular kinds of social relationships and social arrangements.

B. Psychological Explanations of Deviance

    1. Sociologists have been critical of psychological explanations of deviance, which emphasize individual factors as the underlying cause of deviant behavior, because they overlook the context in which deviance is produced.

    2. The **medicalization of deviance** refers to the popularity of explanations of deviant behavior that interpret deviance as the result of individual pathology, an approach that focuses on the physical or genetic roots of deviant behavior.

    3. Sociologists integrate individual factors into explanations of deviance that emphasize the social context of the behavior. For example, although alcoholism has medical consequences, successful treatment requires that the social relationships, social conditions, and social habits of alcoholics be altered.

II. SOCIOLOGICAL THEORIES OF DEVIANCE

A. Functionalist Theories of Deviance

Functionalist theory interprets all parts of society, including deviance, as contributing to the stability of the whole. Deviance creates social cohesion, clarifies society's norms, and affirms the collective identity of the group when those who are defined as deviant are labeled or condemned [Table 6.1].

    1. Durkheim developed his analysis of deviance through his study of suicide, in which he was critical of psychological interpretations of suicide. He developed an alternative, sociological explanation that emphasized the role of social structure in producing deviance, noting that suicide is a social phenomenon.

        a. Durkheim investigated causes of suicide related to time and place, rather than emotional stress, and identified the importance of social attachments in preventing or producing deviant behavior such as suicide.

        b. Durkheim analyzed three types of suicide: anomic suicide, altruistic suicide, and egoistic suicide.

            1) **Anomie** is the condition which exists when social regulations in a society breakdown so that people exist in a state of relative normlessness. **Anomic suicide** occurs when the disintegrating forces in society make individuals feel lost or all alone, as in the case of students on college campuses who commit suicide.

            2) **Altruistic suicide** occurs when there is excessive regulation of individuals by social forces. For example, the terrorists who hijacked and crashed 4 airplanes during the September 11 tragedy were willing to kill themselves to achieve their goals.

            3) **Egoistic suicide** occurs when people feel totally detached from society. For example, the high rate of suicide among elderly men in the United States, who often lose their work roles and have weakened ties to family and community, may be egoistic.

        c. The concept of anomie has implications beyond suicide. Although anomie is reflected in how individuals feel, its origins are in society, where there may be unclear or conflicting norms. Anomie is related to a variety of social problems, including juvenile delinquency.

    2. Robert Merton's **structural strain theory** traces the origins of deviance to the tensions caused by the gap between cultural goals and the means people have to achieve those goals.

        a. Societies are characterized by *culture*, which establishes goals for both people and society, and *social structure*, which provides (or fails to provide) the means for people to achieve these goals.

        b. When the means are out of balance with the goals, deviance is likely to occur. For example, prostitutes accept the goals of society but lack the means to achieve those goals, so they develop creative, although illegitimate, means of economic support.

3. Social control theory, developed by Travis Hirschi, posits that deviance occurs when an individual's or group's attachment to social bonds is weakened. This theory, which assumes there is a common value system within society and that deviance derives from breaking one's allegiance to that system, can help explain why 2 teen boys committed murder and suicide at a Littleton, Colorado school.

4. Functionalists emphasize that social structure, not just individual motivation, produces deviance, and deviance may be functional for society. Although individuals choose to behave in a deviant manner, they make their choices from among socially structured options. Critics of functionalism argue that it does not explain how norms of deviance are established, nor does it explain why some behaviors are defined as normative and others as illegitimate.

B. Conflict Theories of Deviance

1. *Conflict theory* emphasizes the unequal distribution of power and resources in society, arguing that the economic organization of capitalist societies produces deviance and crime [Table 6.1].

    a. The dominant class controls societal resources and uses its power to create values and belief systems that support that power.

    b. The ruling class develops mechanisms to protect their own interests, such as the law. For example, wealthy, powerful individuals and organizations regularly commit **elite deviance** (also called *corporate crime*) within the legitimate context of doing business, yet these acts often go unpunished.

2. Conflict theory also emphasizes the significance of **social control**, or the process by which groups are brought into conformity with dominant social expectations, noting that *social control agents* (such as police and social workers) regulate and administer responses to deviance.

3. The strength of conflict theory is its insight into the significance of power relationships for the definition, identification, and handling of deviance. It offers a powerful analysis of crime among low-income groups, but is less effective in explaining delinquency among middle class adolescents, for example.

C. Symbolic Interaction Theories of Deviance

1. Symbolic interaction theory argues that people behave as they do because of the meanings people attribute to situations. W.I. Thomas used *situational analysis* to understand deviant behavior within its social framework, arguing that deviance is a normal response to the social conditions in which people find themselves.

2. **Differential association theory**, developed by Edwin Sutherland, interprets deviance as learned through interaction with others, offering a powerful explanation for how deviance is culturally transmitted through social groups.

3. **Labeling theory** interprets the responses of others as the most significant factor in understanding how deviant behavior is created and sustained.

    a. Certain social groups and institutions, including the police, courts, health care professionals, and teachers, have the power to label people deviant and impose sanctions.

    b. Once a deviant label is applied, it is difficult for the deviant to recover a nondeviant identity, even if the person did not actually engage in the behavior for which the label was assigned.

4. **Deviant identity** is the definition a person has of himself or herself as deviant. The formation of a deviant identity involves a process of social transformation resulting in the person who was labeled assuming a personal identity consistent with the label.

5. A **deviant career** is the sequence of movements people make through a particular subculture of deviance. Within deviant careers, people are socialized into new roles and may have to demonstrate their commitment to superiors by securing a label.

6. **Deviant communities** such as gangs maintain their own values, norms, and rewards for deviant behavior. Joining a deviant community can shut a person off from conventional society and solidify a deviant career.

7. Labeling theorists question the value of official statistics as indicators of the true extent of deviance because this information is produced by the people who have the power to label and sanction deviance. Because authorities define, classify, and record only certain behaviors as deviant, the death of one person may be classified as a "suicide" while a similar death of someone else may be classified as an "accident."

8. The strength of labeling theory is its recognition that social definitions about presumably deviant behavior have powerful social effects. However, labeling theory neglects to explain why deviance occurs in the first place and fails to explain why officials define only some behaviors as deviant or criminal.

III. **FORMS OF DEVIANCE**
   A.   Mental Illness
       1.   Sociological explanations of mental illness examine the social systems in which mental illness is defined, identified, and treated.
       2.   Research indicates that lower-income people, women, and racial minorities are more likely to be labeled mentally ill.
           a.   These groups may have a higher rate of mental illness resulting from higher levels of stress associated with oppressive social conditions.
           b.   It may be that some behavior is labeled as mental illness for some groups but tolerated in others.

   B.   Social Stigmas
       1.   A **stigma** is an attribute that is socially devalued and discredited, such as a physical disability. That disability can become the **master status** for a person, or the characteristic that overrides all other features of their identity.
       2.   Seen by others as deficient or inferior, stigmatized individuals may get caught in a role imposed by the stigma and attempt to hide their stigmas.

IV. **CRIME AND CRIMINAL JUSTICE**
The concept of deviance is broad and encompasses many forms of behavior, legal and illegal, ordinary and usual. **Crime** is deviant behavior that violates criminal laws. Although each sociological perspective explains crime differently, sociology traces criminal behavior to social conditions rather than the intrinsic characteristics or tendencies of individuals.
   A.   Crime: How Much Is There?
       1.   The *FBI Uniform Crime Reports*, which are published annually, show that violent crime increased until 1990 but has since decreased in all categories except rape and aggravated assault [Figure 6.1].
       2.   National victimization surveys show that people are less likely today than twenty years ago to report that they have been victimized by crime.
       3.   The FBI distinguishes between *personal crimes*, which are crimes directed against people (including murder, aggravated assault, forcible rape, and robbery), and *property crimes*, which involve theft of property without threat of bodily harm (including burglary, larceny, auto theft, and arson).
       4.   **Hate crimes**, which have been increasing in recent years, refer to assaults and other malicious acts motivated by various forms of bias, including those based on race, ethnicity, religion, sexual orientation, or disability.
       5.   The FBI's serious crime list does not include *victimless crimes*, or those that violate laws but have no complainant, such as gambling and prostitution.

6. "White-collar crime" refers to criminal activities by people of high social status who commit their crimes in the context of their occupations, such as illegal stock manipulation and embezzlement. Although this type of crime has serious financial consequences for society, it is the least investigated, least prosecuted, and least likely to generate great public concern.

7. Organized crime, or crime committed by organized groups, typically involves the provision of illegal goods (such as drugs) and services (such as prostitution) to others. Organized crime syndicates are often based on racial-ethnic membership and structured along the same lines as legitimate business corporations.

8. **Organizational deviance** is wrongdoing that occurs within the context of a formal organization and is sanctioned by the norms and operating principles of that organization.

    a. Individual workers within the organization may not be aware that they are engaging in illegitimate behavior because the behavior becomes institutionalized as routine procedure, or "business as usual." This was the case at Bridgestone/Firestone, where executives were aware of a manufacturing flaw in tires that caused certain vehicles to capsize.

    b. Organizations may be fined for such deviant actions, but individual perpetrators within corporations or governments are rarely punished.

B.   Race, Class, Gender, and Crime

1. Certain groups are more likely to commit crimes than others because crime is linked to patterns of social inequality. For example, unemployment is correlated with poverty, both of which are related to participation in crime.

2. Those who are economically deprived often feel no alternative to crime. Arrest rates are strongly correlated with social class, with the poor being more likely than other income groups to be arrested, prosecuted, convicted, and sentenced to prison for crimes.

3. Law enforcement is concentrated in areas populated by lower-income and racial-ethnic minority residents, placing higher-income and White people further from police scrutiny. Interestingly, Black people and groups with the lowest incomes are also more likely to be the *victims* of crime [Figure 6.2 and Figure 6.3].

4. As labeling theory would predict, police discretion in making arrests (especially for minor offenses such as disorderly conduct) is strongly influenced by class and race judgments, with Blacks twice as likely to be arrested for crime as Whites.

5. Except for a few crimes (including fraud, shoplifting, and prostitution), women commit fewer crimes than men, although the number of women arrested for crime has increased slightly in recent years.

    a. Women's lower crime participation may reflect their socialization into less risk-taking roles. Furthermore, the crimes women do commit are generally extensions of their gender roles in society.

    b. Women's increased participation in crime may be related to the changing self-images of women in society; increased employment in jobs that present opportunities to commit crime; and the persistent economic disadvantage women face due to low-wage employment, responsibility for heading households, and reductions in welfare support.

6. Women are less likely than men to be victimized by crime, although women's *fear* of crime is greater, with women of all social groups being most afraid of being victimized by rape [Figure 6.3].

    a. Esther Madriz argues women's fear of crime is the result of an ideology that depicts women as needing protection and defines public spaces as reserved for men, resulting in a system of social control that restricts women's full participation in society.

  b. Although rape is the most underreported crime, women are showing an increased willingness to report; at the same time, there appears to have been an actual increase in the incidence of rape in the United States.

  c. Rape is an act of aggression against women that stems from learned gender roles that teach men to be sexually aggressive and define women as objects for men's sexual pleasure. Rape is further supported by the use of alcohol, widespread acceptance of rape myths, and the peer support for participation in sexual assault often found in all-male organizations.

  d. Those women who have the least power in society -- African American and Latina women, poor women, unmarried women, and young women-- are the most likely to be raped.

C. The Criminal Justice System

Those in socially disadvantaged groups are more likely to be defined and identified as deviant, regardless of their behavior, and more likely to be detained and arrested, found guilty, and punished once they encounter systems of authority [Table 6.2].

  1. Although police presence is generally reassuring to middle-class White people, encounters with police can be terrifying for minority men, who are more likely to be perceived by police as threats, regardless of what they are doing at the time.

  2. **Racial profiling** occurs when police use race alone as the criterion for deciding whether to stop and detain someone on the suspicion that they have committed a crime. For example, eight out of ten vehicle searches conducted by state troopers on the New Jersey Turnpike in the last ten years were in vehicles with Black or Hispanic drivers, and the majority of those searches turned up no contraband.

  3. Police are more likely to use excessive force against racial-ethnic minorities.

  4. When arrested, bail is set higher for African Americans and Latinos than Whites, minority defendants are found guilty more often than Whites once on trial, and minorities who are convicted of crimes are more likely to receive longer sentences and the death penalty than are White men convicted of the same crime.

  5. Despite arguments that the death penalty is a brutish law that constitutes cruel and unusual punishment, it can be used against mentally impaired people and minors who are tried as adults the United States.

  a. In 1972, the Supreme Court ruled in *Furman v. Georgia* that the death penalty was discriminatory because it was applied unevenly by race.

  b. After a period of banning executions in the United States, the Supreme Court upheld the death penalty in *McCleskey v. Georgia* in 1987.

  6. The United States has the highest rate of imprisonment in the world, with 6.3 million people in prison or jail or on probation or parole [Figure 6.4].

  7. Blacks have the highest rate of imprisonment and Hispanics are the fastest growing minority group in prison, reflecting the racial stratification in society.

  8. The rapid increase in the rate of imprisonment has led to the privatization of prisons, or the operation of prisons by private companies, which raises questions about the treatment of prisoners in centers being run for profit.

  9. Although the number of women in prison is relatively small, the rate of imprisonment for women has increased at a faster rate than for men, with the majority of women being imprisoned for drug offenses.

  10. Although the enforcement of drug laws has increased, comparable decreases in drug use have not occurred, especially among Blacks and inner-city youth, suggesting that the threat of imprisonment does not deter crime.

11. Because prisons concentrate on individuals rather than address the structural causes of crime, prisons seem to neither deter nor rehabilitate offenders. In fact, prison helps inmates acquire new criminal skills and make more connections to criminal networks while further detaching them from the norms of society.

12. Some sociologists have argued that the criminal justice system is not meant to reduce crime, but functions to reinforce an image of crime as a threat from the poor and racial minority groups.

V. DEVIANCE AND CRIME IN GLOBAL PERSPECTIVE: TERRORISM AND INTERNATIONAL CRIME NETWORKS

Crime and deviance increasingly cross national borders. Many nations have long experienced terrorism, but this problem was propelled into the American public's mind when hijackers assumed control of four airplanes in the United States on September 11, 2001. Terrorism is often motivated by political, and sometimes by ethnic or religious, conflict. Sociologists understand terrorism not just as individual insanity, but as a form of deviance that emerges from social conditions. Terrorism is linked to other forms of deviance, such as the international drug trade, which generates profits that may be used to finance terrorist acts. Nations around the world are connected by their participation in the international drug trade. For example, the United States and parts of Western Europe provide markets for the consumption of illegal drugs, Columbia is a major drug producer, and China, Brazil, and Mexico are conduits for drug traffic [Map 6.2].

PRACTICE TEST

Multiple Choice Questions

1. Which of the following statements about definitions of deviance is true?
    a. Biological definitions of deviance emphasize social context rather than individual behavior.
    b. Sociological definitions of deviance recognize that not all groups perceive or judge deviance in the same ways.
    c. Psychological definitions of deviance assume that genetics have little or no influence on a person's tendency to participate in deviant behavior.
    d. Medicalized definitions of deviance recognize that established rules and norms are socially created, rather than morally decreed or individually imposed.

2. Body piercing violates customary norms, so it is an example of which type of deviance?
    a. elite
    b. formal
    c. medical
    d. informal

3. According to conflict theory, crime results primarily from the:
    a. competition for social resources in capitalist societies.
    b. lack of shared norms and social integration in modern societies.
    c. individual genetic deficiencies that result in psychological impairment.
    d. cultural transmission of deviant values from one generation to the next.

4. According to the FBI, assaults and other malicious acts motivated by various forms of bias are:
    a. organizational deviance.
    b. victimless crimes.
    c. elite deviance.
    d. hate crimes.

5.   Criminologist Joel Best argues that crimes such as "wilding" and "road rage:"
        a.   are completely random phenomena.
        b.   have markedly increased since 1990.
        c.   are patterned, predictable social random acts of violence.
        d.   are unrelated to the social characteristics of the victims and the perpetrators.

6.   The condition that exists when social regulations break down in a society and people exist in a state of relative normlessness is:
        a.   crime.
        b.   anomie.
        c.   altruism.
        d.   deviance.

7.   According to Durkheim, which type of suicide occurs when people feel totally detached from society due to weakened social ties?
        a.   anomic
        b.   egoistic
        c.   altruistic
        d.   egalitarian

8.   Which of the following crimes is a violation of the law, yet does not appear in the FBI's serious crime index because it does not have a complainant?
        a.   arson
        b.   murder
        c.   burglary
        d.   prostitution

9.   Edwin Sutherland, who argued deviant behavior is behavior learned through interaction with others, developed which theory of deviance?
        a.   social control theory
        b.   social labeling theory
        c.   alternative identity theory
        d.   differential association theory

10.   Ramiro Martinez's investigation of homicide in Latino communities indicates that:
        a.   a high poverty rate is strongly correlated with a higher homicide rate.
        b.   level of educational attainment is the strongest predictor of homicide for Latinos.
        c.   immigration to the United States has weakened the importance of religion for Latinos, resulting in increased participation in immoral and illegal activities such as homicide.
        d.   All of the above statements are true according to Martinez's research.

11.   Members of which of the following groups are most likely to be victimized by robbery and physical assault in the United States?
        a.   Black men
        b.   White men
        c.   Black women
        d.   White women

12. According to Robert Merton, deviance occurs when individuals:
    a. organize a social movement to raise awareness about a problematic behavior, redefine that behavior as deviant, and strengthen sanctions to punish the behavior.
    b. are labeling by powerful social groups and sanctioned within impersonal bureaucracies.
    c. accept the goals of the society but lack the means to legitimately achieve those goals.
    d. break their allegiance to the common value system within society.

13. Functionalist theory posits that:
    a. people choose whether or not to behave in a deviant manner.
    b. social structure, not just individual motivation, produces deviance.
    c. what appears to be dysfunctional behavior may be functional for society.
    d. All of the above are basic assumptions of functionalist theory.

14. Durkheim suggested that which type of suicide results from the excessive regulation of individuals by social forces?
    a. anomic
    b. egoistic
    c. altruistic
    d. communal

15. Mark was born with cerebral palsy and is confined to a wheelchair. In other people's minds, Mark's condition overrides all other features of his identity, thereby creating what type of status?
    a. elite
    b. master
    c. primary
    d. differential

16. W.I. Thomas argued that juvenile delinquency was brought on by the social disorganization of slum life and urban industrialism, reflecting his assertion that:
    a. deviance is an emotionally immature response to the experience of poverty.
    b. adolescents are not cognitively mature enough to manage stressful situations.
    c. poor individuals are genetically predisposed to delinquent or criminal behavior.
    d. deviance is a normal response to the social conditions in which people find themselves.

17. Which of the following statements about race and the American criminal justice system is true?
    a. Police officers are more likely to use excessive force against Black suspects than White suspects.
    b. There is ample evidence that police officers perceive Black and Hispanic men as more of a "threat" than White men, regardless of what the men are actually doing.
    c. When Black men and White men are convicted of committing the same crime against a White victim, Black men are more likely to receive the death penalty at sentencing.
    d. All of the above statements are true.

18. When a person undergoes a process of social transformation in which a new self-image and new public definition of the person as deviant emerges, the person has developed a(n):
    a. primary identity
    b. deviant identity
    c. insider status
    d. victim role

19. Which role do Australia and the United States play in the international drug trade?
    a. major drug producers
    b. major drug consumers
    c. conduits for drug traffic
    d. money laundering locations

20. In 1972, the United States Supreme Court ruled in *Furman v. Georgia* that the death penalty:
    a. can be applied to minors who are tried as adults.
    b. may not be applied to mentally impaired people.
    c. is discriminatory because it is applied unevenly based on race.
    d. is unconstitutional because it constitutes cruel and unusual punishment.

21. Which of the following statements about victimization by crime is true?
    a. Women are more likely than men to be victimized by crime.
    b. White men are more likely than Black men to be victimized by crime.
    c. Poor people are more likely than higher income people to be victimized by crime.
    d. All of the above statements are true.

22. Which of the following statements about women and crime is true according to Esther Madriz?
    a. Women are more afraid of being victimized by rape than by any other crime.
    b. Women's fear of crime is rooted in an ideology that depicts women as vulnerable and in need of protection.
    c. Women's fear of crime is a system of social control that prevents women from enjoying the full rights of citizenship in a free society.
    d. All of the above statements are true according to Esther Madriz's research.

True-False Questions

1. Social control theory assumes there is a common value system within society and breaking one's allegiance to that value system is the main cause of deviant behavior.

2. Sociologists do not define excessive drinking as deviant behavior because it is contributes to social cohesion among young adults on college campuses.

3. One of the primary reasons for the rapid increase in the prison population has been the introduction of minimum mandatory sentences for drug offenders.

4. Once a deviant label has been assigned to a person, that person can recover their nondeviant identity fairly easily if prove that they did not engage in the behavior that led to being labeled.

5. Functionalist theory views the dominant class as controlling societal resources and using its power to create values, belief systems, and laws that support that power.

6. Labeling theorists argue that the official statistics concerning deviant behavior, such as suicide rates, accurately reflect the actual incidence of such behavior.

7. Lower-income people and members of racial minority groups in the United States are more likely than higher-income and White people to be defined as mentally ill.

8. Taking into consideration women of all races and social class backgrounds, it is White, middle class women who have the highest likelihood of being raped in the United States.

9. Durkheim's analysis of suicide suggests that students on college campuses who experience intense feelings of loneliness and hopelessness are at risk for committing anomic suicide.

10. The United States has the highest rate of imprisonment in the world.

Fill in the Blank Questions

1. Mark was born with cerebral palsy and is confined to a wheelchair. In other people's minds, Mark's condition overrides all other features of his identity, creating a _____ status.

2. Racial _____ refers to the common policing practice of using race as the sole criterion on which a person is stopped and detained for suspicion of criminal activity.

3. The FBI classifies larceny, auto theft, and arson as _____ crimes.

4. Deviant _____ maintain their own values, norms, and rewards for deviant behavior, thereby creating a worldview that solidifies the deviant identity of the members.

5. The process whereby deviant behavior is increasingly defined and treated as resulting from an illness is the _____ of deviance.

Essay Questions

1. Using the concepts of deviant identity, deviant career, and deviant community, discuss how a person becomes a gang member.
2. Identify the three types of suicide discussed by Emile Durkheim, and use his analysis to explain why suicide rates are higher for men than for women.
3. Provide evidence to support or refute the following statement: "The American criminal justice system treats all people according to the neutral principles of law."
4. Identify three social factors that help explain why women's participation in crime has been increasing in the United States.
5. Explain why sociologists are critical of the *medicalization of deviance*, providing a specific example of a deviant behavior commonly believed to be the result of individual pathology but having origins in social conditions.

ANSWERS TO PRACTICE TEST

Answers to Multiple Choice Questions

1. D   147   Sociological definitions of deviance: 1) emphasize social context rather than individual tendencies, 2) recognize that not all groups perceive or respond to different forms of deviance in the same ways, and 3) acknowledge that rules and norms are socially created. Psychological, biological, and medical explanations of deviance emphasize individual pathology as the cause of deviance and understate or neglect the importance of social conditions in producing deviance.

2. D   147   Body piercing, a behavior that violates customary norms, is a type of informal deviance. Behavior that violates laws is formal deviance.

3. A   154   Conflict theory views crime as rooted in the economic organization of capitalist societies, which results in competition for social resources. Functionalist theory sees deviance as resulting from a lack of social integration and shared norms. Psychological theories focus on individual deficiencies or impairments as the primary cause of deviant behavior. Differential association theory, derived from

symbolic interaction theory, views deviance as behavior one learns through interaction with others who support alternative values [Table 6.1].

4.   D   161   Hate crimes are malicious acts against people or property that are motivated by bias based on race, ethnicity, religion, sexual orientation, or disability. Victimless crimes are violations of laws that have no complainant, such as prostitution. Organizational deviance is wrongdoing that occurs within the context of a formal organization and is sanctioned by the norms and operating principles of the organization. Elite deviance, also known as corporate crime, refers to the wrongdoing of wealthy and powerful individuals and organizations.

5.   C   158   Joel Best argues that violence is patterned according to the social characteristics of both perpetrators and victims. Violent crime is predictable, not random. Barry Glassner has argued that the media sensationalizes violence, thereby creating a culture of fear, despite a decreased incidence of violent crime since 1990.

6.   B   152   Durkheim defined anomie as the condition that exists when social regulations break down and people exist in a state of relative normlessness. Deviance is behavior that violates norms, and crime is deviant behavior that violates criminal laws. Altruism refers to behavior that is devoted to the interests of others.

7.   B   152   According to Durkheim, egoistic suicide occurs when people become detached from society, as in the case of elderly men who have lost their work roles. Anomic suicide occurs when disintegrating forces in society make individuals feel intensely alone and hopeless. Altruistic suicide occurs due to the excessive regulation of individuals by social forces.

8.   D   162   The FBI's list of serious crimes does not include victimless crimes, or crimes for which there is no complainant (such as illegal drug use). Personal crimes (such as assault and murder) involve bodily harm. Arson and larceny are property crimes.

9.   D   156   Sutherland developed differential association theory, which emphasizes that deviance is learned through interaction with others. This theory developed out of symbolic interaction theory and the work of W.I. Thomas.

10. B   163   Although poverty is correlated with crime, the results of Martinez's research did not show a strong correlation between the poverty rate and Latino involvement in homicide. Instead, the degree of disparity in income between residents was an important predictor of homicide, as was the education level of residents. Martinez did not examine the religious beliefs of Latinos in his study.

11. A   164   As indicated in Figure 6.3, men are more likely than women to be victimized by crime, and Black men are the *most* likely group to be victimized by crime.

12. C   153   According to Merton, deviance results from inconsistency between the goals and means of the society. For example, a prostitute accepts the goal of economic self-sufficiency supported by American values, but because she lacks the means to achieve this goal, she must develop alternative, albeit illegal, means.

13. D   151   As indicated in Table 6.1, functionalist theory posits that individuals choose to engage in deviant behavior when their attachment to social bonds is weakened. Deviance, which results from structural strains in society, can be functional for society because it creates social cohesion and clarifies norms.

14. C   152   According to Durkheim, altruistic suicide occurs due to the excessive regulation of individuals by social forces, as when an individual takes his or her life in the name of a greater cause.

15. B   160   A physical disability may become a master status when that single characteristic overrides all other features of the person's identity. The disability may also be considered a stigma, or an attribute that is socially devalued and discredited.

16. D   156   Using symbolic interaction theory as the basis for what he called situational analysis, Thomas examined people's actions and the subjective meanings they

attributed to their behavior within their social context. Thomas argued deviance is a normal response to the social conditions in which people find themselves.

17. D 166   Police perceive minority men as threats, regardless of their behavior at the time, and are more likely to use excessive force against them. Black and Hispanic men are more likely than White men to be arrested, detained, found guilty once at trial, be given a longer sentence and be sentenced to death than are White men who are found guilty of the same crime.

18. B 157   Deviant identity is the definition a person has of herself or himself as deviant. The formation of a deviant identity involves self-acceptance of the label and role of "deviant." A deviant career is the sequence of movements a person makes through a deviant community, or a group organized around a form of deviant behavior, as they are socialized into the new role.

19. B 171   As illustrated in Map 6.2, the United States provides a major market for the consumption of illegal drugs. Columbia is a major drug producer, while Mexico acts as a conduit for the transportation of drugs. The profits from this drug trade may end up in a bank account in the Cayman Islands or Switzerland.

20. C 167   In the 1972 case, *Furman v. Georgia*, the Supreme Court ruled that the death penalty is discriminatory because it is applied unevenly by race, and a ban on executions ensued. However, the Supreme Court upheld the death penalty in 1987 in *McCleskey v. Georgia*. Today, the death penalty can be applied to mentally impaired people as well as minors who are tried as adults.

21. C 164   Men, racial-ethnic minorities, and poor people are more likely to be victimized by crime [Figure 6.2 and Figure 6.3].

22. D 165   Esther Madriz argues that women's fear of crime, and particularly of being raped, is the result of an ideology that depicts women as needing protection and defines public spaces as reserved for men, resulting in a system of social control that prevents women from enjoying the full rights of citizenship in a free society.

Answers to True-False Questions

1. T 153   Social control theory assumes there is a common value system in society and breaking one's allegiance to that system is the source of deviant behavior.

2. F 149   Sociologists recognize that behavior that is deviant in one situation may not be deviant in another situation. Excessive drinking is often encouraged and rewarded on college campuses, but it violates the norms of the larger society.

3. T 168   Increased enforcement of drug offenses and the introduction of minimum mandatory sentences for drug offenders have led to significant increases in the number of men and women imprisoned in the United States.

4. F 157   According to labeling theory, it is very difficult for a person to recover their nondeviant identity once they have been labeled deviant, even if they did not engage in the behavior for which they were labeled.

5. F 154   Conflict theorists view deviance as the result of competition for social resources within a capitalist system that is controlled by the dominant class. Functionalist theorists note that laws protect all people in the society, and economic interests alone cannot explain all the forms of deviance observed in society.

6. F 159   Labeling theorists do not accept official statistics as accurate reflections of the actual incidence of deviant behavior, because these statistics are produced by people in the social system who define, classify, and record only certain behaviors as deviant. For example, one death may be classified as a suicide, while another, similar death is classified as an accident.

7.	T	160	People with the fewest resources in society (including women, poor people, and members of racial-ethnic minority groups) suffer higher rates of reported mental illness and are most likely to be labeled mentally ill.
8.	F	166	Women who are most powerless in society (including poor women, young women, and racial-ethnic minority women) are more likely to be raped.
9.	T	152	College students who experience feelings of intense loneliness and hopelessness within the social context of relative normlessness may commit anomic suicide.
10.	T	167	As indicated in Figure 6.4, the United States has the highest rate of imprisonment in the world, followed closely by Russia.

Answers to Fill in the Blank Questions

1.	master	225
2.	profiling	207
3.	property	161
4.	communities	157
5.	medicalization	150

CHAPTER 7
SOCIAL CLASS AND SOCIAL STRATIFICATION

BRIEF CHAPTER OUTLINE

Social Differentiation and Social Stratification
> Forms of Stratification: Estate, Caste, and Class
> Defining Class

Why Is There Inequality?
> Karl Marx: Class and Capitalism
> Max Weber: Class, Status, and Party
> Functionalism and Conflict Theory: The Continuing Debate

The Class Structure of the United States
> Layers of Social Class
> Class Conflict
> The Distribution of Wealth and Income
> Diverse Sources of Stratification

Social Mobility: Myths and Realities
> Defining Social Mobility
> The Extent of Social Mobility
> Class Consciousness

Poverty
> Who Are the Poor?
> Causes of Poverty
> Welfare and Social Policy

CHAPTER FOCUS: This chapter provides an overview of the social class system in the United States and explores the fundamental sociological questions of why inequality exists and what consequences inequality has for diverse groups and the society as a whole.

QUESTIONS TO GUIDE YOUR READING
1. What are the three types of stratification systems found around the world, and what characteristics do sociologists use to distinguish among them?
2. What are the major social classes in the United States, and what features are characteristic of each social class?
3. How is a person's social class position determined, and how do race, ethnicity, gender, and age influence the social class placement of people in the United States?
4. How great is class inequality, and how common is social mobility, in the United States?
5. How do the core assumptions underlying functionalist and conflict theories of inequality influence social policy development in the United States?

SOCIOLOGY IN ACTION: AN INTERNET EXERCISE
Go to www.habitat.org to find out more about Habitat for Humanity, an organization that assist lower-income people become homeowners. What does home ownership indicate about a person's social class? What strategies does this organization use to increase home ownership in the U.S. and around the world?

KEY TERMS (defined at page number shown and in glossary)

caste system 177
class consciousness 193
educational attainment 184
false consciousness 194

class 178
culture of poverty 197
estate system 177
feminization of poverty 195

KEY PEOPLE (identified at page number shown)

CHAPTER OUTLINE
I.   **SOCIAL DIFFERENTIATION AND SOCIAL STRATIFICATION**
      Status refers to a socially defined position in a group or a society. **Social differentiation** is the process by which different statuses in any group, organization, or society develop. **Social stratification** is a relatively fixed, hierarchical arrangement in society by which groups have different access to resources, power, and perceived social worth. All societies have a system of structured inequality; however, the basis on which groups are stratified varies cross-culturally.
      A.   Estate, Caste, and Class
            1.   In an **estate system** of stratification, which is most common in agricultural societies, the elite have total control over societal resources, as in the European feudal systems of the Middle Ages.
            2.   In a **caste system** of stratification, one's status is ascribed, or assigned at birth. Examples include the former *apartheid* system in South Africa and the traditional caste system of India.
            3.   In class systems, one's status is partially achieved, or determined by one's personal achievements. Although the class system of the United States is open, allowing for movement from one class to another, relatively few people experience much mobility over time. The social class a person is born into still has major consequences for that person's life.
      B.   Defining Class
            1.   **Social class** (or **class**) is the social structural position that groups hold relative to the economic, social, political, and cultural resources of society. Class is both an attribute of individuals and a feature of society.
            2.   Max Weber identified **life chances** as the opportunities that people in a particular class have in common by virtue of membership in that class, including access to jobs, health care, housing, and education.
            3.   Because social class is a structural phenomenon that cannot be directly observed, sociologists measure it by using indicators, or measurements that assess a concept, including income, education, occupation, and place of residence.
II.   **WHY IS THERE INEQUALITY?**
      A.   Karl Marx: Class and Capitalism
            1.   Karl Marx (1818-1883), who analyzed the class system under capitalism, defined classes in terms of their relationship to the *means of production*, or the system by which goods are produced and distributed.
            2.   Marx identified two primary social classes under capitalism -- the *capitalist class*, which owns the means of production, and the *working class*, or proletariat, which labors for wages.

3.   Within the two major classes are two other classes -- the *petty bourgeoisie*, or small business owners and managers, who identify with the capitalists, and the *lumpenproletariat*, or those who become unnecessary as workers and are discarded. Today, this class includes the homeless and permanently poor.

4.   Marx predicted that class struggles would occur because the two main classes would become increasingly polarized as wealth became more concentrated; thus, the exploitive character of capitalism would lead to its own destruction.

5.   Capitalism provides the *infrastructure* of society and other social institutions reflect capitalist interests; for example, the family and education socialize people into appropriate work roles.

6.   The dominant ideas of society are promoted by the ruling class, resulting in an **ideology** that supports the status quo.

7.   Marx did not foresee the emergence of a large, highly differentiated, and culturally influential middle class like the one that exists in the U.S. today.

B.   <u>Max Weber: Class, Status, and Party</u>

1.   Max Weber (1864-1920) agreed with Marx that social class has a powerful effect on people's lives, but argued that there were *three* dimensions to stratification.

    a.   *Class* (the economic dimension) refers to how much access an individual or group has to the material goods of society, and is measured by income, property, and other financial assets.

    b.   *Status* (the cultural dimension) is the social judgment of, or recognition given to, a person or group.

    c.   *Party*, or what we now call power (the political dimension), is the ability to influence people, even in the face of opposition. It is also reflected in one's ability to negotiate through social institutions, such as the criminal justice system.

2.   Weber noted that a person can rank high on one or two dimensions of stratification and low on another. For example, ministers are accorded high social status but do not typically earn high incomes.

C.   <u>Functionalism and Conflict Theory: The Continuing Debate</u>

1.   Functionalist theory views society as an interdependent system of institutions organized to meet society's needs. It emphasizes cohesion and stability.

    a.   Davis and Moore argue that inequality is a mechanism to ensure that the most talented people go into the most demanding positions.

    b.   The higher rewards attached to these positions ensure that people will make the sacrifices needed to acquire the necessary training to achieve **social mobility**.

2.   Conflict theory emphasizes that society is a system held together through conflict and coercion, focusing on the friction in society rather than the coherence.

    a.   Stratification is a system of domination and subordination whereby the unequal distribution of rewards reflect the class interests of the powerful, rather than the survival needs of the whole society.

    b.   The more stratification in the society, the less likely the society will benefit from the talents of all its citizens because inequality limits the life chances of those at the bottom, who experience blocked opportunities.

3.   Implicit in the argument presented by each perspective is criticism of the other. The fundamental, contradictory assumptions that drive each academic theory have practical implications for the development of social policy.

III.   THE CLASS STRUCTURE OF THE UNITED STATES

The class structure of the United States is an elaborate, open system that can be conceptualized as a ladder. Social class is the common position that groups hold in a status hierarchy. **Social**

attainment is the process whereby people end up in a particular position in the stratification system, influenced by such factors as class origins, educational level, and occupation. One's **socioeconomic status (SES),** or an individual's position in the stratification system, is derived primarily from income, occupational prestige, and educational attainment. **Income** is the amount of money a person receives in a given period. The **median income** is the midpoint of all household incomes in a particular society [Figure 7.1]. **Prestige** is the value assigned to people and groups by others. **Occupational prestige** is the subjective evaluation people give to jobs as determined through nationwide surveys of the American public. Occupations such as judge, physician, professor, lawyer, and scientist are accorded the highest prestige, while electrician, newspaper columnist, insurance agent, and police officer are in the middle range of prestige ratings. Those occupations typically considered to have the lowest prestige are farm laborer, maid or servant, janitor, and garbage collector. These rankings reflect social judgements about the value of these jobs to society, rather than the worth of the people who hold these jobs. **Educational attainment** is typically measured as years of formal education. The amount of occupational prestige attributed to jobs is strongly related to the amount of education required by the job; thus, one's status generally increases as education level increases.

A.   Layers of Social Class

1.   The *upper class* in the United States constitute a very small proportion of people who control vast amounts of property and wealth, most of which is inherited. In Marx's terms, these elites own the means of production. The *nouveau riche*, such as owners of successful dot com companies, have moved into the upper class through the recent acquisition of wealth.

2.   The *upper-middle class* includes those with high incomes and high social prestige, such as well-educated professionals and business executives.

3.   The *middle class* is probably the largest group in the United States, or at least 45 percent of Americans identify themselves as middle class.

4.   The *lower-middle class*, also known as the working class, includes lower-income bureaucratic workers, service workers, and workers in the skilled trades.

5.   The *lower class* is comprised primarily of poor and displaced people who have little formal education and are often unemployed or working for minimum wage. People of color and women are over-represented in this class. Contrary to popular belief, forty percent of the poor work.

6.   The **urban underclass** refers to people who are likely to be permanently unemployed and dependent on public assistance or crime for economic support. Sociologist William Julius Wilson argues that major structural changes in the economy have left racial minorities in especially vulnerable positions, thereby intensifying the problems of urban poverty.

B.   Class Conflict

1.   Rather than defining social class in terms of a hierarchy, or "ladder," conflict theorists define classes in terms of their structural relationship to each other and to the economic system.

2.   This theory emphasizes power relations in society, noting that classes compete with each other for resources and the capitalist class exploits the working class.

3.   The position of the middle class, or the *professional-managerial* class (including managers and professionals) is unique because members have substantial control over other people, especially in the workplace, but have minimal control over the economic system. This theory suggests that as capitalism progresses, members of the middle class will be pushed down into working class jobs.

4.   Although the middle class has not been eliminated as Marx predicted, classes have become more polarized, and many members of the middle class have experienced downward social mobility due to economic restructuring.

5. Using Marx's definition, the working class would include many white-collar workers (such as secretaries, nurses, and salespeople) because they have little control over their work lives and little power to challenge the decisions of those who supervise them.

6. Because the middle and working classes shoulder much of the tax burden for social programs, they tend to develop resentment toward the poor, who are blamed for their own poverty. At the same time, privileges for the wealthy elite are perpetuated through declines in corporate taxes.

C. The Distribution of Wealth and Income in the United States

1. Class inequality in the United States is enormous and has intensified as elites have gained more power and greater control over wealth [Figure 7.2].

2. Sociologists distinguish between **wealth**, which is the monetary value of everything one owns (including stocks, bonds, property, insurance, and investments); and **income**, which is the amount of money brought into a household from various sources during a given period of time (including wages, investment income, and dividends).

3. The distribution of wealth provides evidence of significant class inequality. For example, median income (in constant dollars) has actually declined since 1970.

   a. The top one-fifth of the population has received 47 percent of all income, while the bottom fifth has received 4.2 percent of the total income.

   b. The richest 10 percent of American households have reaped 73 percent of the growth in the stock market in recent years [Figure 7.2].

   c. With the wealthiest 1 percent of the population owning 38 percent of all net worth, the concentration of wealth is higher in the United States than in any other industrialized nation.

   d. With one-third of all Americans having no financial assets at all once debt is subtracted, and debt continuing to increase in the typical American household, the American dream is increasingly unattainable.

4. At all income, occupational, and educational levels, Black families have lower levels of wealth than similarly situated White families. Because the advantages of wealth accumulate over time, providing equality of opportunity in the present has not mediated the consequences of years of discriminating against Black Americans in housing, lending, and other social policies.

5. Without significant wealth holdings, families of any race or ethnicity are less able to transmit assets from one generation to the next, which is one of the main supports for social mobility.

6. Class divisions in the United States are real, apparently permanent, and becoming more marked as economic restructuring concentrates more wealth in fewer people's hands; downsizing redistributes formerly middle-class employees into jobs with lower pay, less prestige, and few (or no) benefits; and reductions in government programs eliminate much of the safety net for people in need.

D. Diverse Sources of Stratification

1. Class position is manifested differently depending on one's race and gender, and class significantly differentiates group experiences within a given racial or gender group. For example, Latinos are broadly defined as those who trace their origins to regions originally colonized by Spain, yet some Latinos identify as White, others as Black, and others by their specific national origins.

   a. The class structure among African Americans has historically existed alongside the White class structure, with the Black middle class having relatively high prestige *within* Black communities.

b. Although the Black and Latino middle classes have expanded as people of color gained increased access to higher education and middle-class occupations, many in this group have a tenuous hold on middle-class status, and residential segregation by race persists in the United States.

2. The *myth of the model minority* reflects a stereotype based on the belief that a minority group member must adopt dominant group values to succeed. Asian Americans are often stereotyped in this way because of their presumed thrift, educational achievement, and hard work. This myth obscures the high rates of poverty among many Asian American groups as well as the significant obstacles to success that Asian Americans encounter.

3. In the past, women were thought to derive their class position from their husband or father, but sociologists now challenge this assumption. Based on their own income and occupation, the majority of American women are working-class. The median income for women working full-time, year-round in 1999 was $27,370 (compared to $37,574 for men).

4. Age is also a significant source of stratification; thus, being born in a particular generation can significantly influence one's life chances. For example, the age group most likely to be poor today is children. The elderly were most likely to be poor in the past, which reflects the greater affluence of older people in the United States today [Figure 7.3].

IV. **SOCIAL MOBILITY: MYTHS AND REALITIES**
A. Defining Social Mobility
   1. **Social mobility** refers to a person's movement over time from one class to another. Mobility may be *intergenerational* (occurring between generations), as when a son or daughter rises above the class of his or her mother or father, or *intragenerational* (occurring within a single generation), as when a person's status changes during his or her lifetime due to business success (or failure).
   2. Societies differ in the extent to which social mobility is permitted, with *closed class systems* strictly limiting or prohibiting movement from one class to another, and *open class systems* fostering mobility through individual achievement.

B The Extent of Social Mobility
   1. Social mobility is more limited than the American dream suggests, with most people remaining in the same class as their parents as the privileges and disadvantages of class position reproduce themselves across generations.
   2. Increases in educational attainment account for a considerable amount of class mobility, which explains many of the recent gains by African Americans.
      a. African American families are more likely than White families to prepare their daughters for careers and less likely to encourage marriage as a primary goal.
      b. Working-class African American parents are likely to steer their daughters toward traditionally female occupations, and White working-class parents socialize their daughters to marry and form greater attachments to family and community rather than go away to college.
   3. Factors that affect the whole society, such as changes in the occupational system and demographic characteristics, are more likely to influence changes in a person's social status than are individual characteristics unique to that person.
   4. Although most attention is focused on upward mobility in the United States, *downward mobility* is becoming more common as income distribution becomes more skewed toward the top and the middle class experience a decline.

C.   Class Consciousness
    1.   **Class consciousness** is both the perception that a class structure exists and the feeling of shared identification with one's class and others who share the same life chances.
        a.   Many argue that Americans are not very class conscious because of their strong cultural belief in upward mobility and personal focus on getting ahead individually.
        b.   Research indicates that Americans do recognize class divisions and generally believe that classes are organized around opposing interests.
        c.   The elite are a cohesive group who are quite class conscious and protective of their institutional power and common interests.
        d.   People in the working-class are more likely than those in the middle class to believe that others in higher classes control their lives.
        e.   The single most important determinant of where one sees oneself in the class system is whether one does mental or manual labor.
    2.   Karl Marx used the term **false consciousness** to refer to the class consciousness of subordinate classes who had internalized the views and belief systems of the dominant class.
        a.   The myth of classlessness supports class inequality by promoting the idea that everyone has the same chance of success, so any inequality that exists must be fair and just.
        b.   Beliefs that people are biologically, socially, or culturally different tend to justify the higher position of some groups, providing legitimacy for the system of inequality.

V.   **POVERTY**
The **poverty line** is the amount of money required to support the basic needs of a household. In 1999, the poverty line was $17,184 for a family of four, an amount determined by multiplying a low-cost food budget by a factor of three. This official definition of poverty is used to determine eligibility for government assistance in the United States.
A.   Who Are the Poor?
    1.   There are over 32 million poor people in the United States, representing 12.7 percent of the population. The majority of the poor are White, although disproportionately high rates of poverty are found among racial-ethnic minorities.
    2.   The majority of the poor have always been women and children, and their proportion has been increasing in a trend known as the **feminization of poverty**.
        a.   This trend results from the growth in the number of single-female headed households and persistent wage inequality between men and women.
        b.   Women are increasingly likely to be without the contributing income of a spouse, and for longer periods of time, contributing to the fact that over half of all families headed by women are poor [Figure 7.4].
        c.   Budget cutbacks in federal support programs such as Food Stamps and housing assistance further contribute to the feminization of poverty.
    3.   The majority of the poor live in center cities, and within cities, poverty rates are highest in the most racially segregated neighborhoods [Map 7.1].
    4.   Although estimates of homelessness vary widely, it is clear that homelessness increased in the United States over the last twenty years.
        a.   Families constitute the fastest growing segment of the homeless population.
        b.   The main factors contributing to homelessness are unemployment, eviction, inadequate low-income housing supply, and reductions in public assistance.

B.   Causes of Poverty

    1.   The **culture of poverty** argument views poverty as a cultural way of life that is transmitted across generations. Many people blame the poor for being poor and argue that individual motivation and ability allow anyone in the U.S. to succeed.

    2.   Contrary to popular opinion, cycling in and out of poverty due to a household crisis (such as divorce, illness, unemployment, or family death) is more common than intergenerational welfare dependency, and most of the able-bodied poor do work, but they earn wages at or below the poverty line.

    3.   Most sociologists argue that poverty is caused by complex economic and social factors, including increased unemployment, declining wages, reductions in government support programs, increased divorce rates and lack of affordable child care, and continued wage discrimination for women.

C.   Welfare and Social Policy

    1.   In 1935, the Aid to Families with Dependent Children (AFDC) program was established as part of the Social Security Act, based on the government's recognition that some people are victimized by economic circumstances beyond their control and deserving of public assistance.

    2.   In 1996, AFDC was eliminated by the 1996 Personal Responsibility Act, which introduced limits on the length of time a person can receive welfare benefits and mandated that all recipients find paid employment, a policy known as *workfare*.

    3.   Although many former welfare recipients were able to find work when the economy was strong, most of these jobs do not provide livable wages, so working has not lifted them out of poverty. In fact, higher levels of welfare benefits can actually hasten recipients' exit from poverty by giving them the support they need to get job training and childcare.

    4.   Other recipients of government subsidies, such as the elderly who receive Social Security, have not been subject to the same public suspicion and stigma as welfare recipients, who are generally stereotyped as lazy and undeserving.

PRACTICE TEST

Multiple Choice Questions

1.   Which of the following statements about the *estate system* of stratification is true?

    a.   The apartheid system of South Africa was a stark example of this type of system.

    b.   Because there is little differentiation between classes in this type of system, considerably less social inequality exists than in other systems.

    c.   One's status in this type of system is determined largely by one's personal achievements, allowing for social mobility within one's lifetime.

    d.   Historically, this type of system was found in feudal societies where nobles controlled the land and peasants performed the labor.

2.   Social differentiation refers to the:

    a.   assignment of class position according to one's sex.

    b.   systematic inequalities between nations that result from differences in wealth, power, and prestige in the international economy.

    c.   process by which different statuses in any group or society develop based on which characteristics are deemed important in that society.

    d.   process whereby the most talented individuals, who perform the jobs that are most important in a society, receive the greatest rewards.

3. According to Marx, which social class owns and controls the means of production?
   a. capitalists
   b. proleteriat
   c. petty bourgeoisie
   d. lumpenproletariat

4. According to Max Weber, the three most important dimensions of stratification in industrialized societies are:
   a. class, status, and party.
   b. race, class, and gender.
   c. power, party, and prestige.
   d. economic, political, and religious.

5. Which of the following factors have contributed to the feminization of poverty in recent years?
   a. an increase in the percentage of elderly people in poverty
   b. the persistence of wage discrimination for female workers
   c. an increase in the average number of children born to poor women
   d. All of the above contribute to the feminization of poverty.

6. In the United States, socioeconomic status (SES) is derived primarily from which three variables?
   a. income, occupation, and education
   b. occupation, wealth, and consciousness
   c. income, prestige, and political affiliation
   d. occupation, education, and religious affiliation

7. The degree of occupational prestige associated with a particular job is strongly correlated with which of the following variables?
   a. extent of opportunity for promotion in the job
   b. degree of danger involved in performing the job
   c. number of years of education required for the job
   d. degree to which the job makes a valuable contribution to the public good

8. Sociologists refer to those who become upper class through independent effort and have newly acquired wealth as the:
   a. capitalists.
   b. Ivy League.
   c. nouveau riche.
   d. traditional elites.

9. Sociologists refer to those people who are most likely to be permanently unemployed and dependent on public assistance or crime for economic support as the:
   a. lower-middle class
   b. working class
   c. surplus class
   d. underclass

10. According to Weber, life chances include the opportunity to have which of the following things?
    a. political affiliation with the Republican party
    b. high self-esteem
    c. home ownership
    d. All of the above are opportunities included in Weber's definition of life chances.

11. According to conflict theory, those who have substantial control over other people, especially in the workplace, but have minimal control over the economic system, are in which class?
    a. upper-elite
    b. working-laborer
    c. welfare-dependent
    d. professional-managerial

12. The amount of money brought into a household from various sources, such as wages, investments, and dividends, during a given period refers to a person's:
    a. debt.
    b. wealth.
    c. income.
    d. surplus.

13. The monetary value of everything a person owns, including property, stocks, bonds, and insurance, refers to a person's:
    a. debt.
    b. wealth
    c. income.
    d. surplus.

14. Which of the following groups has recently experienced an expansion of the middle class due to increased opportunities for higher education and improved access to professional jobs?
    a. African Americans
    b. Native Americans
    c. Puerto Ricans
    d. None of these groups have experienced an expansion of the middle class due to persistent racial discrimination in the United States.

15. In the United States, the age group most likely to be poor today is:
    a. elderly people over age 65.
    b. children under age 18.
    c. adults age 21 to 40.
    d. adults age 41 to 60.

16. The myth of the model minority, which is based on the assumption that a minority group member must adopt dominant group values to succeed, has been most frequently applied to which racial-ethnic minority group in the United States?
    a. Hispanic Americans
    b. African Americans
    c. Native Americans
    d. Asian Americans

17. When an individual moves from one class to another in his or her own lifetime, it is referred to as:
    a. generational fortune.
    b. professional success.
    c. intragenerational mobility.
    d. intergenerational mobility.

18. Which theory asserts that upward mobility is available to any individual in the United States if they are motivated to acquire the necessary education and skills?
   a. conflict
   b. feminist
   c. functionalist
   d. symbolic interaction

19. According to Vanneman and Cannon, the *most* important determinant of where an individual in the United States sees herself or himself in the class system is whether s/he:
   a. does mental or manual labor.
   b. graduates from high school.
   c. owns or rents a home.
   d. is single or married.

20. Research on class consciousness in the United States indicates that:
   a. the development of a strong class consciousness among Americans is impeded by a strong cultural belief in the possibility of upward mobility.
   b. the working class is considerably more class conscious than the middle class, as reflected by their perception that their lives are controlled by others.
   c. the upper class is quite class conscious, as reflected by their collective efforts to protect their shared interests.
   d. All of the above statements concerning class consciousness in the United States are true.

21. Oscar Lewis' suggestion that poverty is a way of life for the poor that is transmitted from one generation to the next is referred to as the:
   a. restructuring of the economy.
   b. deindustrialization of society.
   c. welfare dependency model.
   d. culture of poverty.

22. Measured by their own incomes and occupations, rather than by their husbands', a majority of women in the United States would be members of which social class?
   a. working
   b. middle
   c. upper
   d. under

23. The fastest growing segment of the homeless population in the United States is:
   a. single adult women.
   b. runaway adolescents.
   c. families with children.
   d. men who are mentally ill.

24. Which of the following changes to the American welfare system were instituted under the Personal Responsibility and Work Reconciliation Act adopted in 1996?
   a. All recipients were limited to receiving benefits for no more than 2 years.
   b. Teenage recipients were required to stay in school and live with an adult while receiving welfare benefits.
   c. Recipients were required to place their children in foster care if they could not financially support them without government assistance.
   d. This Act includes all of the above stipulations for welfare recipients.

25.   Which of the following statements about poverty in the United States is true?
        a.   Approximately one-fourth of all families headed by women are poor.
        b.   Approximately one-fifth of the total population is poor.
        c.   The majority of the poor live in isolated rural areas.
        d.   The majority of the poor are White.

True-False Questions

1.   In the United States, women have significantly higher rates of poverty than do men.

2.   White families are more likely than Black families to prepare their daughters for paid employment and less likely to stress marriage as a primary goal.

3.   The estate system of stratification is found primarily in agricultural societies.

4.   According to Max Weber, a person's position in the stratification system is almost solely determined by their income.

5.   The majority of upper class people in the United States acquire their wealth through independent efforts, such as establishing a successful business.

6.   As adults, most individuals in the United States remain in the same social class as their parents.

7.   The income gap between Blacks and Whites in the United States has remained relatively unchanged since 1970.

8.   The concentration of wealth is higher in the United States than in any other industrialized nation.

9.   "Median income" refers to the minimum amount of income that a family needs to earn to support their basic needs, such as housing, food, and clothing.

10.   The feminization of poverty refers to the increased percentage of poor women who became eligible for welfare benefits under the 1996 Personal Responsibility and Work Opportunity Act.

Fill in the Blank Questions

1.   According to Marx, _____ consciousness develops when subordinate classes internalize the views and belief systems of the dominant class, which justify inequality.

2.   According to _____ theory, social inequality ensures that the most talented people go into the most demanding positions in society by rewarding them for investing in education and training.

3.   The United States is a(n) _____ class system because social mobility is permitted and an individual's placement in the system may change over time.

4.   In 1999, the official _____ in the United States was $17,184 for a family of four people.

5.   In a _____ system of stratification, one's position is determined through ascribed status, as in the former apartheid system in South Africa.

Essay Questions

1. Define *life chances* and explain how the social class position of one's family of origin contributes to one's life chances in adulthood.
2. Explain why there are differences in wealth between Black and White Americans at all educational, income, and occupational levels.
3. Identify three factors that have contributed to the trend known as the feminization of poverty, and suggest one possible solution for addressing this problem.
4. Discuss why the myth of social mobility persists in the United States despite considerable evidence to the contrary.
5. Identify the most significant factor(s) underlying social mobility for those people who do achieve upward mobility in the United States.

ANSWERS TO PRACTICE TEST

Answers to Multiple Choice Questions

1. D 177 The estate systems of stratification is usually found in agricultural societies. It is characterized by stark inequality between those who own the land (elites) and those who work on it (commoners or peasants). The estate system characterized the feudal societies of Europe during the Middle Ages.
2. C 176 Social differentiation is the process by which different statuses in a group or society develop. Social stratification refers to the relatively fixed, hierarchical arrangement in society that distributes social resources unequally across groups.
3. A 179 According to Marx, the two primary classes under capitalism are the capitalists, who own and control the means of production, and the working class, or proletariat, who sell their labor. The petty bourgeoisie are the skilled craftspeople who identify with the capitalist class and the lumpenproletariat are the group of dispossessed workers.
4. A 180 Weber identified three important dimensions of stratification: economic (class or income), cultural (status or prestige), and political (party or power).
5. B 195 The persistence of wage discrimination, high rates of divorce and the associated lack of men's financial contributions to the household, and reductions in government assistance programs have intensified the feminization of poverty.
6. A 183 In the United States, socioeconomic status is determined by three indicators – income, education, and occupation.
7. C 184 Occupations that require high levels of education, such as judge, physician, and scientist, are accorded high occupational prestige. Jobs such as maid and laborer are typically associated with the least prestige. Nurses and police officers are in the middle range.
8. C 184 The nouveau riche are people who have recently acquired substantial wealth through independent effort, rather than inheritance, including the owners of successful dot com companies.
9. D 186 The underclass includes those people who experience chronic unemployment and are likely to be dependent on government assistance or crime for economic support. Marx identified disposed workers like these as the lumpenproletariat.
10. C 178 Weber identified life chances as the opportunities that people have in common by virtue of belonging to a particular class. Life chances include the opportunity for having a certain income, possessing goods, and having access to particular jobs.

11.	D	186	According to conflict theory, the professional-managerial class have substantial control over other people but minimal control over the economic system, placing them in a position of identifying with the capitalist class yet laboring for wages.
12.	C	188	Income is the amount of money brought into a household in a given period.
13.	B	188	Wealth refers to the total monetary value of everything one owns. Net worth refers to a person's or family's total assets minus their debts.
14.	A	191	African Americans have experienced an expansion of the middle class through higher education and increased access to middle-class jobs; however, many middle-class African Americans have a tenuous hold on their class position. Puerto Ricans have the highest rate of poverty among Latinos, and Native Americans have the highest poverty rate of all groups in the United States.
15.	B	192	In the past, the elderly were the most likely group to be poor, but today, children are the age group most likely to be poor. Seventeen percent of American children live in poverty [Figure 7.3].
16.	D	191	Asian Americans are often referred to as the "model minority;" however, many Asian American subgroups experience high rates of poverty, and even those groups that have assimilated into the dominant culture continue to experience prejudice and discrimination.
17.	C	192	Intra generational mobility occurs when an individual's class status changes over his or her lifetime. Intergenerational mobility occurs when an individual's class changes from his or her parents' class. Social mobility, which may be upward or downward, occurs less frequently than is commonly believed.
18.	C	181	Functionalist theorists view upward mobility as available to those who acquire education and job skills, whereas conflict theorists argue there is blocked mobility in the system because the lower and working classes are not provided with the same opportunities as other classes [Table 7.2].
19,	A	194	According to Vanneman and Cannon, the most important determinant of one's class identification in the U.S. is whether one does manual or mental labor.
20.	D	194	Research on class consciousness, or the perception that a class structure exists and the feeling of identification with one's class, indicates that the working class is more class conscious than the middle class.
21.	D	197	The culture of poverty thesis states that poverty is a subcultural way of life that is transmitted from one generation to the next. This thesis explains poverty as the result of dysfunctional values. Structural explanations of poverty suggest that changes in social institutions, such as economic restructuring, higher divorce rates, and wage discrimination, are the root causes of poverty.
22.	A	191	Most women in the United States would be considered working class by their own incomes and occupations, because women are disproportionately located in low-status, low-wage jobs, despite having educational levels comparable to men.
23.	C	197	Families with children are the fastest growing segment of the homeless population in the United States.
24.	B	200	The public perception of welfare recipients as lazy and sneaky is based primarily on myths. Research on the effects of welfare reform indicates that higher levels of welfare benefits can hasten an individual's exit from poverty by providing enough financial support for job training and childcare. The Personal Responsibility and Work Conciliation Act placed a 5 year limit on receiving benefits and required that recipients secure a job within 2 months or agree to do community service work without being paid. The Act also requires teen mothers who receive benefits to stay in school and live in another adult's household. Additionally, women who refuse to identify the fathers of their children risk losing their benefits regardless of their eligibility for assistance.

25. D 195 The majority of the poor are White, although racial-ethnic minorities are disproportionately represented among the poor, and most poor people live in urban areas. About 12.7 percent of the total population of the United States is poor, and over half of households headed by women are poor.

Answers to True-False Questions

1. T 195 Women and children have always had higher rates of poverty than men, but this disparity has been intensified in the United States through the process known as the feminization of poverty.
2. F 193 Black families are more likely than White families to prepare their daughters for paid employment, and less likely to stress marriage as a primary goal, reflecting a long history of high rates of employment among African American women.
3. T 177 In a caste system of stratification, one's social status is ascribed, or assigned at birth. An example of this system is the traditional caste system of India.
4. F 179 Marx emphasized the importance of class for one's placement in the class system, arguing that it was determined solely by one's relationship to the means of production (as owner or laborer). Weber identified three dimensions as important – economic (class), cultural or social (status), and political (party).
5. F 184 Most of the wealth owned by the majority of the upper class is inherited. The nouveau rich have earned their wealth through personal achievement.
6. T 193 The majority of people in the United States occupy the same class position as their parents.
7. T 189 The income gap between Blacks and Whites has remained virtually unchanged since 1970 [Table 7.1]. At all education, income, and occupation levels, Black families have lower levels of wealth than similarly situated White families.
8. T 188 The concentration of wealth in the United States has increased in recent years, and it is higher than in any other industrialized nation.
9. F 183 The median income is the midpoint of all household incomes in a society. The poverty line, which was $17,184 for a family of four in 1999, is the minimal amount of income needed to support the household members' basic needs.
10. F 195 The feminization of poverty refers to the fact that an increasing proportion of the poor are women and children. *Fewer* women with children received welfare benefits after the passage of welfare reform legislation in 1996.

Answers to Fill in the Blank Questions

1. false   194
2. functionalist 181
3. open   193
4. poverty line   194
5. caste   177

CHAPTER 8
GLOBAL STRATIFICATION

BRIEF CHAPTER OUTLINE

Global Stratification
> Rich and Poor
> First, Second, and Third Worlds
> The Core and Periphery
> Race and Global Inequality

Consequences of Global Stratification
> Population
> Health
> Education
> Gender

Theories of Global Stratification
> Modernization Theory
> Dependency Theory
> World Systems Theory

World Poverty
> Defining World Poverty
> Who Are the World's Poor?
> Women and Children in Poverty
> Poverty and Hunger
> Causes of World Poverty

The Future of Global Stratification

CHAPTER FOCUS: This chapter emphasizes the interconnectedness of nations around the world by examining the economic and political relationship of the United States and other world powers to less developed nations. It includes a detailed discussion of the causes and problems of global poverty.

QUESTIONS TO GUIDE YOUR READING
1. How do sociologists measure the wealth of nations, and how reliable is this measure for industrialized and non-industrialized nations?
2. Which measure of world stratification combines levels of development and the political orientation of the country, and how are countries classified according to this model?
3. Using power as the main dimension of stratification in the world system, how are countries classified, and which countries are located in each position?
4. How can sociologists use the Human Poverty Index to assess the standard of living in countries around the world, and what does the index indicate about the world's poor?
5. What is the gender development index, and what does it indicate about the status of women around the world?

SOCIOLOGY IN ACTION: AN INTERNET EXERCISE
Go to www.peacecorps.gov/indexf.cfm to find out when and why the Peace Corps was established. What strategies does this organization use to address the important global issues identified in this chapter?

KEY TERMS (defined at page shown and in glossary)
absolute poverty 220
core countries 211
extreme poverty 220

commodity chain 219
dependency theory 217
first-world countries 210

gender development index 215
human poverty index 220
multinational corporations 218
newly industrializing countries 225
per capita gross national product 208
relative poverty 220
semiperipheral countries 211
world systems theory 318

global stratification 206
modernization theory 215
neocolonialism 217
new international division of labor 212
peripheral countries 212
second-world countries 210
third-world countries 210

KEY PEOPLE (identified at page shown)
Anthony Marx 212
W.W. Rostow 216
Max Weber 216

Karl Marx 217
Immanuel Wallerstein 218

I.   **GLOBAL STRATIFICATION**

Worldwide, there are not only rich and poor individuals, but there are also rich and poor countries. There is a system of **global stratification** in which units are countries; thus, nations cannot be seen independently of economic and social processes that link them together in a world-based economy. Several measures of well being, such as life expectancy and infant mortality, illustrate great inequities resulting from stratification.

A.   <u>Rich and Poor</u>
1.   One of the most common ways to measure the wealth of nations is to use the **per capita gross national product (per capita GNP)**, which measures the total volume of good and services produced by a country each year, divided by the size of the population.
a.   Per capita GNP is only reliable in countries that are based on a cash economy, because it does not measure non-cash transactions such as bartering, making the measure less reliable for poorer countries.
b.   The per capita GNP of the United States, the tenth richest nation in the world using this measure, was $33,812 in 1998 [Figure 8.1].
2.   The world's poorest countries, located mostly in Eastern and Central Africa, are largely rural, depend on subsistence agriculture, and have high fertility rates.

B.   <u>First, Second and Third Worlds</u>
Another dimension of world stratification combines levels of development with political orientation. This classification system, used during the Cold War, does not account for more recent political changes, such as the collapse of the Soviet Union.
1.   **First-world countries** consisted of industrialized, capitalist countries with market-based economies and democratically elected governments. They included the U.S., New Zealand, Australia, Japan, and countries in Western Europe.
2.   **Second-world countries** were socialist countries with state-managed economies and Communist governments, including the former Soviet Union, China, Eastern Europe, Cuba, and North Korea.
3.   **Third-world countries** were the remaining countries that were poor, underdeveloped, largely rural, dependent on subsistence agriculture, and had increasing levels of poverty.

C.   <u>The Core and Periphery</u>
Another dimension of stratification in the world system is *power*, or the ability of a country to exercise control over other countries, especially by influencing the economic system.
1.   **Core countries** such as the U.S. and Japan are the industrialized, developed countries of the first world. They control and profit the most from the system.

        2.   **Semiperipheral countries**, such as Spain, Turkey, and Mexico, are the semi-industrialized nations that play a middleman role, extracting profits from the poor countries and passing them on to the core countries.

        3.   **Peripheral countries** such as Haiti are the largely agricultural, poor countries of the world, with little power or influence in the world system. They often have important resources that are exploited by the core countries.

    D.   <u>Race and Global Inequality</u>

        1.   In addition to the U.S. and Japan, the rich core countries that dominate the world system are largely European, where the majority of the population is White.

        2.   The poorest countries of the world, mostly in Asia, Africa, and South America, have populations comprised primarily of people of color, who have long been exploited by imperialism and colonialism as cheap sources of labor.

        3.   In the global capitalist system, a **new international division of labor** has emerged that relies on employing cheap labor, which is usually found in non-Western countries.

        4.   Anthony Marx's comparison of Brazil and the United States has shown that how race is defined within a country influences the ability of racial minority groups to organize and fight for equality.

II.   CONSEQUENCES OF GLOBAL STRATIFICATION

    A.   <u>Population</u>

        1.   More than sixty percent of the people in the world live in mostly rural countries where the average income is less than $760 per year. These countries have the highest birth and death rates and rapidly growing populations.

        2.   The richest countries of the world, which are largely urban, contain only fifteen percent of the world's population. These countries are experiencing population declines because fertility rates are low, but the elderly population is growing.

        3.   Rapid population growth caused by high fertility rates can cause significant differences in the quality of life across countries, because this growth produces a large proportion of economic dependents in society, which strains public services such as schools and hospitals. Rich countries with very low birth rates experience a shortage of workers, who must be imported from other countries.

    B.   <u>Health</u>

There are significant differences in the basic health standards of countries depending on their position in the global stratification system. Higher income countries have lower childhood death rates, high life expectancy, and fewer children born underweight. In low-income countries, the problems of poor sanitation, contaminated water, high childhood death rates, and low life expectancy are closely related.

    C.   <u>Education</u>

        1.   In high-income countries, literacy and school attendance are taken for granted, and education is nearly universal.

        2.   The percent of elementary-age children in school is significantly lower in middle and lower income nations; however, even in poor areas, education is improving.

        3.   Most education around the world, including basic literacy and math skills, occurs in family settings or religious congregations. This informal education does not give most people the skills and knowledge needed to operate successfully in an increasingly technological world.

    D.   <u>Gender</u>

Around the world, women experience poverty more than men, a situation that is reflected in the **gender development index**. The index measures gender inequality in terms of life expectancy, educational attainment, and income, revealing the relative well being or deprivation of women in nations around the world.

III. THEORIES OF GLOBAL STRATIFICATION

A. Modernization Theory

1. **Modernization theory** views the economic development of a country as a process whereby traditional societies become more complex and differentiated by changing their attitudes, values, and institutions.

2. Based largely on functionalist theory and the work of Max Weber, this perspective argues that the Industrial Revolution occurred in Northern Europe because the Protestant residents there were hardworking people who valued thrift and individual achievement.

3. Similar to the "culture of poverty" theory, modernization theory views countries as poor because they have poor attitudes and poor institutions; thus, proponents of this theory recommend development as the solution to poverty.

4. Modernization theory has been criticized for not explaining the development, or lack thereof, in all nations; blaming countries for being poor; and arguing that government should not make economic decisions or develop policies that restrict business or free trade.

B. Dependency Theory

1. Derived from the work of Karl Marx, **dependency theory** argues that the poverty of low-income countries is a result of their colonization and economic exploitation by powerful countries.

2. **Neocolonialism** is a form of international control of poor countries by rich countries, without direct political or military involvement. In this process, rich industrialized nations set prices for raw materials produced by poor countries at very low levels so that the poor countries are unable to accumulate enough profit to industrialize.

3. **Multinational corporations**, who buy resources and labor in the countries with the lowest prices, play an important role in keeping dependent nations poor.

4. Critics of dependency theory argue that some colonies, such as Hong Kong, have done well economically. Critics also emphasize that it is not clear that the involvement of multinational corporations always impoverishes nations.

C. World Systems Theory

1. **World systems theory** argues that there is a world economic system that must be understood as a single unit, not in terms of individual countries.

2. This theory, derived from conflict theory and most closely associated with the work of Immanuel Wallerstein, argues that a global system of stratification has developed based on historical and strategic imbalances in the economic system.

3. This theory divides the world into three groups of interrelated nations.

   a. *Core countries* are the rich, powerful, capitalistic countries that control the world system.

   b. *Semiperipheral countries* occupy an intermediate position in the world.

   c. *Peripheral countries* are poor, largely agricultural, and manipulated by core countries that extract resources and profits from them.

4. This focuses on the economic interconnectedness of countries worldwide and the **new international division of labor**, which contributes to the global production of goods through a **commodity chain**, or the network of production and labor processes by which a product becomes a finished commodity.

5. The growing phenomenon of international migration is the result of refugees seeking asylum as well as the demand for cheap labor in *world cities*, or cities closely linked to international commerce.

6. Critics of world systems theory note that it is not clear that the world system always works to the advantage of core countries and to the detriment of

peripheral countries, and furthermore, low-wage sweatshops are found in *all* nations, including core countries such as the United States.

IV. WORLD POVERTY

A. Defining World Poverty

1. The definition of poverty in the United States identifies **relative poverty**, or the amount of income considered necessary for a family of four to maintain a suitable standard of living. Nearly 13 percent of Americans live at or below the official poverty line of $17,184.

2. **Absolute poverty** is the situation in which individuals live on less than $365 per year, thus, they do not have enough money for basic survival.

3. **Extreme poverty** is the situation in which individuals live on less that $275 per year. There are 6 million people who live at or below this level of poverty.

4. The United Nations uses the **Human Poverty Index**, which indicates the degree of deprivation of a population in four dimensions of life: health and life expectancy, knowledge, economic well-being, and social inclusion [Figure 8.2].

B. Who are the World's Poor?

Using the World Bank's definition of international poverty, 1.2 billion people, or 26 percent of the world's population, live in poverty. Although there has been progress in reducing poverty in East Asia, poverty has increased substantially in Africa, Latin America, South and Central Asia, and Eastern Europe. In sub-Saharan Africa, the poor live in marginal areas where poor soil, erosion, continuous warfare, and political instability have created extremely harsh conditions.

C. Women and Children in Poverty

1. There is no country in the world in which women are treated as well as men. The disproportionate burden of poverty carried by women in many poor countries is referred to as *double deprivation*.

   a. The United Nations Commission on the Status of Women estimates that women constitute almost 60 percent of the world's population, perform two-thirds all working hours, receive one-tenth of the world's income, and own less than one percent of the world's wealth.

   b. In poor countries, women suffer greater health risks than do men because fertility rates are higher in poor countries and women spend a greater part of their lives pregnant, nursing and raising small children. Women also suffer because of patriarchal cultural norms, such as feeding men before women, which increase women's rates of malnutrition and anemia.

2. Children are also hit particularly hard in poor countries, where they do not have the luxury of a protected childhood or an education, but must work to help the family by performing domestic chores, begging, stealing, laboring in sweatshops, or being sold into prostitution by their families.

D. Poverty and Hunger

An estimated 1.2 billion people in the world are unable to obtain enough food to meet their nutritional needs, and each day, about 30,000 people die as a consequence of chronic, persistent hunger. Malnutrition, which stunts physical and mental development, is dangerously high despite the fact that the food supply around the world is plentiful, because food is not distributed to those who need it.

E. Causes of World Poverty

Poverty is not necessarily caused by too rapid population growth, although high fertility rates and poverty are related. Poverty is not caused by an unmotivated, lazy population; in fact, people in poor countries work very hard to survive. Poverty results from several tragic situations, including unstable governments, collapsed economies, and changes in the world economic system that increased unemployment and drove wages down in commodity-producing nations.

V.   THE FUTURE OF WORLD STRATIFICATION

In some areas of the world, particularly East Asia, but also in Latin America, many countries have shown rapid growth and have emerged as developed countries. In **newly industrialized countries** (NICs) such as Korea, Malaysia, Thailand, Taiwan, and Singapore, governments have invested in social and economic development and individuals have saved and invested. Despite these changes, some nations are facing enormous economic and social problems, including ethnic hatred leading to mass genocide, government collapse, bankruptcy, and plummeting standards of living. Although capitalist expansion may assist some countries, it is likely that other countries, which are suffering from years of neglect, will be placed at a further disadvantage.

PRACTICE TEST

Multiple Choice Questions

1.   Which of the following is a measure of the total volume of goods and services produced by a country each year?
    a.   annual commodity product
    b.   annual human poverty index
    c.   annual global economic index
    d.   annual per capita gross national product

2.   The majority of the wealthy countries are located in which part of the world?
    a.   Western Europe
    b.   Eastern Europe
    c.   South America
    d.   South Asia

3.   The classification scheme used during the Cold War categorized the United States as a:
    a.   peripheral country.
    b.   first-world country.
    c.   second-world country.
    d.   semiperipheral country.

4.   Which of the following features are characteristic of third-world countries?
    a.   They are largely urban.
    b.   They are semi-industrialized.
    c.   They have very high fertility rates.
    d.   All of the above are characteristics of third-world countries.

5.   Using power as the main dimension of stratification in the world system, the semi-industrialized nations of Spain and Turkey would be classified as _____ countries.
    a.   core
    b.   modern
    c.   peripheral
    d.   semiperipheral

6. Using power as a dimension of world stratification, most of the countries of Western Europe would be classified as _____ countries.
   a. semiperipheral
   b. traditional
   c. peripheral
   d. core

7. Those largely agricultural countries that lack power or influence in the world system, but often possess important resources that are exploited by rich nations, are classified as _____ countries.
   a. core
   b. modern
   c. peripheral
   d. semiperipheral

8. Which of the industrialized nations has the highest rating on the human poverty index; that is, which is the poorest industrialized nation?
   a. Japan
   b. Russia
   c. Sweden
   d. United States

9. In which of the following poor regions of the world has poverty been reduced since 1987?
   a. East Asia
   b. South Asia
   c. Latin America
   d. Sub-Saharan Africa

10. Which of the following is a dimension of the gender development index?
    a. level of educational attainment
    b. rate of home ownership
    c. family size
    d. None of the above indicators are used to construct the gender development index.

11. Modernization theory focuses on the:
    a. economic interconnection of countries worldwide and the emergence of an international division of labor whereby products are produced globally.
    b. role of neocolonialism in controlling and exploiting poor countries to prevent them from accumulating enough wealth to become industrialized.
    c. adoption of new technologies and market-driven attitudes that promote saving and investing in traditional societies.
    d. contribution of multinational corporations to maintaining poverty in dependent nations by keeping wages low.

12. Based on the work of Karl Marx, _____ theory asserts that the poverty of low-income countries is a result of colonization and economic exploitation by rich, powerful countries.
    a. dependency
    b. modernization
    c. world systems
    d. global production

13. Which of the following is a dimension of deprivation used to calculate the human poverty index?
   a. economic well-being
   b. life expectancy
   c. knowledge
   d. All of the above are dimensions of deprivation used to calculate the index.

14. The United Nations identifies the situation in which individuals live on less than $275 per year as:
   a. global stratification.
   b. double deprivation.
   c. extreme poverty.
   d. chronic poverty.

15. Sociologists generally agree that people who suffer from chronic hunger:
   a. cannot purchase adequate food because they are not motivated to work enough to earn sufficient wages to support themselves and their families.
   b. experience malnutrition that may stifle mental and physical growth but rarely die as a result.
   c. cannot secure enough food because they live in countries that are so overpopulated that the demand is far greater than the available food supply.
   d. None of the above is an accurate explanation for chronic hunger around the world today.

16. In the United States, the poverty level is determined by the annual income for a family of four that is considered necessary to maintain a suitable standard of living, which reflects ___ poverty.
   a. chronic
   b. relative
   c. absolute
   d. extreme

17. Which of the following nations would be considered a *newly industrializing country* based on its recent, rapid economic growth?
   a. United States
   b. Australia
   c. Africa
   d. Korea

18. The reason(s) that women in poor countries experience *double deprivation* is that they:
   a. perform only one-third of all working hours.
   b. constitute only half of the world's population.
   c. consume less food and suffer more malnutrition than do men.
   d. All of the above contribute to double deprivation.

19. The richest countries in the world have approximately what percent of the world's population?
   a. 15
   b. 25
   c. 50
   d. 75

20. Anthony Marx argues that the lack of clearly defined racial categories in Brazil has:
    a.   resulted in a society where racial differences have no influence on individual opportunities or social status.
    b.   upset the elite class, who has repeatedly demanded that the government establish an official racial classification system.
    c.   denied dark-skinned people the opportunity to develop a strong group identity that would serve as the basis for group solidarity.
    d.   encouraged dark-skinned people to collectively pressure the government to recognize them as a distinct social group with a unique cultural history.

True-False Questions

1.   With the exception of Russia, the United States has a higher rate of child poverty than all other industrialized nations in the world.

2.   Most of the basic education provided to people in poor countries occurs in informal settings such as the family and religious congregations.

3.   According to the World Bank's definition of international poverty, approximately one-fourth of the world's population lives in poverty.

4.   Modernization theory, which is derived from conflict theory, views traditional societies as poor because they have been colonized and otherwise exploited by rich countries.

5.   World systems theory argues that the poverty of low-income countries is a result of having poor institutions and poorly motivated individuals who do not save or invest their money.

6.   Dependency theory classifies nations based on their degree of control over the global economic system.

7.   The populations of the poorest countries in the world are largely rural and comprised mainly of people of color.

8.   According to a global classification system used during the Cold War, countries with Communist governments and state managed economies were categorized as first world countries.

9.   In low-income countries, high childhood death rates are attributable to poor sanitation and contaminated water supplies as well as food shortages.

10.   One of the main problems facing rich countries today is that declining birth rates have led to a shortage of workers.

Fill in the Blank Questions

1.   The form of international control whereby rich countries lend money to poor countries, resulting in the greater dependence of poor countries on rich countries, is called _____.

2.   Companies such as Nike are _____, or large companies whose stockholders are from the industrialized countries, but whose materials are purchased in countries where resources are cheapest and whose goods are manufactured in countries where labor costs are lowest.

3. World systems theorists call the global network of production and labor processes by which a product becomes a saleable item the _____.

Essay Questions

1. Explain why the classification system that categorizes countries as First World, Second World, and Third World is not as useful today as it was during the Cold War.
2. Use the concepts of the *commodity chain* and the *new international division of labor* to explain how clothing is produced in today's global economy.
3. Discuss how population characteristics are related to poverty levels around the world, specifically identifying how rich and poor nations differ on each relevant characteristic.

ANSWERS TO PRACTICE TEST

Multiple Choice Questions

1.	D	208	One of the most common ways to measure the wealth of nations is by using the annual per capita gross national product (per capita GNP), which measures the total volume of goods and services produced per year.
2.	A	212	Most of the wealthy countries are in Western Europe. The poorest countries in the world are in Africa, Asia, and South America.
3.	B	210	First world countries consist of the industrialized, capitalist nations such as the U.S., Japan, Australia, and the countries of Western Europe.
4.	C	210	Third World countries are poor, largely rural, and have high fertility rates.
5.	D	212	Semiperipheral countries such as Spain, Turkey, and Mexico are semi-industrialized. They play a middleman role in the world economy, extracting profits from poor countries.
6.	D	211	Core countries, such as the United States, control and profit the most from the world system. They rank highest on the power dimension of global stratification.
7.	C	212	Peripheral countries have little power or influence in the world system, but they have important resources that are exploited by the core countries.
8.	B	221	Figure 8.2 indicates that among the industrialized nations, Russia has the highest rating on the human poverty index, while Sweden has the lowest rating.
9.	A	220	There has been a decline in poverty in Asia, mostly attributable to reduced poverty in the People's Republic of China. Sub-Saharan Africa has the highest poverty rate in the world.
10.	A	215	The gender development index measures women's well-being using three dimensions of deprivation: life expectancy, educational attainment, and income.
11.	C	215	Table 8.2 indicates that modernization theory emphasizes the role of technology and people's value systems in fostering the economic development of a country.
12.	A	217	Table 8.2 indicates that dependency theory explains the poverty of low-income countries as a result of their exploitation by the rich, powerful countries.
13.	D	220	The four dimensions of the human poverty index are knowledge, life expectancy, social inclusion, and economic well being.
14.	C	220	The United Nations identifies the situation in which individuals live on less than $275 per year as extreme poverty. Absolute poverty is the situation in which individuals live on less than $365 per year. The disproportionate burden of poverty carried by women in countries around the world is double deprivation.
15.	D	223	Poor people are motivated to acquire food and other necessities; in fact, they work hard to survive. There is enough food to feed the world's population, but

food is not distributed in such a way that it reaches all of the people who need it. In addition to causing widespread malnutrition, chronic hunger kills people.

16. B 220 Relative poverty is the amount of income that a family in the United States needs to maintain a suitable standard of living. The official poverty level is $17, 184.

17. D 225 Korea, Malaysia, Thailand, Taiwan, and Singapore, which have shown rapid economic growth and emerged as developed nations, are referred to as the newly industrializing countries.

18. C 221 Women constitute 60 percent of the world's population, perform two-thirds of work hours, and receive only one-tenth of the world's income. Women are more likely than men to suffer from malnutrition, and experience greater illness and death associated with pregnancy, birth, and childrearing.

19. A 214 The richest countries in the world have about 15 percent of the world's population, and population growth occurs at a slower rate in rich countries than in poor countries due to declining fertility rates.

20. C 213 Anthony Marx's comparison of racial categories in Brazil and the United States indicates that being clearly labeled as Black has supported the development of group solidarity and collective action among people of color in the U.S. In Brazil, where elites declared the country a racial democracy, skin color still influences individual opportunities and social status, but the lack of clearly defined racial categories has denied Afro-Brazilians an important source of collective identity.

Answers to True-False Questions

1. T 223 Among the industrialized nations, only Russia has a higher child poverty rate than the United States {Figure 8.3].

2. T 215 In high-income countries, education is nearly universal, but in poor countries, school attendance is low and most basic education occurs in informal settings such as the family and religious congregations.

3. T 220 Twenty-six percent of the world's population, or 1.2 billion people, live in poverty.

4. F 217 Dependency theory is derived from conflict theory and views poverty as the result of neocolonialism and the expansion of capitalism [Table 8.2].

5. F 218 Modernization theory argues that poverty is the result of having poorly developed institutions, low technological development, and unmotivated populations who do not save or invest money [Table 8.2].

6. T 217 Dependency theory argues that core countries are able to exert greater control over the world economic system, particularly by lending money to peripheral countries, because debt perpetuates their dependence on the rich countries.

7. T 212 Those countries that suffer a poor standard of living, have low levels of education and high death rates, and are generally at the bottom of the global stratification system are comprised largely of people of color.

8. F 210 According to a global classification system used during the Cold War, countries with Communist governments and state managed economies, such as the former Soviet Union, were second world countries. First world countries consisted of the industrialized capitalist countries, such as the United States and Japan.

9. T 214 Less than 50 percent of the people in the poor nations have adequate sanitation, and only 57 percent have access to clean water. Young children are highly susceptible to waterborne illnesses such as cholera, which may result in death.

10. T 214 Many of the richest countries are experiencing population declines, creating a shortage of young people to meet the society's labor needs, which may be addressed by importing workers from other countries.

Answers to Fill in the Blank Questions

1.	neocolonialism	217
2.	multinational corporations	218
3.	commodity chain	219

CHAPTER 9
RACE AND ETHNICITY

BRIEF CHAPTER OUTLINE

Race and Ethnicity
    Ethnicity
    Race
    Minority and Dominant Groups
Racial Stereotypes
    Stereotypes and Salience
    The Interplay Among Race, Gender, and Class Stereotypes
Prejudice, Discrimination and Racism
    Prejudice
    Discrimination
    Racism
Theories of Prejudice and Racism
    Social Psychological Theories of Prejudice
    Sociological Theories of Prejudice and Racism
Diverse Groups, Diverse Histories
    Native Americans
    African Americans
    Latinos
    Asian Americans
    Middle Easterners
    White Ethnic Groups
Patterns of Racial and Ethnic Relations
    Assimilation and Pluralism
    Colonialism
    Segregation and the Urban Underclass
    The Relative Importance of Class and Race
Attaining Racial and Ethnic Equality: The Challenge
    Civil Rights
    Radical Social Change
    Affirmative Action: Race-Specific versus Color-Blind Programs for Change

CHAPTER FOCUS: This chapter discusses the causes and consequences of racial and ethnic prejudice and discrimination. It also examines the social and historical circumstances in which various racial-ethnic groups developed in the United States.

QUESTIONS TO GUIDE YOUR READING
1.   Which characteristics do sociologists use to define minority groups, and which groups would be defined as minority groups in the United States according to this definition?
2.   What is the difference between prejudice and discrimination, and how do both concepts support social inequality?
3.   How do class and gender interact with race and ethnicity in the development of stereotypes?
4.   What evidence exists to support the assertion that race is a socially constructed category rather than a biologically determined category?
5.   How is the current social situation of various minority groups related to their initial employment and immigration patterns?

SOCIOLOGY IN ACTION: AN INTERNET EXERCISE

Go to www.naacp.org and www.blackpanther.org to compare the mission statements of two organizations committed to supporting the rights of Black Americans, the National Association for the Advancement of Colored People (NAACP) and the Black Panther Party. How are their philosophies and tactics for promoting racial equality similar? How are they different?

KEY TERMS (defined at page number and in glossary)

affirmative action 254	assimilation 239
authoritarian personality 239	contact theory 240
cultural pluralism 248	discrimination 237
domestic colonialism 248	ethnic group 230
ethnocentrism 236	gendered racism 240
institutional racism 238	minority group 233
prejudice 235	race 232
racial formation 233	racial profiling 238
racialization 231	racism 238
residential segregation 238	salience principle 234
scapegoat theory 239	segregation 249
stereotype 234	stereotype interchangeability 235
urban underclass 249	

KEY PEOPLE (identified at page number shown)

Robert Blauner 248   William Julius Wilson 249

CHAPTER OUTLINE

I.   **RACE AND ETHNICITY**

    A.   Ethnicity

        1.   An **ethnic group** is a social category of people who share common cultural characteristics such as language, religion, and customs.

        2.   Ethnic groups develop because of their unique historical and social experiences, which become the basis for the group's *ethnic identity*, or the definition the group has of itself as sharing a common cultural bond.

        3.   Ethnic groups can develop a more or less intense ethnic identity at different points in time. For example, prejudice, hostility, and exclusionary practices from other groups often strengthen ethnic identity.

    B.   Race

        Like ethnicity, race is a socially constructed category. Societies assign people to races not by logic and fact, but based on opinion and social experiences, making the definition of race a *social* process.

        1.   The categories used to presumably divide groups into races are not fixed; they vary from society to society and over time. For example, the U.S. Bureau of the Census has classified various groups differently over time [Table 9.1].

        2.   The biological characteristics that have been used to define different racial groups vary both within and between groups. For example, in Brazil, only those people of African descent are classified as Black, regardless of skin color.

        3.   The biological differences presumed to define different racial groups are rather arbitrary, for example, skin color rather than hair or eye color. In fact, most of the variability in truly biological characteristics, such as blood type, is *within* (rather than between) racial groups.

4. Different groups use different criteria to define racial groups. For example, some Native American tribes recognize as members only those people who are of 75 percent ancestry, while other tribes recognize 50 percent ancestry.

5. **Racialization** is a process whereby some social category, such as social class or nationality, takes on what are perceived in the society to be race characteristics. For example, Adolph Hitler labeled Jews, a religious ethnic group, as a race.

6. A **race** is a group treated as distinct in society on the basis of certain characteristics, some of which are biological, that have been assigned social importance; thus, race is *socially constructed*.

7. **Racial formation** is the process by which a group comes to be defined as a race through support from official institutions such as the law and schools. For example, Latinos are defined as a "race" in the United States despite the varied backgrounds and experiences of specific groups within the established category.

C. Minority and Dominant Groups

1. A **minority group** is any distinct group in society that shares common group characteristics and is forced to occupy low status in society because of prejudice and discrimination.

   a. Not all racial or ethnic groups are minorities; for example, although Irish Americans were once minorities, they are not a minority group today.

   b. Minority status does not necessarily depend on numerical representation; for example, Black people in South Africa under the *apartheid* system were a numerical majority but a social minority.

2. The group that assigns a racial or ethnic group to subordinate status in society is the *dominant group* by virtue of their power to establish such designations.

3. A racial or ethnic group typically has four primary features.

   a. It possesses characteristics that are popularly regarded as different from those of the dominant group.

   b. It suffers prejudice and discrimination by the dominant group.

   c. Membership is frequently ascribed rather than achieved, although either form of status can be the basis for being identified as a minority.

   d. Members feel a strong sense of solidarity or "we feeling."

II. **RACIAL STEREOTYPES**

A. Stereotypes and Salience

1. A **stereotype** is an oversimplified set of beliefs about members of a social group or social stratum that is used to categorize individuals of that group. They are presumed to describe the "typical" member of the group.

2. The categorization of people into groups and the subsequent application of stereotypes are based on the **salience principle**. Salience implies that we categorize people on the basis of what initially appears prominent and obvious about them, such as skin color, gender, and age.

B. The Interplay Among Race, Gender and Class Stereotypes

1. *Gender stereotypes* about women are more likely to be negative than those about men. The mass media convey and support cultural stereotypes of women as subservient and overly emotional, and of men as insensitive and macho.

2. *Social class stereotypes* are based on assumptions about one's social position. These include the characterizations of upper class people as snooty and phony and of lower income people as dirty, lazy, and violent.

3. The principle of **stereotype interchangeability** holds that stereotypes, especially negative ones, are often interchangeable from one targeted group to another. For example, ethnic jokes often interchange groups as the butt of the humor, but stereotype the groups in the same ways; for example, as lazy and inept.

4.   Whatever group occupies low social status at a given time is stereotyped, and the stereotype is used to explain observed behavior and justify the low social status.

III.   **PREJUDICE, DISCRIMINATION, AND RACE**

   A.   Prejudice

      1.   **Prejudice** is the evaluation of a social group, and individuals within that group, based on conceptions about the social group that hold together despite facts that contradict it.

      2.   Prejudice involves both prejudgment and misjudgment. A prejudiced person will have negative attitudes about members of an *outgroup*, or any group other than one's own, as well as positive attitudes about members of one's own *ingroup*.

      3.   Prejudice based on race or ethnicity is called *racial-ethnic prejudice. Gender prejudice* is a negative evaluation of someone based on gender, and *class prejudice* is a negative evaluation of someone solely on the basis of social class.

      4.   Prejudice is revealed in **ethnocentrism**, or the belief that one's group is superior to all other groups, and has a marked effect on people's political views and voting behavior.

      5.   Stereotypes and prejudices are learned and internalized through the socialization process, where children imitate their parents, peers reinforce negative attitudes, and the mass media either ignore or strongly stereotype minorities.

   B.   Discrimination

     Discrimination is the negative and unequal treatment of the members of some social group solely because of their membership in that group. *Racial-ethnic discrimination* is the unequal treatment of a person on the basis of race or ethnicity. Discrimination toward Blacks in housing, for example, is especially prominent in the United States. Pervasive discrimination in housing has resulted in persistent **residential segregation**, or the spatial separation of racial and ethnic groups into different neighborhoods.

   C.   Racism

      1.   **Racism** is the perception and treatment of a racial or ethnic group, or member of that group, as intellectually, socially, and culturally inferior to one's own group. Racism may be overt, subtle, or covert.

      2.   **Institutional racism** is negative treatment and oppression of one racial or ethnic group by society's existing institutions based on the presumed inferiority of the oppressed group.

          a.   Institutional racism occurs when dominant groups have the economic and political power to subjugate the minority group, even if they do not have the explicit intention of being prejudiced or discriminatory.

          b.   Institutional racism is evident in the American criminal justice system by examining the practice of **racial profiling**, whereby police use the criterion of race to determine suspicion of criminal activity.

      3.   Institutional racism exists at the level of social structure and is therefore a *social fact* that is external to the attitudes and behaviors of individuals.

IV.   **THEORIES OF PREJUDICE AND DISCRIMINATION**

   A.   Social Psychological Theories of Prejudice

      1.   **Scapegoat theory** argues that historically, members of the dominant group in the United States have harbored various frustrations in their desire to achieve social and economic success. This frustration results in anger and aggression being directed toward minority groups.

      2.   Another social psychological theory focuses on the personality traits of prejudiced individuals. The **authoritarian personality** is characterized by a tendency to rigidly categorize other people, submit to authority, rigidly conform,

be very intolerant of ambiguity, and be inclined to superstition. Individuals with an authoritarian personality are more likely to be prejudiced.

B. Sociological Theories of Prejudice and Racism
    1. Functionalist theory argues that social stability requires the assimilation of racial-ethnic minorities and women.
        a. **Assimilation** is a process by which a minority becomes socially, economically, and culturally absorbed within the dominant society.
        b. How rapidly a group assimilates into a society will depend partly on its unique history and the group members' desire to assimilate.
    2. Symbolic Interaction theory examines the role of social interaction in reducing racial-ethnic hostility and the social construction of race and ethnicity. **Contact theory** argues that interaction between Whites and minorities will reduce prejudice on the part of both groups if three conditions are met.
        a. The contact must be between individuals of equal status.
        b. The contact between equals must be sustained over time.
        c. Participants must agree on social norms favoring equality.
    3. Conflict theory assumes that class-based conflict is an inherent part of social interaction; therefore, class inequality must be reduced to lessen racial and ethnic conflict in society. **Gendered racism** theory, a variety of conflict theory, focuses on the interactive or combined effects of race and sex in the oppression of women of color.

V. DIVERSE GROUPS, DIVERSE HISTORIES

The histories of various racial and ethnic groups in the United States are similar in some ways, yet unique in others. The groups' histories are related by the common experience of White supremacy, economic exploitation, and political disenfranchisement. Members of some White ethnic groups, such as Irish Americans have also been victims of prejudice and discrimination.

A. Native Americans
    1. At the time of the first European contacts with Native Americans in the 1640s, there was considerable linguistic, religious, governmental, and economic heterogeneity among the original 500 nations of Native Americans. Much of this tribal culture has since been destroyed.
    2. Government policies forced many Native Americans into inhospitable country, leading to starvation. Massive numbers of indigenous people were also killed by disease and wars of extermination.
    3. Today, about 55 percent of Native Americans live on or near a reservation, a system associated with abject poverty, very high unemployment, and severely limited access to education, health care, and other basic services.

B. African Americans
    1. Slaves were forcibly imported from Africa to provide free labor for sugar and tobacco plantations in the United States.
    2. Until recently, our knowledge of slavery has been distorted by its dependence on the records and observations made by White male slave owners. More recent research includes the accounts, records, and narratives of the slaves themselves.
    3. In the early part of the twentieth century, the formation of ghettos subjected Black Americans to grim urban conditions. However, these ghettos also encouraged the development of Black community resources, including voluntary organizations, social movements, and artistic and cultural achievements.

C. Latinos
Latino Americans include Chicanos and Chicanas (Mexican Americans), Puerto Ricans, Cubans, and other recent Latin American immigrants to the United States, as well as Latin Americans who have lived in the United States for generations. There is great

structural and cultural diversity within the Hispanic population, which has grown considerably in recent years.

1.   Chicanos, or Mexican Americans, lost claims to huge land areas (which became Texas, New Mexico, and parts of other Midwestern states) in the Mexican-American War of 1846-1848.

   a.   American immigration policy in the 1920s disproportionately restricted Mexican immigration.

   b.   In the early twentieth century, irrigation and its resulting year-round crop production increased the need for field labor, leading to the exploitation of migrant workers from Mexico as a cheap source of labor.

2.   The Jones Act extended United States citizenship to Puerto Ricans in 1917, and the Commonwealth of Puerto Rico was established in 1952 with its own constitution. In the 1960s and 1970s, unemployment in Puerto Rico became so severe that in the U.S. government attempted to reduce the population by encouraging forms of population control, including female sterilization.

3.   Cuban migration to the United States is recent in comparison to other Hispanic groups. Many of the immigrants who arrived shortly after the 1959 revolution led by Fidel Castro were middle and upper class landowners and professionals. The most recent wave of Cuban immigration occurred in 1980 when the Cuban government opened the port of Mariel to anyone who wanted to leave. The second group of immigrants has not been unable to achieve much social mobility.

D.   Asians

Asian Americans hail from many countries and have diverse cultural backgrounds.

1.   Chinese Americans began migrating to the United States during the mid-nineteenth century in response to a demand for labor. They performed much of the most difficult and dangerous work of building the Central Pacific Railroad. Ethnic antagonisms led to the establishment of several urban Chinatowns on the West Coast, which were ethnic enclaves that provided support to residents.

2.   The first generation of Japanese immigrants, who arrived between 1890 and 1924, were generally employed in agriculture or small Japanese businesses. The second generation of Japanese Americans became better educated than their parents, lost their Japanese accents, and generally assimilated.

   a.   By executive order of President Roosevelt, much of the West Coast Japanese American population had their assets frozen, their real estate confiscated by the government, and were forced to move into relocation centers during World War II.

   b.   In 1987, the United States government offered an official apology for their actions and awarded $20,000 to each former detainee.

3.   In 1934, the Filipino Islands became a commonwealth of the United States and immigration quotas were imposed upon the Filipinos. Over 200,000 Filipinos immigrated to the United States between 1966 and 1980, most of who were professional workers with high levels of education.

4.   Korean Americans, who are largely concentrated in Los Angeles, California, tend to be former professionals who experience downward social mobility when they migrate to the United States. Conflict between African American residents and Korean business owners exists in many urban communities today.

5.   Vietnamese people began to arrive in the United States after the fall of South Vietnam in 1975, and a second wave of Vietnamese arrived after China attacked Vietnam in 1978. Despite initial discrimination, most Vietnamese heads of households in the United States are now employed full-time.

E. Middle Easterners

Immigrants from countries such as Syria, Lebanon, Egypt, and Iran speak no single language and follow no single religion, yet they are grouped together socially. Many are from working class backgrounds, but those who are professionals have not always been able to secure employment in their original occupations, leading to downward mobility once they immigrate to the United States.

F. White Ethnic Groups

1. White Anglo-Saxon Protestants (WASPs) who immigrated from England, Scotland, and Wales were the first ethnic group to have widespread contact with Native American Indians. WASPs dominated the newly emerging society earlier than any other White ethnic group.

    a. The original WASP immigrants were skilled workers with a strong Protestant Ethic, or desire to work and achieve wealth.

    b. WASPs began to direct prejudice and discrimination toward other European immigrants during the mid- to late-nineteenth century. The dominance of WASPs in the U.S. has declined somewhat since 1960.

2. There were two waves of immigration of White Ethnic groups in the 19th century, with immigrants from Northern and Western Europe arriving in the United States from 1850 to 1880 and immigrants from Eastern and Southern Europe arriving from 1890 to 1914. The Irish arrived in large numbers in the mid-nineteenth century as a consequence of food shortages and massive starvation in Ireland.

3. Another large immigrant group was Jewish people. Over 40 percent of the world's Jewish population now lives in the United States.

4. In 1924, the National Origins Act imposed *ethnic quotas* that permitted immigrants to enter only in proportion to their numbers already in the country.

VI. **PATTERNS OF RACIAL AND ETHNIC RELATIONS**

A. Assimilation and Pluralism

1. The assimilation model asserts that to overcome adversity and oppression, minorities need only to imitate the dominant White culture.

2. Although many Asian American groups have followed this pattern and been identified as the "model minority," they are still subject to prejudice and discrimination, and some Asian American groups have high rates of poverty.

3. This model is problematic because it does not consider the amount of time that it takes for certain groups to assimilate. For example, groups from rural areas typically take longer to assimilate than do groups with urban backgrounds.

4. The assimilation model does not take into account that Blacks arrived in the United States involuntarily and were enslaved, so their histories cannot be compared to Whites who voluntarily immigrated.

5. Many White ethnics entered the United States at a time when the economy was rapidly growing and labor was in high demand, thereby providing more opportunities for attaining education and job skills despite discrimination.

6. The assimilation model raises the question of whether a society can maintain **cultural pluralism**, defined as different groups in society maintaining their distinctive cultures while coexisting peacefully with the dominant group. The Amish in Pennsylvania are an example of successful cultural pluralism.

B. Colonialism

Robert Blauner, who developed the **domestic colonialism** model and applied it to Blacks in the United States, asserted that Black Americans are an internal colony because: 1) the dominant group forcibly entered the community; 2) the affairs of the colonized group are administered and determined by the colonizers (the dominant group); 3) racism and racial stereotypes are used to explain and justify the colonizer's domination over the minority group; and 4) the colonizers do not allow the minority group to freely express its culture and values. This suppression of the group's native culture may result in the development of cultural nationalism among the colonized group.

    C.   <u>Segregation and the Urban Underclass</u>
        1.   **Segregation** refers to the spatial and social separation of racial and ethnic groups.
            a.   *De jure segregation*, or legal segregation, is prohibited by law today.
            b.   *De facto segregation*, or "in fact" segregation, still exists, particularly in housing and education.
        2.   According to Wilson, segregation has contributed to the creation of an **urban underclass**, or a grouping of people, largely minority and poor, who live at the absolute bottom of the socioeconomic ladder in urban areas. The problems of the inner city, such as joblessness and crime, arise from inequalities in the social structure and have dire consequences at the individual level, including teen pregnancy and AIDS.

    D.   <u>The Relative Importance of Class and Race</u>
    Wilson contends that the importance of social class has increased as the significance of race in determining Black people's access to privilege and power in the United States has declined. Wilson's critics note that race still matters, because Blacks at every level of education still earn less than Whites.

VII.   ATTAINING RACIAL AND ETHNIC EQUALITY: THE CHALLENGE

Throughout the world, conflicts stemming from facial and ethnic differences are frequently the basis for economic inequality, cultural conflict, and war [Map 9.2].

    A.   <u>Civil Rights</u>
    The civil rights movement in the United States, which was based on the philosophy of passive resistance promoted by Dr. Martin Luther King, was probably the single most important source for change in race relations in the twentieth century. This major movement intensified after the 1954 Supreme Court ruled in *Brown v. Board of Education* that separate education for Blacks and Whites is unconstitutional. In 1957, President Eisenhower called out the National Guard to assist the entrance of nine Black students into Little Rock Central High in Arkansas.

    B.   <u>Radical Social Change</u>
        1.   By the late 1960s, militant leaders had grown increasingly dissatisfied with the limitations and slow process of the civil rights agenda, and the militant Black Power movement emerged.
            a.   Political activist Stokely Carmichael saw inequality stemming from the institutional power that Whites had over Blacks
            b.   Prior to his assassination in 1965, Malcolm X advocated a form of pluralism by demanding separate business establishments, banks, churches, and schools for Black Americans.
            c.   When militant groups such as the Black Panthers advocated fighting oppression with armed revolution, the United States government responded by imprisoning and killing some group members.
        2.   The Black Power movement dramatically altered the nature of political struggle and race and ethnic relations in the United States and influenced the development of other groups concerned with institutional racism, including the Chicano organization, *La Raza Unida*, and the American Indian Movement (AIM).

    C.   <u>Affirmative Action: Race Specific versus Color-Blind Progress for Change</u>
        1.   *Color-blind policies* advocate that all groups be treated alike, with no barriers to oppression posed by race, gender, or other group differences.

2. *Race-specific policies* recognize that certain racial groups occupy a unique status because of a long history of discrimination and the continuing influence of institutional racism.

3. **Affirmative action**, a heavily contested program for social change, is a race-specific policy for reducing job and educational inequality. It includes two components:
   a. recruiting minorities from a wide base in order to ensure consideration of groups that have been traditionally overlooked, but without rigid quotas based on race or ethnicity.
   b. using admission slots (in education) or designated contracts or jobs (in employment) to assure minority representation.

4. The Legal Defense Fund argues that Affirmative Action does not constitute discrimination against the dominant group in society; however, legal opinion on affirmative action is inconclusive.

5. In 1996, the University of California Board of Regents, through Proposition 209, eliminated race, but not social class, as a basis for admissions.

PRACTICE TEST

Multiple Choice Questions

1. The process whereby some social category such as nationality or religion takes on what are perceived in the society to be race characteristics is referred to as:
   a. discrimination.
   b. stratification.
   c. racialization.
   d. assimiliation.

2. Sociologists refer to a social category of people who share common cultural elements, such as language, religion, norms, and customs, such as Irish Americans or African Americans, as a(n):
   a. dominant group.
   b. racial minority.
   c. ethnic group.
   d. underclass.

3. According to sociologists, which of the following statements about race is (are) true?
   a. Race is a fixed, biologically-based category that varies little over time.
   b. Definitions of race do not vary significantly within or across groups because they are based on a universal set of physical characteristics.
   c. A race is a group of people who have been defined as distinct on the basis of certain identifiable characteristics.
   d. All of the above statements about race are true.

4. Which immigrant group was initially tolerated because they provided cheap labor for the expanding railroad system, but later became the targets of prejudice and discrimination because Whites began to view them as competing for scarce jobs on the West coast in the 1800s?
   a. Cuban
   b. Chinese
   c. Africans
   d. Filipinos

5.   Sociologists refer to any socially distinct group that presumably shares common characteristics and is forced to occupy low status in society because of prejudice and discrimination as a:
   a.   dominant group.
   b.   racial minority.
   c.   minority group.
   d.   ethnic enclave.

6.   The basic premise of contact theory is that:
   a.   individuals who have particular personality traits, such as tendencies toward rigidly categorizing other people, submitting to authority, and being intolerant of ambiguity, are more likely to be prejudiced.
   b.   WASPs deserve to receive a greater proportion of society's rewards because they have been living and working in the United States longer than any other group.
   c.   prejudice between Whites and Blacks can be reduced through providing ample opportunities for sustained interaction between equal members of both groups.
   d.   the urban underclass developed as a result of economic and political policies designed to reduce public services (such as police patrols) in urban areas as a way to save money.

7.   As defined by sociologists, minority groups typically have which of the following characteristics?
   a.   Members feel a strong sense of solidarity.
   b.   Membership is usually ascribed rather than achieved.
   c.   Most members share an easily identifiable characteristic.
   d.   Racial and ethnic groups typically have all of the above characteristics.

8.   Sociologists refer to an oversimplified set of beliefs about members of a social group that is used to categorize individuals of that group and justify discrimination as:
   a.   prejudice.
   b.   stereotype.
   c.   victimization.
   d.   discrimination.

9.   Which concept implies that we categorize people on the basis of what appears initially prominent and obvious about them, such as skin color, gender, and age?
   a.   salience principle
   b.   victim hypothesis
   c.   racialization theory
   d.   authoritarian personality model

10.   Conflict theory argues that the best solution for reducing racial-ethnic inequality is to:
   a.   reduce the amount of contact racial and ethnic minorities have with Whites.
   b.   encourage minority groups to better assimilate into the dominant culture.
   c.   establish stricter punishments for people who insult or assault minorities.
   d.   reduce the degree of class inequality in society.

11.   Sociologists define the overt negative and unequal treatment of the members of some social group solely because of their membership in that group as:
   a.   prejudice.
   b.   discrimination.
   c.   differentiation.
   d.   ethnocentrism.

12. The current spatial segregation of racial and ethnic groups into different housing areas of the United States represents which type of segregation?
    a. de jure
    b. de facto
    c. quid pro quo
    d. in loco parentis

13. Which theory argues that members of the dominant group in the U.S. have historically harbored frustrations in their desire to achieve social and economic success, which they directed toward minority group members?
    a. assimilation
    b. resentment
    c. scapegoat
    d. contact

14. The largest community of Jewish people in the world lives in which nation?
    a. Israel
    b. Poland
    c. Germany
    d. United States

15. When the United States annexed the land that became Texas in the mid-1800s, which ethnic group became defined as a race and subsequently stereotyped as lazy and corrupt?
    a. Cubans
    b. Italians
    c. Mexicans
    d. Puerto Ricans

16. Which of the following statements about WASPs is (are) true?
    a. WASPs immigrated primarily from Ireland and Poland.
    b. The original WASP immigrants were skilled workers with a strong work ethic.
    c. The dominance of WASPs in U.S. society has increased somewhat since 1960.
    d. All of the above statements about WASPs are true.

17. Which of the following is **not** a feature of domestic colonialism according to Robert Blauner?
    a. The dominant group gradually enters an area and assumes control of the population's government by consent of the colonized people.
    b. The dominant group determines the agenda and administers the affairs of the colonized people.
    c. The colonizers use stereotypes to explain and justify their control over the colonized people.
    d. The colonizers suppress the colonized group's expression of cultural values and practices.

18. The 1924 National Origins Act:
    a. explicitly prohibited African Americans from marrying people of a different race.
    b. allowed the United States to legally establish Puerto Rico as a Commonwealth.
    c. allowed an increase in immigration for groups fleeing war in their own nations.
    d. imposed ethnic quotas restricting immigrants to enter the country only in proportion to their current representation.

19. Those policies that recognize the unique status of racial groups because of a long history of discrimination and the continuing influence of institutionalized racism are:
    a. color-blind.
    b. race-specific.
    c. domestic-based.
    d. culturally-oriented.

20. The majority of Cuban people who immigrated to the United States following the Cuban revolution led by Fidel Castro were:
    a. impoverished people who had little education and few job skills.
    b. working-class people who were moderately educated, skilled craftspeople.
    c. middle-class people who were highly educated professionals and land owners.
    d. None of the above groups migrated to the United States after the Cuban revolution because President Kennedy feared retribution from Castro if he allowed refugees to enter.

21. By executive order of President Roosevelt, which of the following groups had their assets frozen, their real estate confiscated by the American government, and were ordered into relocation centers in the United States during World War II?
    a. Japanese Americans
    b. German Americans
    c. African Americans
    d. None of the above groups experienced relocation, because the United States government has never violated American citizens' rights in this way.

22. Which of the following statements about Native Americans in the contemporary United States is (are) true?
    a. Only 10 percent of the Native American population still lives on a reservation.
    b. There is more than 50 percent unemployment among Native American men.
    c. Only African Americans have a higher poverty rate than Native Americans.
    d. All of the above statements about Native Americans are true.

True-False Questions

1. One necessary characteristic of a minority group is that it be comprised of fewer members than are in the dominant group.

2. The mass media most commonly stereotype lower-income men as overly emotional and talkative.

3. Prejudice is an individually held attitude, while discrimination is an overt behavior.

4. Imposed in 1924, the National Origins Quota Act prohibited Chinese people from immigrating to the United States.

5. The authoritarian personality is characterized by a tendency to challenge authority and be very tolerant of ambiguity.

6. Social psychologists argue that people with an authoritarian personality are more likely to be prejudiced.

7. Functionalist theory argues that the best solution for reducing racial-ethnic inequality is to encourage segregation, which reduces opportunities for adversarial groups to interact.

8. Over half of the Filipino population that migrated to the United States between 1966 and 1980 were well-educated professionals.

9. The Emancipation Proclamation of 1863 affected the status of Blacks in society by encouraging the development of political action groups that supported social movements for equality.

10. The United States classifies immigrants from Middle Eastern countries such as Syria, Lebanon, and Iran as one cohesive ethnic group because they share a common language and religious affiliation.

Fill in the Blank Questions

1. Prejudice is revealed in _____, or the belief that one's own group is superior to all other groups.

2. The principle of stereotype _____ holds that the same negative stereotypes are often applied to various groups who are the targets of racial or ethnic prejudice.

3. The social majority, or _____ group, assigns particular racial and ethnic groups to subordinate status in society.

4. Although _____ segregation is prohibited in the United States today, _____ segregation in housing and education persists.

5. Racial profiling is an example of _____ racism, which exists at the level of social structure rather than individual attitudes or behavior.

Essay Questions

1. Compare and contrast the experiences of, and outcomes for, three minority groups in the United States based on the circumstances (such as time period and primary reason for immigrating) in which they immigrated.
2. Provide evidence to support the statement, "Race and ethnicity are socially constructed."
3. Identify the three conditions that contact theory argues must be met to reduce prejudice between Whites and minority groups, and suggest one way that these conditions could be established in an educational or workplace setting.
4. Explain how domestic colonialism has contributed to the establishment and growth of the urban underclass in the United States.
5. Explain four problems with using the assimilation model to understand the experiences of African American people.

ANSWERS TO PRACTICE TEST

Answers to Multiple Choice Questions

1. A 231 The process whereby some social category such as nationality takes on what are perceived in the society to be race characteristics is racialization. An example of this process was Hitler's labeling Jews, an ethnic religious group, as a race.
2. C 230 Sociologists designate a category of people who share common cultural elements as an ethnic group. Only those racial and ethnic groups that are assigned to a low status in society and subject to discrimination are considered minority groups.

3. C 232 Sociologists view race as a socially constructed, rather than biologically-determined, category. The designation of a category of people as a "race" is a social process. Racial classifications vary cross-culturally and over time.

4. C 245 Chinese immigrants were a source of cheap labor for the railroad system; however, they were forced out of railroad employment in the late 1800s and subsequently faced considerable prejudice and discrimination because Whites viewed them as competition for scarce jobs in the West.

5. C 233 A minority group is forced to occupy low status in society because of prejudice and discrimination. The group granted the authority to designate other groups as minorities is referred to as the dominant group.

6. C 240 Contact theory posits that prejudice can be reduced by facilitating regular, sustained interaction between members of different racial-ethnic groups.

7. D 233 Sociologists identify four typical characteristics of minority groups: membership is ascribed rather than achieved, members possess characteristics that are popularly regarded as different from those of the dominant group, members suffer prejudice and discrimination, and members share a strong sense of solidarity or belonging.

8. B 234 An oversimplified set of beliefs about members of a social group that is used to categorize individuals of that group and justify inequality is a stereotype. Stereotypes are presumed to describe "typical" members of a social group. Prejudice is the negative evaluation of a group, whereas discrimination is the negative treatment of individuals belonging to a group based solely on their membership in that group.

9. A 234 The salience principle implies that we categorize people on the basis of what appears initially prominent and obvious about them, such as skin color and sex.

10. D 240 Conflict theory views racial and ethnic inequality as rooted in class inequality. This theory advocates challenging current social arrangements that are based on differences in power and access to valued resources. Conflict theory views social change as emerging from the active resistance of minority groups [Table 9.2].

11. B 237 The negative and unequal treatment of the members of some social group solely because of their membership in that group is discrimination. Prejudice is an attitude based on the negative evaluation of a group. Prejudice is revealed in ethnocentrism, or the belief that one's own values, norms, and practices are superior to those of other groups.

12. B 249 *De jure* segregation, or legal segregation, is prohibited in the United States, but *de facto* segregation persists, particularly in education and housing.

13. C 239 Scapegoat theory asserts that members of the dominant group have historically harbored frustrations in their desire to achieve social and economic success, which they then direct toward minority group members. Contact theory, which is associated with symbolic interaction theory, focuses on reducing prejudice through fostering positive, sustained social interaction between members of different racial groups. Functionalist theory advocates the assimilation of minority groups into the dominant culture as a mechanism for fostering social equality and social stability.

14. D 247 Forty percent of the world's Jewish population lives in the United States, making it the largest population of Jews in the world.

15. C 244 Mexicans became defined as a distinct racial-ethnic group based on their geographic origin, which exemplifies the process known as racialization. White Americans stereotyped them as lazy and corrupt.

16.	B	246	The original WASPs (White Anglo Saxon Protestants) were skilled workers with a strong Protestant work ethic. They immigrated primarily from England, Wales, and Scotland. The WASP influence in the United States has slightly declined.
17.	A	248	Blauner asserts that domestic colonialism is characterized by the forced and involuntary entry of the dominant group, the management of the colonized group's affairs without their consent, the use of stereotyping to explain and justify domination, and the suppression of the group's native culture.
18.	D	247	The National Origins Quota Act of 1924 set the first real ethnic quotas, limiting the number of new immigrants from each country to their current representation in the United States. Consequently, those from western and northern Europe were allowed to immigrate in higher numbers than those from southern and eastern Europe, who, although White, tended to be people with darker skins.
19.	B	254	Race-specific policies such as Affirmative Action recognize that racial-ethnic groups such as African Americans have a unique status because of a long history of discrimination and the continuing influence of institutional racism. Color-blind policies such as the Civil Rights Act of 1964 advocate treating members of all groups exactly the same, without regard to race or ethnicity.
20.	C	244	Cuban immigration is relatively recent compared to the immigration of other Hispanic groups. A majority of Cubans who fled the country after the revolution led by Castro were well-educated professionals and landowners. Cubans who immigrated in the 1980s have not achieved much economic or social mobility.
21.	A	245	By executive order of President Roosevelt, Japanese Americans were forced into relocation centers after the bombing of Pearl Harbor during World War II. In 1987, the United States government issued a formal apology to Japanese Americans and awarded $20,000 to each former detainee.
22.	B	242	Today, about 55 percent of Native Americans live on or near a reservation, a system that has poorly served them. Native Americans have the highest poverty rate of any group in the country, with over 50 percent unemployment for men.

Answers to True-False Questions

1.	F	233	A minority group need not be numerically smaller than the dominant group. For example, Blacks are the numerical majority in South Africa, but were a social minority under the apartheid system.
2.	F	235	The mass media tend to reinforce stereotypes by portraying women as overly emotional and talkative, men as insensitive and macho, and lower-income people as dirty, lazy, and inept.
3.	T	235	Prejudice is a negative evaluation, or attitude, while discrimination is a behavior.
4.	F	247	The National Origins Quota Act of 1924 set the first real ethnic quotas, limiting the number of new immigrants from each country to their current representation in the United States. The Chinese Exclusion Act of 1882 prohibited the immigration of unskilled Chinese laborers to the United States.
5.	F	231	The authoritarian personality is characterized by rigid categorization of other people, submission to authority, and intolerance of ambiguity.
6.	T	231	An individual with an authoritarian personality is more likely to be prejudiced.
7.	F	239	Functionalist theorists do not support segregation; in fact, they advocate that minority groups fully assimilate into the dominant culture to promote social equality, stability, and harmony.
8.	T	246	Demographers predict that Filipinos will constitute the largest group of Asian Americans within the next thirty years. Over two-thirds of those who immigrated to the United States from 1968 to 1980 were well-educated professionals.

9.   F   243   The Emancipation Proclamation of 1863 legally ended slavery, but the emerging sharecropping system continued exploiting Black Americans for their labor. The Great Black Migration to northern cities, which occurred from the 1900s to the 1920s, led to the development of urban ghettos such as Harlem in New York City. Although Black Americans suffered from grim urban conditions, they also developed resources such as volunteer organizations, political action groups, and cultural achievements that supported social movements for equality.

10.   F   246   Although Middle Easterners are categorized as an ethnic group in the United States, members come from a variety of countries, speak several different languages, and do not always have a common religious affiliation.

Answers to Fill in the Blank Questions

1.	ethnocentrism	321
2.	institutional	326
3.	interchangeability	320
4.	dominant	318
5.	acculturation	337

CHAPTER 10
GENDER

BRIEF CHAPTER OUTLINE

Defining Sex and Gender
      Gender: Diversity Across Cultures
      Sex Differences: Nature or Nurture?
The Sociological Construction of Gender
      The Formation of Gender Identity
      Sources of Gender Socialization
      The Price of Conformity
      Race, Gender and Identity
      Gender Socialization and Homophobia
      The Institutional Basis of Gender
Gender Stratification
      Sexism and Patriarchy
      Women's Worth: Still Unequal
      The Persistence of Gender Segregation
      Balancing Work and Family
Theories of Gender
      The Frameworks of Sociology
      Feminist Theory
Gender in Global Perspective
      Contemporary Attitudes
      Legislative Change

CHAPTER FOCUS: This chapter examines how social institutions and social forces support a system of gender stratification that systematically disadvantages women relative to men in the United States and around the world. It also introduces feminist theory as an analytical framework for understanding the position of women in society.

QUESTIONS TO GUIDE YOUR READING
1.   What are the primary agents of gender socialization in the United States, and how do they influence the formation of gender identity for males and females?
2.   What evidence exists to support the claim that the cultural categories of "femininity" and "masculinity" are socially constructed?
3.   How do race, ethnicity, age, and social class intersect with gender in the labor market, and what consequences does job segregation have for women in the United States?
4.   How has the legal system contributed to increased equality for women in education and employment, and how effective has this legislation been in reaching its goals?
5.   What consequences has women's increased participation in the paid labor force had for them, their families, and the society at large?

SOCIOLOGY IN ACTION: AN INTERNET EXERCISE
Go to www.ifba.com and www.wusa.com to learn more about the International Female Boxers Association and the Women's United Soccer Association, a professional soccer league for women. How has women's participation in sports, especially at the professional level, challenged assumptions about gender roles? What benefits does participation in organized sports provide for women?

KEY TERMS (defined at page number shown and in glossary)

biological determinism 260
discrimination 275
feminist theory 279
gender apartheid 271
gendered institutions 269
gender socialization 262
hermaphroditism 261
human capital theory 274
liberal feminism 279
patriarchy 272
sex 259
socialist feminism 279

comparable worth 284
dual labor market theory 274
gender 259
gender identity 262
gender segregation 275
gender stratification 270
homophobia 268
labor force participation rate 272
multiracial feminism 279
radical feminism 279
sexism 272

CHAPTER OUTLINE

Gender affects one's physical appearance and clothing, communication style, attitudes on many social and political issues, education level, type of employment, income, and likelihood of being imprisoned or dying a violent death.

I. **DEFINING SEX AND GENDER**

Sex refers to one's biological identity as male or female. **Gender** is the socially learned expectations and behaviors associated with members of each sex. Sociologists view the process of becoming a man or a woman as the result of social and cultural expectations that pattern people's behavior. From the moment of birth, gender expectations influence how boys and girls are treated, with boys being given greater independence and girls being more protected by others.

A. Gender: Diversity Across Cultures

1. Gender roles associated with masculinity and femininity vary greatly across cultures. For example, Western industrialized societies tend to define masculinity and femininity as opposites. In China, however, the law formally defines marriage as a relationship between equal companions who share family and household responsibilities.

2. Substantial differences in the construction of gender across social classes and racial-ethnic subcultures within a single society may also exist. For example, the Navajo Indians historically defined three possible gender roles, including the *berdache*, who were anatomically male, lived as women, and were not considered homosexual.

B. Sex Differences: Nature or Nurture?

1. Biology is only one component of the differences between women and men. The important question for sociologists is how biology and culture interact to produce a person's gender identity.

2. **Biological determinism** refers to explanations that attribute complex social phenomena to physical characteristics.

   a. Although many believe that men are more aggressive than women because of hormonal differences, reductions in testosterone levels do not predict changes in men's aggression.

   b. Although hormonal differences between males and females in childhood are minimal, boys exhibit significantly more aggression than girls.

   c. Biological explanations of inequality between men and women tend to flourish during periods of rapid social change, helping maintain the status quo by supporting claims that differences are "natural."

3. A person's sex is determined by chromosomal structure and established at conception.

a. In addition to the presence of different genitalia, differences exist in male's and female's average length and weight at birth as well as average resting heart rate, blood pressure, and muscle mass in adulthood.

b. **Hermaphroditism** is a condition produced when irregularities in chromosomal formation or fetal differentiation produce persons with mixed biological sex characteristics. Case studies of hermaphrodites reveal the extraordinary influence of social factors on identity.

4. *Transgendered* people are those who deviate from the binary system of gender, including transsexuals and cross-dressers. Trangendered people experience enormous pressure to fit within normative gender expectations.

II. THE SOCIAL CONSTRUCTION OF GENDER

Through **gender socialization**, men and women learn the expectations associated with their sex. This process affects self-concept, social and political attitudes, perceptions of others, and feelings about relationships with others. Even people who set out to challenge traditional gender expectations often find themselves yielding to the powerful influence of socialization.

A. The Formation of Gender Identity

One result of gender socialization is the formation of **gender identity**, or one's definition of oneself as female or male. Two traits commonly associated with masculine gender identity are *competition* and *dominance*. The general pattern is for boys to be more physically aggressive, men to develop a more competitive orientation than women, and girls and women to show more concern with including others in social interaction.

B. Sources of Gender Socialization

Gender socialization is reinforced whenever gender-linked behaviors receive approval or disapproval from others.

1. Parents are one of the most important sources of gender socialization. For example, parents tend to assign different chores to sons and daughters. In play activities, gender norms are applied even more strictly to boys than to girls.

2. Socialization also comes from *peers*. Through play, children learn patterns of social interaction, cognitive and physical development, analytical skills, and the values and attitudes of the culture. Research indicates that boys' play is more likely to encourage violence, individualism, and hierarchy.

3. Schools are particularly strong influences on socialization because of the amount of time children spend in them. Teachers tend to pay more attention to boys and often express different expectations for boys and girls.

4. Religion is an often overlooked but significant source of gender socialization. Religious doctrines have a strong effect on the formation of gender identity. In the United States, the major Judeo-Christian religions place strong emphasis on gender differences and explicitly affirm the authority of men over women.

5. The *media* communicate strong gender stereotypes, often delivering unrealistic portrayals of women and men.

a. Advertisements, an important outlet for the communication of gender images to the public, tend to disseminate particularly idealized, sexist, and racist images of women and men.

b. *Popular culture*, including greeting cards, books, songs, films, and comic strips, all contain images that represent the presumed cultural ideals of womanhood and manhood.

C. The Price of Conformity

1. A high degree of conformity to stereotypical gender expectations takes its toll on both men and women, often with negative health consequences, including eating disorders for women and steroid use for men.

2.   Male socialization discourages intimacy and encourages aggression, risk-taking, independence, self-reliance, and repression of emotion, all of which contribute to men's higher rate of injury and early death from accidents and violence.

3.   Violence associated with gender roles is endemic in the United States and around the world. Sexual assault, harassment, and domestic violence are all linked to the association of gender with men's power.

4.   Women who rigidly conform to a feminine gender role defined as passive and dependent experience higher rates of depression and other forms of mental illness, as well as more physical health problems, than women who adopt a variety of traits and balance multiple social roles.

5.   Gender expectations relax with age; for example, older women have more self-confidence and view themselves as more competent than younger women.

D.   Race, Gender and Identity

    1.   Because gender identity is merged with racial identity, men and women's roles are conditioned by the social context of their experiences as members of particular racial-ethnic groups.

    2.   African Americans are more likely to find value in both sexes displaying a variety of traits, including assertiveness, self-reliance, and gentleness.

        a.   Given their long history of paid employment, African American women's socialization emphasizes both self-sufficiency and nurturing.

        b.   For African Americans, manhood is defined by self-determination, responsibility, and accountability to family and community, but power over others is not highly valued.

    3.   Latino men bear the stereotype of *machismo*, or exaggerated masculinity associated with sexist behavior; however, *machismo* is also associated with dignity, honor, and respect within Latino culture.

E.   Gender Socialization and Homophobia

Homophobia is the pervasive fear and hatred of homosexuals. This learned attitude plays an important role in gender socialization because it encourages stricter conformity to traditional expectations, especially for males, and it becomes deeply embedded in people's definitions of themselves as men and women.

F.   The Institutional Basis of Gender

    1.   Gender is not just a matter of identity or an attribute of individuals, but also a characteristic of social institutions, where gender is a system of privilege and inequality that systematically disadvantages women relative to men.

    2.   **Gendered institutions** are the total pattern of gender relations, including stereotypical expectations, interpersonal relationships, and the different placement of women and men in the hierarchies of social institutions.

        a.   Women who work in organizations dominated by men report that there are subtle ways that men's importance in the organization is communicated, often resulting in women feeling like outsiders.

        b.   Military academies such as VMI and the Citadel have been constructed on a strict gender order in which masculinity was built into the schools.

III.   **GENDER STRATIFICATION**

Gender stratification refers to the hierarchical distribution of social and economic resources according to gender. For example, two-thirds of illiterate people worldwide are women. Gender stratification is an institutionalized system that rests on a specific belief system that supports the inequality of women and men. Although gender stratification varies cross-culturally, research indicates that women are more nearly equal to men in societies where six conditions exist:

- women's work is central to the economy
- women have access to education
- ideological or religious support for gender inequality is not strong
- men make direct contributions to household work and child care
- work is not highly segregated by sex
- women have access to formal power and authority in public decision-making

Gender stratification is multidimensional; that is, women may have freedom in some areas of life but not others. In Sweden, for example, both women and men participate in the workforce and the household, and women have a strong role in the political system, yet women's wages lag behind men's [Figure 10.2]. Japanese women are well educated and have high labor force participation, yet there are rigid gender roles within the family. Extreme gender stratification, such as the exclusion of women from public life in Afghanistan under the Taliban's rule, has been labeled **gender apartheid**.

A.   Sexism and Patriarchy

    1.   An *ideology* is a belief system that tries to explain and justify the status quo. **Sexism** is an ideology, but it is also a set of institutional practices and beliefs through which women are controlled because of the social significance assigned to presumed differences between the sexes.

    2.   Like racism, sexism distorts reality by making behaviors seem natural when they are rooted in entrenched systems of power and privilege.

        a.   An example of sexist ideology is the idea that men should be paid more than women because men are the primary breadwinners. When the idea becomes embedded in the wage structure, people need not continue to believe in the idea for it to continue to have real consequences.

        b.   The common belief that that women take men's jobs away and racial-ethnic minorities advance more rapidly than Whites is a distortion of facts, because most women work in gender- and race-segregated jobs, and women are still less likely than men to get promotions and raises.

    3.   **Patriarchy**, which refers to a society or group in which men have power over women, is common throughout the world. In patriarchal societies, husbands have authority over wives and men hold most of the positions of public power.

B.   Women's Worth: Still Unequal

    1.   Gender stratification is especially obvious in the persistent earnings gap between women and men. The gap has closed since the 1960s, but women who work year-round and full-time still earn an average of 74 percent of what men earn. In 1999, the median income for men was $37,574 and $27,370 for women [Figure 10.3].

    2.   The **labor force participation rate** is the percentage of those in a given category who are employed either part-time or full-time. By 2000, 60 percent of women and 75 percent of men were in the labor force.

    3.   The labor force participation rate among women has changed most dramatically among White women, because Black women were already more likely to work for pay. The employment of married women with children has tripled since 1960.

    4.   Changes in family patterns in contemporary society mean that more women are the sole supporters of their dependents, and a majority of women report working to support themselves or their families.

    5.   The Equal Pay Act of 1963 was the first federal law to require that men and women receive equal pay for equal work, yet wage discrimination persists.

    6.   There are four main explanations for the continued difference in wages by sex.

        a.   **Human capital theory**, which assumes that the economic system is fair and competitive, explains gender differences in wages as the result of differences in the individual characteristics workers bring to the job.

Human capital variables include age, prior experience, number of hours worked, marital status, and education level.

     b.   **Dual labor market theory**, which contends that women and men earn different amounts because they tend to work in different segments of the labor market, reflects the devaluation of women's work, because there are usually low wages in jobs where women are most concentrated.

        1)   In the *primary labor market*, jobs are stable, wages are good, benefits are likely, and opportunities for advancement exist.

        2)   In the *secondary labor market*, there is high job turnover, low wages, short or non-existent promotion ladders, few benefits, poor working conditions, arbitrary work rules, and capricious supervision. Fast food workers are in this category.

        3)   There is also an *informal sector* of the labor market where there is even greater wage inequality, no benefits, and little, if any, oversight of employment practices. People who are paid under-the-table to perform services for a fee are in this sector.

     c.   *Occupational segregation* refers to a pattern in which different groups of workers are separated into different occupations, or different specialties within a single occupation, that are linked to wage differences. **Gender segregation**, a specific form of occupational segregation, refers to the distribution of men and women in different jobs.

        1)   The greater the proportion of women in a given occupation, the lower the pay.

        2)   Women are concentrated in a smaller range of occupations than men; for example, two-thirds of all employed women work as either sales clerks; clerical, food service, health service, or child care workers; hairdressers, or maids.

     d.   A fourth explanation of the gender wage gap is overt **discrimination**, or practices that single out some groups for different and unequal treatment, including *sexual harassment* and other forms of intimidation used by dominant groups to perpetuate their own advantage.

C.   The Persistence of Gender Segregation

    1.   When jobs are defined as "women's work," they become devalued and associated with less prestige and income. For example, elementary school teachers, whose job is associated with caring for children, are paid less than airplane mechanics.

    2.   Only a small proportion of women work in occupations traditionally thought to be men's jobs (such as soldier), and very few men work in occupations historically considered to be women's work (such as nursing). This pattern reinforces the belief that there are significant differences between the sexes.

    3.   When people cross the boundaries established by occupational segregation, they may be considered gender deviants. These workers feel strong pressure to assert gender-appropriate behavior, such as wearing make-up for women. Perceptions of gender appropriateness influence the likelihood of women's success at work.

    4.   Internal gender segregation refers to a pattern whereby women not only work in different jobs than men, but are also are segregated into particular fields or job types within specific occupations. For example, female physicians are most concentrated in the least prestigious specialties in medicine -- pediatrics and gynecology -- and least concentrated in neurosurgery, cardiology, and oncology.

    5.   Some explanations of gender segregation emphasize that women and men are socialized differently, thus, they choose different jobs. Another explanation is that structural obstacles discourage women from entering male-dominated jobs

and from advancing once they are employed in those jobs. For example, the *glass ceiling* places subtle yet decisive barriers to women's advancement.

D.   Balancing Work and Family
Although women's participation in the workplace continues to increase, women still have primary responsibility for meeting the needs of home and family, a phenomenon Arlie Hochschild calls the "second shift." The social speedup that comes from increased hours of employment for men and women, combined with household demands, is a source of considerable stress for women in the contemporary United States.

IV.   **THEORIES OF GENDER**
A.   The Framework of Sociology
1.   *Functionalist theory* argues that men and women fill complementary roles that support an arrangement that works to the benefit of society.
2.   *Conflict theory* views women as disadvantaged by power inequalities between women and men that are built into the social structure.
3.   Feminist scholars, drawing on symbolic interaction theory and using the *ethnomethodological approach*, have developed what is known as the *"doing gender"* perspective, which interprets gender as something that is accomplished through the ongoing social interactions that people have with each other. This microlevel approach does not address the structural basis of women's oppression.

B.   Feminist Theory
Feminist theory refers to analyses that seek to understand the position of women in society for the purpose of bringing about liberating social changes. The link between theory and action is critical to feminist theory. There are four major frameworks within feminist theory [Table 10.1].
1.   **Liberal feminism** argues that inequality for women originates in past traditions that pose barriers to women's advancement. It emphasizes individual rights and equal opportunities as the basis for social justice and social reform.
2.   **Socialist feminism** is a more radical perspective that views women's oppression as originating in the system of capitalism. Because capitalism exploits women as a cheap source of labor, equality for women will only come when the economic and political system is changed.
3.   **Radical feminism** interprets patriarchy as the primary cause of women's oppression and asserts that the origin of women's oppression lies in men's control over women's bodies. Radical feminists do not believe that change can come through the existing system, which is male-dominated.
4.   **Multiracial feminism**, which clearly emphasizes the interactive effects of race, class, and gender in systems of domination, argues there is no single, universal experience associated with being a woman. This theory notes that different privileges and disadvantages accrue to women and men as a result of their location in a racially stratified and class-based society.

V.   **GENDER IN GLOBAL PERSPECTIVE**
The global division of labor is acquiring a gendered component, with female workers in the poorest nations providing a cheap source of labor for manufacturing products sold in the rich, industrialized countries. Worldwide, women work as much or more than men [Table 10.2], but receive 30 to 40 percent less pay, own only one percent of all property, and are seriously underrepresented in government [Map 10.2]. There is marked inequality in the domestic sphere in Japan, while China is unusual in that there is far greater sharing of household responsibilities between men and women. Work is not the only measure of women's inferior status throughout the world. The United Nations has concluded that violence against women is a "global epidemic" that takes many forms, including domestic violence, rape, infanticide, murder, and genital

mutilation. The high rates of violence against women are supported by cultural norms, women's economic and social dependence on men, and discriminatory political practices.

VI. GENDER AND SOCIAL CHANGE

The women's movement has changed how women's issues are perceived in the public consciousness, as well as generated laws that protect women's rights.

A. Contemporary Attitudes

  1. Public attitudes toward gender roles have changed noticeably; for example, only 16 percent of women and 20 percent of men now disapprove of women being employed while they have young children.

    a. Research indicates that mother's employment does not have a direct, negative effect on children.

    b. One of the most significant changes in women's lives is the increased stress they experience when they combine family and paid work.

  2. People's beliefs about appropriate gender roles have evolved as women's and men's lives have changed, with younger men and single men expressing more egalitarian views than older, married men.

B. Legislative Change

  1. Legislation that prohibits overt discrimination against women has been in place for nearly 40 years, including the Equal Pay Act of 1963 and the Civil Rights Act of 1964, which forbid discrimination in employment on the basis of race, color, national origin, religion, or sex.

  2. Title IX of the Educational Amendments of 1972 forbid gender discrimination in any educational institution receiving federal funds, which radically altered the opportunities available to women students, particularly in athletics.

  3. Passage of anti-discrimination policies does not guarantee their universal implementation. For example, male athletes still outnumber female athletes by more than two to one, and male athletes receive more scholarship support than female athletes.

  4. Although a strong legal framework for gender equality exists in the workplace, equity has not yet been achieved.

    a. Because most women work in different jobs than men, the principle of equal pay for equal work does not fully address workplace inequities.

    b. Some scholars have suggested implementing **comparable worth**, or policies that pay women and men equivalent wages for jobs involving similar levels of skill. This policy creates job evaluation systems that assess the degree of similarity between different kinds of jobs.

  5. Many victories in the fight for gender equity are now at risk, such as *affirmative action*, a method for opening opportunities to women and racial-ethnic minorities that specifically redresses past discrimination by taking proactive measures to recruit and hire previously disadvantaged groups.

  6. Gender inequality could be addressed by increasing the number of women in positions of public power, although feminists note that increasing women's representation in institutions will not lead to significant change without also reforming the sexism in those institutions.

PRACTICE TEST

Multiple Choice Questions

1. Meg Lovejoy's research on eating disorders indicates that:
    a. Black women are more likely than White women to develop eating disorders because they have such a strong desire to achieve culturally valued standards of beauty.
    b. Eating disorders are prevalent for both Black and White women, but they manifest themselves as overeating in Black women and excessive dieting in White women.
    c. Lesbian women are less likely than heterosexual women to develop eating disorders because they reject dominant cultural beauty norms in order to distinguish themselves as homosexual.
    d. The "culture of thinness" that affects the development of women's body image is now affecting many more young men, whose participation in excessive dieting has increased significantly over the past decade.

2. Research indicates that which of these nations is unusual in that there is far greater sharing of paid work and household responsibilities between men and women?
    a. United States
    b. Korea
    c. Japan
    d. China

3. Which perspective generally attributes the complex social phenomena associated with gender to differences in physical characteristics between men and women?
    a. patriarchal domination
    b. social constructionism
    c. biological determinism
    d. chromosomal geneticism

4. The first federal law to require that men and women receive equal pay for equal work was the:
    a. Affirmative Action Executive Order
    b. Civil Rights Act
    c. Equal Pay Act
    d. Title IX statute

5. Among the Navaho Indians, the *berdache* were considered:
    a. hermaphrodites who were forced to live as women because they were anatomically deformed.
    b. homosexuals because they were biologically male and married other men.
    c. ordinary men who adopted many female characteristics and lived as a third gender.
    d. men who were born anatomically male but underwent surgery to become female because they experienced a gender identity crisis as children.

6. Which of the following physical differences exists between males and females?
    a. average length and weight at birth
    b. average muscle mass and bone density in old age
    c. average heart rate and blood pressure in adulthood
    d. All of the above physical differences are found between males and females.

7. Which feminist framework locates the origins of women's oppression in the capitalist system and argues that the transformation of the gender division of labor will only come about with changes in the social class division of labor?
   a. liberal feminism
   b. radical feminism
   c. socialist feminism
   d. multiracial feminism

8. Social psychological research on gender identity indicates that compared to men, women generally:
   a. develop a more competitive orientation, especially in mixed-sex groups.
   b. show more concern with including others in conversation and activities.
   c. inhibit other people in conversations by frequently interrupting.
   d. All of the above statements about gender-linked behavioral traits are true.

9. Research indicates that men who thoroughly internalize gender expectations and highly conform to rigid standards of masculinity are:
   a. more likely to die from accidents.
   b. less likely to smoke and drink alcohol.
   c. more likely to have closer intimate relationships with their wives.
   d. All of the above outcomes are linked to men's overconformity to the masculine role.

10. The pervasive fear and hatred of homosexuals in American culture that supports rigid definitions of gender roles is:
    a. hermaphroditism..
    b. homoeroticism.
    c. homosapiens.
    d. homophobia.

11. Military academies have been constructed on a strict gender order in which masculinity is built into the schools in the behaviors expected from cadets and the opportunities given to, or denied, women. This example illustrates the concept of gendered:
    a. roles.
    b. identities.
    c. institutions.
    d. personalities.

12. To radical feminists, the origins of women's oppression lies in:
    a. changes in the gendered division of labor that occurred as a result of industrialization in capitalist societies.
    b. men's control over women's bodies, which is maintained through sexual and physical assault.
    c. traditional socialization practices that restrict women's opportunities in the public sphere.
    d. the global exploitation of women of color as a cheap source of labor.

13. Which of the following groups of men are most likely to find value in women displaying a variety of "masculine" and "feminine" traits and to support women's right to work outside the home?
    a. African American men
    b. Asian American men
    c. Hispanic men
    d. White men

14. Research finds that women are more nearly equal to men in societies where:
    a. work is highly segregated by sex.
    b. women's work is central to the economy.
    c. religious support for gender inequality is strong.
    d. All of the above conditions contribute to greater gender equality.

15. Which of the following characteristics is **not** protected by the Civil Rights Act of 1964?
    a. sex
    b. age
    c. race
    d. religion

16. The set of institutionalized practices and beliefs that distort reality by making presumed differences between men and women seem natural, even though they are rooted in social systems that distribute power unequally, is:
    a. homophobia.
    b. devaluation.
    c. matriarchy.
    d. sexism.

17. Which perspective suggests that people "do gender" through the daily interactions they have with one another and through the interpretations they have of other's actions and appearances as consistent with "being a man" or "being a woman?"
    a. functionalist
    b. human capital
    c. dual labor market
    d. symbolic interaction

18. Which perspective explains gender differences in wages as the result of differences in the individual characteristics (such as education level) that workers bring to their jobs?
    a. symbolic interaction
    b. dual labor market
    c. human capital
    d. glass ceiling

19. Which segment of the labor market is associated with high job turnover, short or non-existent promotion ladders, few or no benefits, poor working conditions, and arbitrary work rules?
    a. secondary
    b. primary
    c. overt
    d. dual

20. The pattern in which different groups of workers are systematically separated into different occupations that are usually linked to different wages is occupational:
    a. worth.
    b. ceiling.
    c. segregation.
    d. participation.

21. The purpose of the federal legislation commonly referred to as Title IX was to:
    a. forbid discrimination against women in any educational program, including sports, at any school that receives government funding.
    b. increase the percentage of women working in traditionally male occupations by enforcing quotas that required those employers to hire more women.
    c. redress past discrimination in education by providing government funding for colleges to recruit and retain female students in science, math, and engineering.
    d. forbid discrimination in employment practices, including hiring and promotion.

22. Which theory has asserted that men fill instrumental roles and women fill expressive roles in society, thereby creating an efficient social arrangement?
    a. conflict theory
    b. feminist theory
    c. functionalist theory
    d. gendered institutions theory

23. For which group of women in the United States has the labor force participation rate changed most dramatically in recent years?
    a. Black
    b. White
    c. Asian
    d. Puerto Rican

24. Which feminist framework asserts that gender is learned through traditional patterns of socialization and change can best be accomplished through legal reform?
    a. liberal feminism
    b. radical feminism
    c. socialist feminism
    d. multiracial feminism

25. The principle of paying women and men equivalent wages for different jobs that involve similar levels of skill is:
    a. affirmative action.
    b. comparable worth.
    c. doing gender.
    d. glass ceiling.

True-False Questions

1. Human capital variables include factors such as one's weight, height, and heart rate.

2. The term "transgendered" refers to an individual who is sexually attracted to people of the same sex.

3. According to dual labor market theory, women are more likely than men to work in the primary labor market.

4. Studies of gender identity development and social interaction indicate that boys tend to communicate their wishes to others by using commands, whereas girls use more polite directives.

5. On average, women in the United States today earn sixty percent of what men earn.

6. The major Judeo-Christian religions place strong emphasis on gender equality, with explicit support for an equal division of labor and decision making between men and women in both the public and private spheres.

7. National opinion polls indicate that women are more likely than men to agree that homosexuality is morally wrong and AIDS is the victim's fault.

8. Research indicates that women who rigidly conform to the traditional feminine gender role experience higher rates of depression than do women who occupy multiple roles.

9. The wage gap between men and women is lowest – that is, women's wages are nearly equal to men's wages – in Japan, a country that strongly supports egalitarian gender roles.

10. Girls who choose toys defined as "masculine" or play activities associated with boys are more negatively regarded and seriously sanctioned than are boys who choose "girl's" toys or activities.

Fill in the Blank Questions

1. Gender _____, a system of stratification characterized by extreme segregation and the exclusion of women from public life, was instituted in Afghanistan when the Taliban seized power in 1996.

2. Most societies have some form of gender _____, or the hierarchical distribution of economic and social resources according to gender.

3. The term _____ refers to a society or group in which men have power over women, often in both the public and private spheres.

4. Analyses that seek to understand the position of women in society for the purpose of bringing about liberating social changes are included in the framework known as _____ theory.

5. Sexual harassment and other means of intimidation are examples of overt _____, or practices that single out women for different and unequal treatment.

Essay Questions

1. Explain how the mass media contribute to gender socialization in the United States, giving specific examples to support your points.
2. How does the economic and social status of women in the United States compare to women in other nations around the world?
3. Compare and contrast human capital theory and dual labor market theory as explanations for the persistence of pay differences between women and men.
4. Identify the various forms of violence that are committed against women around the world, and discuss what factors contribute to the "global epidemic" of violence against women.
5. Provide several examples of laws that have increased women's opportunities in the United States, and discuss the limitations of legal remedies for promoting gender equality.

ANSWERS TO PRACTICE TEST

Answers to Multiple Choice Questions

1. B 268 Although men develop eating disorders, they tend to use steroids rather than diet excessively. Both Black and White women experience problems that result in eating disorders, but Black women are more likely to overeat, while White women are more likely to diet excessively. White women are strongly affected by the "culture of thinness." Although Black women tend to reject Eurocentric standards of beauty, racism fosters health problems.

2. D 280 The Chinese Marriage Act of 1950 states that marriage is a union of equal companions who are expected to share child care and household responsibilities. In China, both men and women work long hours in paid employment. In Japan, there is significant gender inequality in the domestic sphere.

3. C 260 Biological determinism refers to explanations that attribute complex social phenomena to physical characteristics. Sociologists believe that gender is socially constructed because what appears to be natural is only what people have been taught is normal through socialization.

4. C 273 The Equal Pay Act of 1963 was the first piece of federal legislation to prohibit paying men and women different wages for the same work. The Civil Rights Act of 1964 prohibited gender discrimination in employment. Title IX of the Educational Amendments explicitly forbid gender discrimination in schools.

5. C 260 The berdache were anatomically normal men who were defined as a third gender. They married other men but were not considered homosexuals.

6. D 262 At birth, males tend to be longer and weigh more than females. In adulthood, men have a lower resting heart rate, higher blood pressure, and higher muscle mass and density than women.

7. C 279 Socialist feminist locates the origins of women's oppression in the capitalist system, which exploits them both as women and laborers.

8. B 262 Gender identity refers to one's definition of oneself as female or male. It is commonly associated with competition and dominance for males and cooperation and concern for others for females.

9. A 265 Rigid conformity to traditional gender roles is associated with risk-taking behavior for men, particularly involvement in activities correlated with poor health outcomes and early death. Overconformity to the masculine role encourages emotional repression and self-reliance and discourages intimacy.

10. D 268 Homophobia is the pervasive fear and hatred of homosexuals. It encourages conformity to gender roles by acting as a mechanism of social control.

11. C 269 Gendered institutions are the total pattern of gender relations – stereotypical expectations, interpersonal relationships, and the different placement of women and men in the hierarchies of social institutions, such as the military. Gender identity refers to one's definition of oneself as female or male. Gender roles are the set of social expectations for masculinity and femininity.

12. B 279 Radical feminism locates the origins of women's oppression in men's control over women's bodies, which is reflected in violence against women [Table 10.1].

13.   A   268   African American women and men tend to value traits such as assertiveness, athleticism, and gentleness in both sexes. Black women have a long history of paid employment, and Black men are more likely to support equal rights for women than are other groups of men.

14.   B   270   In societies where women's work is central to the economy, work is not highly segregated by sex, men contribute to housework and childcare, women are well educated, and ideology supporting gender inequality is weak, there is greater gender equality.

15.   B   284   The Civil Rights Act of 1964 forbid discrimination in employment on the basis of sex, race, national origin, and religion, *but not age*.

16.   D   272   Sexism is an institutionalized set of practices and beliefs that define differences between women and men as "natural." An ideology is a belief system that tries to explain and justify the status quo. Homophobia is the pervasive fear and hatred of homosexuality. A matriarchy is a society in which women are assigned power. Devaluation refers to assigning lower value to work done by a particular group, resulting in lower wages and prestige being associated with that work.

17.   D   279   Symbolic interaction theory emphasizes subjective perception and social interaction. "Doing gender" is a feminist perspective that interprets gender as something that is accomplished through ongoing social interaction [Table 10.1].

18.   C   274   Human capital theory explains gender differences in wages as the result of differences in the individual characteristics that workers bring to the job, such as education level and experience. The glass ceiling refers to the subtle yet decisive barrier to advancement that women find in the workplace.

19.   A   274   Dual labor market theory contends that jobs in the secondary labor market (such as cashier) have low wages, few benefits, and poor working conditions. Jobs in the primary labor market (such as management) are relatively stable and have good wages and benefits. Women are disproportionately represented in the secondary labor market.

20.   C   275   Occupational segregation refers to a pattern whereby workers are systematically distributed in different occupations by some characteristic such as sex or race.

21.   A   284   Title IX of the Educational Amendments of 1972 forbid gender discrimination in any educational institution receiving federal funds. Adoption of this bill radically altered the opportunities available to female students, most notably in athletic activities. The Civil Rights Act forbids employment discrimination on the basis of race, color, religion, national origin, or sex. Affirmative Action is a method for addressing past discrimination through intentional efforts to recruit and retain socially disadvantaged groups.

22.   C   279   Functionalist theory traditionally argued that men fill instrumental roles and women fill expressive roles, creating an efficient arrangement that benefits society. Feminist theorists have been very critical of this assumption.

23.   B   273   The labor force participation rate among White women has increased most dramatically in recent years, since Black and Asian women have historically had high rates of labor force participation. Two-thirds of mothers are now in the paid labor force. Puerto Rican and Cuban women are the least likely to be employed.

24.   A   279   Liberal feminism is a framework that views traditional socialization practices as the main cause of women's inequality, and suggests change through the legal system. As indicated in Table 10.1, radical and socialist feminism suggest that substantial change cannot occur within the current social system because society is characterized by patriarchy and class inequality. Multiracial feminism posits that there is no universal female experience, and change will come through forming alliances with other groups.

25.	B	284	Comparable worth is the principle of paying women and men equivalent wages for jobs involving similar levels of skill. Comparable worth policy suggests creating pay scales on the basis of job conditions rather than the sex composition of the workforce. Affirmative Action redresses past discrimination through intentional efforts to recruit and retain women and racial-ethnic minorities. The glass ceiling refers to the fact that women are substantially blocked from senior management positions in the workplace. Doing gender refers to social interaction that confirms perceptions of gender roles.

Answers to True-False Questions

1.	F	274	Human capital refers to characteristics that individual workers bring to the workplace, including age, education level, and experience.
2.	F	261	People who are attracted to others of the same sex are defined as having a homosexual sexual orientation. Transgendered people are those who deviate from the binary (either/or) system of gender, including transsexuals and cross-dressers.
3.	F	274	Jobs in the primary labor market are relatively stable, have good wages and benefits, and offer opportunities for advancement. Men are more likely than women to work in the primary labor market.
4.	T	263	Research indicates that there are differences in the patterns of behavior displayed by boys and girls, and men and women, in groups. Boys are more likely to use threats and commands, and less likely to comply with other's wishes. Girls are more likely to use polite directives and take turns speaking.
5.	F	272	On average, women who work full time, year-round earn approximately 74 percent of what employed men earn in the United States.
6.	F	264	Judeo-Christian religions explicitly affirm men's authority over women, thereby supporting gender inequality in society.
7.	F	260	Public opinion polls reveal a gender gap in social and political attitudes, with women more likely than men to say abortion should be legal in all circumstances and laws covering the sale of firearms should be more strict. Men are more likely than women to agree with the statements, "homosexuality is morally wrong" and "AIDS is the victim's fault."
8.	T	267	Women who rigidly conform to traditional gender roles experience higher rates of depression and other forms of mental illness, while women who balance their lives with multiple roles report greater self-esteem and more gratification.
9.	F	271	The wage gap is lowest in Turkey, where women earn nearly the same wages as men [Figure 10.2]. In Japan, there is significant inequality in the domestic sphere.
10.	F	263	Gender norms concerning play activities are more strictly applied to boys than to girls, resulting in boys who choose more "feminine" toys being more negatively regarded and more strongly discouraged than girls who choose "masculine" toys.

Answers to Fill in the Blank Questions

1.	apartheid	271
2.	stratification	270
3.	patriarchy	272
4.	discrimination	275
5.	feminist	279

CHAPTER 11
AGE AND SEX

BRIEF CHAPTER OUTLINE

Age Stratification
>   Age Groups as Minorities
>   Age Prejudice and Discrimination
>   Explaining Age Stratification

The Social Significance of Aging
>   Physical and Physiological Bases of Aging
>   Age Stereotypes

Growing Up/ Growing Old: Aging and the Life Course
>   Childhood
>   Youth and Adolescence
>   Adulthood
>   Retirement
>   Old Age
>   Death and Dying

Sex, Social Structure, and Social Stratification
>   Sexual Politics
>   Technology, Sex, and Cyberspace
>   The Influence of Race, Class, and Gender
>   Sex and Culture: A Global Perspective

Sexuality and Sociological Theory
>   Sex: Functional or Conflict-Based?
>   The Social Construction of Sexual Identity

Contemporary Sexual Attitudes and Behavior
>   Changing Sexual Values
>   Sexual Practices of the American Public

Sex and Social Issues
>   Birth Control
>   New Reproductive Technologies
>   Abortion
>   Pornography
>   Sexual Violence

Age, Sex, and Social Change
>   The Graying of America
>   The Sexual Revolution

CHAPTER FOCUS: This chapter examines age and sex as socially structured features of society that are linked to systems of stratification. It provides an overview of the stages of the life course and discusses how aging and sexual values are related to social change.

QUESTIONS TO GUIDE YOUR READING
1.   Why do sociologists consider age and sex important features of social stratification?
2.   How do social factors influence the way that individuals experience the physical process of aging?
3.   How has the changing age composition of the population influenced policy development in the United States?

4.	What are the four main stages of the life course in the United States, and what characteristics are associated with each stage?

5.	What does research indicate about the sexual values and behavior of the American public?

SOCIOLOGY IN ACTION: AN INTERNET EXERCISE

Go to www.graypanthers.org and www.aarp.org to learn more about the Gray Panthers and the American Association of Retired Persons, respectively. What images of aging and old age are promoted by these organizations? What is the particular focus of each organization? How does each organization attempt to address the needs and concerns of elderly people in the United States?

KEY TERMS

CHAPTER OUTLINE

I.	**AGE STRATIFICATION**

All societies practice **age differentiation**, or the division of labor or roles in a society on the basis of age. Although differentiation of roles by age is a feature of all societies, the specific roles given to different age groups vary from society to society. Virtually every social institution has age barriers that must be surpassed to enjoy the full benefits of that institution. For example, in the United States, there are minimum age requirements for holding national political offices. **Age stratification**, which refers to the hierarchical ranking of different age groups in society, exists because social processes ensure that people of different ages differ in their access to society's rewards, power, and privileges. Age is an *ascribed status*, or one assigned at birth; however, most ascribed statuses (such as race) remain constant over one's lifetime, whereas age changes steadily. Each person remains part of a particular **age cohort**, or aggregate group of people born during the same period who share the same historical experiences. The shared historical experiences of age cohorts result in discernible generational patterns in social attitudes and commonality of life chances, which clearly reveals Mills' concept of the sociological imagination. For example, someone graduating from high school after World War II entered a labor market where jobs and expanding opportunities were widely available; but today, many young people are trapped in low-level jobs with little opportunity for advancement.

A.	Age Groups as Minorities

1.	A minority group is a group with relatively less power and fewer social and economic resources than more dominant groups. Age minorities in the United States include the young and the old.

2.	Viewing oneself as a minority group can be the basis for mobilizing for group rights, a strategy that has been effectively used by the nation's older population.

3.	Despite certain parallels, the similarities between the aged and racial and ethnic minorities should not be overstated, because a person is in a racial or ethnic minority group for life, but is only aged for part of his or her life. As a group, the elderly have more political power than other minority groups and benefit from receiving far more subsidized support in the form of medical care, insurance programs, and senior discounts at private businesses.

B. Age Prejudice and Discrimination

1. **Age prejudice** refers to a negative attitude about an age group that is generalized to all people in that group. Prejudice against the elderly is prominent, as manifested in negative stereotypes such as "old geezer" and "fuddy duddy."

2. **Age discrimination** is the differential and unequal treatment of people based solely on their age. Age discrimination cases have become one of the most frequently filed cases through the Equal Employment Opportunity Commission (EEOC), the federal agency that monitors civil rights violations in employment.

3. **Ageism**, a term sociologists use to describe the institutional practice of age prejudice and discrimination, is structured into the institutional fabric of society, as evidenced in cultural belief systems that devalue the elderly and social systems of care that are inadequate to meet aging people's needs.

C. Explaining Age Stratification

1. Functionalists argue that adulthood is functional to society because adults are seen as the group contributing the most fully to society, while older people are less useful. This theory suggests that as people age, they gradually withdraw from participation in society and are simultaneously relieved from responsibility, providing for an orderly transition from one generation to the next [Table 11.1].

2. Conflict theory focuses on the competition over scarce resources between age groups. This theory argues that barring youth and the elderly from the labor market is a way of eliminating both of these groups from competition for jobs, which benefits middle-aged workers.

3. Symbolic interaction theory analyzes the different meanings attributed to social entities, focusing on which symbolic meanings become attached to different age groups and to what extent these meanings explain how society ranks them.

II. **THE SOCIAL SIGNIFICANCE OF AGING**

A. Physical and Physiological Bases of Aging

1. Depression is not an inevitable consequence of aging. Experiencing stressful events (such as the death of a spouse) and lacking inadequate social support are the most common causes of depression among the elderly

2. **Dementia** is the term used to describe a variety of diseases that involve some permanent damage to the brain, usually involving mental disorientation and memory loss. *Alzheimer's disease*, a degenerative form of dementia that involves neurological changes in the brain, occurs in approximately 10 percent of the population over age sixty-five.

3. Physical changes are an inevitable part of the aging process; however, the social dimensions of aging are just as important in determining how particular groups experience the aging process. For example, menopausal women in the United States are culturally depicted as cranky, overly emotional, irritable, and prone to depression, yet research indicates that a majority of menopausal women do not experience the stereotypical symptoms associated with menopause.

4. **Life expectancy** is the probable number of years a particular group is likely to live, on average, given aggregate statistical patterns. It is based on the age at which half the people born in a particular year die. Life expectancy is clearly shaped by social factors, with men and racial-ethnic minorities having shorter life expectancies than women and White people, respectively.

B.   Age Stereotypes
1. Much of the meaning of growing old in the United States is embedded in social stereotypes, or oversimplified categorizations of beliefs about the characteristics of members of a group, which are reinforced through popular culture.
2. **Age stereotypes** are preconceived judgments about what different age groups are like. For example, teenagers are perceived as lazy, irresponsible, and sloppy, while the elderly are perceived as forgetful, conservative, meddlesome, inactive, unproductive, lonely, incompetent, and disinterested in sex.
3. Perceptions of aging are socially constructed; that is, people subjectively define their age in terms of how they *feel* instead of by their chronological age.

III.   **GROWING UP/GROWING OLD: AGING AND THE LIFE CHANGES**

In the contemporary United States, the life span is divided into four phases: childhood, youth and adolescence, adulthood, and old age. Sociologists use a **life course perspective** to connect people's personal attributes, the roles they occupy, the life events they experience, and the sociohistorical context in which their individual biographies unfold. Transitions to different phases in the life span are often marked by cultural rituals called *rites of passage*. Rites of passage such as baptism, christening, confirmation, bar mitzvah and bas mitzvah, and *quinceanara* ceremonies celebrate or memorialize events in an individual's life and publicly announce the individual's passage from one phase of the life span to another.

A.   Childhood
1. Today, the United States is defined as a child-centered society, which is reflected in the high valuation of youth in the media and popular images of childhood as a period of play, fantasy, and freedom from responsibility.
2. In contrast, the exploitation of child labor was so pervasive in the nineteenth century that legislation prompted dramatic social change.
3. By the middle of the nineteenth century, children became redefined as precious but no longer economically useful, at least among the middle class.
4. The United States is becoming an increasingly dangerous place for the many children affected by violence, homelessness, and poverty. In fact, the United States ranks first among 17 industrialized nations in child and youth poverty.

B.   Youth and Adolescence
1. Adolescence is a relatively new category in the life span. Until the twentieth century, children moved directly into adult roles, but adolescence came to be regarded as a separate stage of life as the period of formal education lengthened.
2. The boundaries of adolescence are imprecisely defined, but most regard the lower boundary as the transition from elementary to junior high school, and the upper boundary as the transition into some adult role such as college, marriage, parenthood, or full-time employment.
3. Establishing a central identity is a main concern in the adolescent period. Young people typically try to mark their unique identity through the establishment of *youth subcultures*, which are characterized by relatively distinct habits, customs, norms, and language that define youth in contrast to other generations.

C.   Adulthood
1. The role of adult carries with it more responsibility, rights, and privileges than any other stage in the life cycle.
2. In the past, the normative transition to adulthood was to finish school, get a job, get married, and start a family. Because social conditions now make it difficult for many people to follow this path, the sequencing of events and length of time it takes to become an adult have changed for many people [Table 11.2].

3.   As adulthood unfolds, the traditional norms of our society suggest that both men and women, but particularly men, should have achieved most of their life goals by the time they reach middle age.

    a.   The *midlife crisis* is popularly conceived as a time of trauma during which people become fixated on what they have failed to achieve or the things they never attempted.

    b.   Research indicates that midlife is actually experienced as happy and positive by most people. Stress at midlife, as in other periods, is caused by unexpected events, such as divorce or death of a partner.

D.   <u>Retirement</u>

Along with becoming a grandparent, one of the most significant markers of approaching old age is retirement from work. Retirement can be a difficult period of adjustment for some, but maintaining social contacts generally eases stress for both men and women. The disadvantages experienced by racial-ethnic minorities and women in the labor force are reproduced in retirement, when these groups typically have fewer financial resources.

E.   <u>Old Age</u>

1.   Aging is not an entirely negative process, but old age is a difficult period that is made worse by negative images of the elderly in American society and the inadequacy of social institutions to care for the aged.

2.   Although the elderly do face problems, most studies have found no differences among the young and the elderly on measures of satisfaction and happiness.

3.   It is a myth that elderly people lose interest in, and capacity for, sexual activity, although sexual partners become less available with advancing age.

4.   The loss of a life partner is one of the most difficult adjustments older people must make, but having social support through extensive friendship and familial networks helps alleviate the stress experienced during old age.

5.   Elder care in the Unite States is provided in two major ways: institutions for the elderly and private care in the home.

    a.   Most elderly people are cared for informally by families, with female relatives providing a majority of long-term care.

    b.   Two-thirds of elderly men live with their spouses, but women are more likely to be living alone after age 65 due to their longer life expectancy.

    c.   About one-tenth of all elderly live in nursing homes, and 75 percent of nursing home residents are women, many of whom are over age 80, ill, disabled, and frail.

    d.   The cost of nursing home care is subsidized by two federal programs -- **Medicaid**, a health insurance program for the poor, and **Medicare**, a government program that provides health insurance for the elderly.

    e.   With the expansion of Medicaid and Medicare programs, nursing homes have become a profitable enterprise for privately owned companies, raising issues of profitability versus humane, affordable care.

6.   Physical and mental abuse of the elderly has only recently surfaced as a notable social problem, and it remains difficult to gauge the true extent of the problem.

    a.   The most common form of elder abuse is neglect, followed by physical abuse and sometimes, financial exploitation.

    b.   Female care givers are most likely to neglect the elderly, while sons are most likely to directly physically abuse them, perhaps because the social strains of care giving produce considerable stress and frustration in the absence of adequate institutional support systems for families.

F.   Death and Dying

    1.   Sociologists note that even death is socially structured, because patterns of stratification that reveal themselves in life are also apparent in death. For example, African American men are seven more times likely to die from homicide than White men, and infant death is twice as likely to occur among racial-ethnic minorities as Whites.

    2.   A person dies within social institutions that are organized to handle death. For example, most Americans die in hospitals, and the multibillion dollar funeral home industry is organized to "manage" the death experience for others.

    3.   Prior to the twentieth century and the emergence of undertaking as a profession, death was usually taken care of at home, and it was largely the work of women from the family and community.

    4.   The **hospice movement** has developed as an alternative to hospital-based, technologically controlled death to provide more personal, home-based care for dying people and their families.

IV.   **SEX, SOCIAL STRUCTURE, AND SOCIAL STRATIFICATION**

Sex is not only a physiological experience, but also a socially meaningful experience that creates intimacy between people and contributes to our social identity. Like other social characteristics, sexual orientation is structured by social institutions and linked to systems of social stratification.

- **Human sexual attitudes and behavior vary in different cultural contexts**, resulting in different sexual behaviors being defined as normal or deviant.
- **Sexual attitudes and behavior change over time**, as reflected by the earlier age at which young people are having sex and the increase in the number of people who have sex before marriage.
- **Sexual identity is learned** through the socialization process and interaction with others; for example, **sexual scripts** teach us what is appropriate behavior for our gender, such as norms about heterosexuality and marriage.
- **Social institutions channel and direct human sexuality** by defining some forms of sexual expression as more legitimate than others and granting certain privileges, such as the right to marry, only to heterosexual couples.
- **Sex is influenced by the economic institutions of society**, as evidenced in the use of sex to sell products (such as cars and personal care items) as well as the sale and purchase of sex itself.
- **Public policies regulate sexual and reproductive behavior**, as reflected in government decisions about which reproductive technologies to endorse and whether to provide federal funding for abortion and sex education.

A.   Sexual Politics

    1.   **Sexual politics** refers to the link that exists between sexuality and power, both in personal relationships and social arrangements.

    2.   Sexual politics is reflected in the sexual exploitation of women in society, the high rates of violence against women and sexual minorities, and the privilege and power accorded to those presumed to be heterosexual.

    3.   Both the gay and lesbian liberation movement and the feminist movement have put sexual politics at the center of the public's attention by challenging gender role stereotyping and sexual oppression.

B.   Technology, Sex, and Cybersex

    1.   The widespread availability of the birth control pill has supported the emergence of new sexual norms associating sex with intimacy, emotional ties, and physical pleasure, but not necessarily with reproduction.

2. The Internet has introduced new forms of sexual relationships as people seek sexual stimulation through pornographic Web sites and on-line chatrooms; however, expanded opportunities to engage in *cybersex* have also introduced new risks and forms of deviance that are difficult to regulate.

C. The Influence of Race, Class, and Gender
1. Sexual behavior follows gendered patterns in addition to patterns established by race and class relations.
   a. The "double standard" is the idea that men are expected to have a stronger sex drive than women, so women who are openly sexual may be labeled "loose."
   b. Men are socialized to see sex in terms of performance and achievement, whereas women are taught to associate sex with intimacy and affection.
   c. Certain sexual stereotypes are associated with particular racial, ethnic, and social class groups; for example, Latin men are stereotyped as "hot lovers," African American men as overly virile, Asian American women as compliant and submissive, and working-class women as "sluts."
2. Class, race, and gender hierarchies have historically been justified by claiming that people of color and women are sexually promiscuous and uncontrollable.
   a. One way that White slaveowners expressed their ownership was through the sexual abuse of Black women, who were depicted as sexual animals.
   b. Black men were stereotyped as highly sexed, lustful beasts who were a threat to White women, which supported lynching.
   c. Sexual abuse was also part of the conquest of American Indians by Whites, and the rape of women following wars is all too common.
3. Women who work in the sex industry (such as prostitutes and topless dancers) may have no other option for supporting themselves. Women who sell sex are usually condemned for their behavior, which is not as true for their male clients.

D. Sex and Culture: A Global Perspective
1. Cross-cultural studies show that sexual norms develop within particular cultural meaning systems; for example, there is considerable cross-national variation in the degree to which men and women experience jealousy when their partners kiss, flirt, or become otherwise sexually involved with another person.
2. As the world has become more globally connected, an international sex trade has flourished, linking economic development, world poverty, tourism, and the subordinate status of women in many societies.
   a. The *international sex trade* (also referred to as "sex trafficking") refers to the use of women worldwide as sex workers in an institutional context where sex is a commodity used to promote tourism, cater to business and military men, and support a huge nightclub industry.
   b. The international sex trade has been strongly implicated in the spread of AIDS worldwide as well as the exploitation of women in countries where women have limited economic opportunities.

IV. **SEXUALITY AND SOCIOLOGICAL THEORY**
A. Sex: Functional or Conflict-Based?
1. Functionalist theory views sexuality in terms of how it contributes to the stability of social institutions; for example, norms that restrict sex to marriage encourage the formation of heterosexual families.
2. Conflict theorists view sexuality as part of the power relations and economic inequality in society. Because sex is linked to other forms of subordination and exploitation, rape and sexual harassment are understood to be the result of power

imbalances between men and women, and the international sex trade is linked to women's poverty and low social status around the world.

    B.   <u>The Social Construction of Sexual Identity</u>

        1.   Symbolic interaction theory uses a **social construction perspective** to interpret sexual identity as learned, not inborn.

            a.   Although hormonal fluctuations, sexual physiology, and genetic factors are elements in sexual desire, sociologists question the extent to which biology shapes sexual identity.

            b.   Sexual identity is learned through the socialization process, develops through social experiences, and is constructed over the life course through a process of self-definition.

        2.   **Sexual orientation**, or how individuals experience sexual arousal and pleasure, is classified as *heterosexual, homosexual,* or *bisexual* in the United States.

        3.   **Compulsory heterosexuality**, a concept developed by Adrienne Rich, is the idea that heterosexual identity is not a choice, because social institutions define heterosexuality as the only legitimate form of sexual identity and enforce it through social norms and sanctions, including peer pressure, socialization, law, economic policies and even violence. **Heterosexism** refers to the belief that heterosexuality is the only legitimate sexual orientation.

        4.   **Coming out** refers to the process of defining oneself as gay or lesbian, which is a series of events in which a person comes to see herself or himself as having a gay identity and may publicly reveal that identity to others. That a person's sexual identity may change over their lifetime indicates that identity is socially created.

V.   **CONTEMPORARY SEXUAL ATTITUDES AND BEHAVIOR**

Overall, Americans are more sexually liberal and show greater tolerance for diverse sexual lifestyles and practices than in the past.

    A.   <u>Changing Sexual Values</u>

        1.   Sexual values change significantly over time; for example, only 21 percent of Americans approved of premarital sex in 1969, now 60 percent do.

        2.   Although the American public has become somewhat more accepting of gays and lesbians, **homophobia** -- the fear and hatred of homosexuals -- is still rampant.

        3.   Significant gender differences are evident on many topics. For example, young men and women give different reasons for engaging in sexual intercourse for the first time [Figure 11.1], and men are more likely than women to think that homosexual relations are morally wrong.

        4.   Sexual attitudes are also shaped by race-ethnicity, age, education, and religious identification; for example, sexual liberalism is associated with higher education, youth, urban lifestyle, and political liberalism on other social issues.

    B.   <u>Sexual Practices of the American Public</u>

Most surveys investigate sexual attitudes because self-report data about sexual practices are often unreliable. Laumann and colleagues conducted the most comprehensive survey of sexual practices in the United States in the early 1990s. The results indicated that:

- *Young people are becoming sexually active earlier.* Over 20 percent of 15 year old males and females report having intercourse [Figure 11.2].
- *The proportion of young people who are sexually active has increased,* particularly among young women.
- *Having only one sexual partner in one's lifetime is rare.*
- *A significant number of people have extramarital sex.*
- *A significant number of people are lesbian or gay.*
- *For those who are sexually active, sex is relatively frequent.*

VI. SEX AND SOCIAL ISSUES

Although most people think of sex in terms of interpersonal relationships, sexual norms are deeply intertwined with various social problems in the United States. For example, teen pregnancy, pornography, and sexual violence can generate personal troubles that have their origins in the structure of society.

A. Birth Control
   1. Birth control availability is now less debated than in the past, but this form of reproductive technology is still related to the position of women in society.
      a. Men mostly define the laws and make scientific decisions about what types of birth control will be available.
      b. Women are seen as more responsible for contraception; at the same time, birth control technology breaks the link between sex and reproduction, freeing women from some traditional constraints on their behavior.
   2. In 1960, the federal Food and Drug Administration approved the marketing of a new oral contraceptive, the birth control pill. The Supreme Court first defined birth control as a right, not a crime, in *Griswold v. Connecticut* in 1965. This right was not extended to unmarried people until 1972 in *Eisenstadt v. Baird*.
   3. **Eugenics** sought to apply scientific principles of genetic selection to "improve" the offspring of the human race. The eugenics movement, an explicitly racist and class-based trend, emerged as the birth rate fell among the White upper and middle classes in the early twentieth century.

B. New Reproductive Technologies
   Although new reproductive technologies (such as surrogacy, in vitro fertilization, cloning, and gene splicing) have increased sexual freedom, they have also raised social policy questions concerning the removal of biological parents from the reproductive process. Although the concept of reproductive choice is important to most people, choice is conditioned by the constraints of race, class, and gender inequalities in society.

C. Abortion
   1. Abortion is one of the most seriously contended political issues in the United States, although the majority of the American public supports abortion rights, at least in some circumstances [Figure 11.3].
   2. The right to abortion was first established in constitutional law by the *Roe v. Wade* Supreme Court decision issued in 1973, which established that the government may restrict access to abortion in different trimesters of pregnancy.
   3. Data on abortion show that it occurs across social groups, although certain patterns do emerge, with young women and Black and Hispanic women more likely than older women and White women to have abortions.
   4. Attitudes toward abortion are clearly rooted in more general attitudes about sexuality, family life, gender roles, and women's right to control their bodies.

D. Pornography
   There is little social consensus about the acceptability and effects of pornography. Debate about pornography often focuses on the legal definition of obscenity. Public agitation over pornography has divided people into those who think it is solidly protected by the First Amendment, those who want it strictly controlled, those who think it should be totally banned for moral reasons, and those who want it banned because it harms women.

E. Sexual Violence
   1. The women's movement has been successful in identifying and raising public awareness about the problems of rape, sexual harassment, domestic violence, incest, and other forms of sexual coercion and violence.

2. Feminists argue that sexual violence is a form of power relations that is shaped by the social inequality between men and women, and note these are forms of deviant and criminal behavior, not expressions of human sexuality.

3. Various forms of sexual coercion can be understood in the context of how social institutions shape human behavior. For example, *date rape* -- forced and unwanted sexual relations by someone who knows the victim – often affects young women on college campuses, particularly in organizations (such as fraternities) that define masculinity as competitive and women as sexual prey.

4. Black, Hispanic, and poor women are most likely to be victimized by violence, although White women are as likely to be victimized by an intimate partner.

VII. AGE, SEX, AND SOCIAL CHANGE
A. The Graying of America
1. Never before have so many people in the United States lived so long, which has profound implications for how society is organized [Figure 11.4].
2. The *contract between generations* refers to the expectation that parents care for children who in turn care for their children, and those children and grandchildren then care for their parents and grandparents during old age. Changes in families (including smaller family size, delayed childbearing, and geographic mobility) are altering these patterns of intergenerational care, but social institutions are poorly designed to handle the demands associated with the *graying of America*.
3. As different generations vie for government entitlement programs that provide economic and social assistance, the issue of **generational equity** arises. This debate concerns whether one age group or generation is unfairly taxed to support the needs and interests of another generation.

B. The Sexual Revolution
The **sexual revolution** refers to the widespread changes in men's and women's roles, the narrowing of differences in the sexual experiences of women and men, and a greater public acceptance of sexuality as a normal part of social development. These changes have brought new freedoms and new dangers in the expression of sexuality, as well as an increase in commercialized sex.

PRACTICE TEST

Multiple Choice Questions

1. Sociologists generally agree that sexual identity:
   a. develops in early childhood and changes little over one's lifetime.
   b. is the driving force behind all human activities.
   c. is biologically determined at birth.
   d. None of the above statements are true from a sociological perspective.

2. According to Vasquez, men who disdain sports, work in personal service occupations such as hairdresser, or dress in ways considered feminine are at risk for assault because they engage in:
   a. compulsory heterosexuality.
   b. gender betrayal.
   c. sexual violation.
   d. homosexuality.

3. The sexual revolution in the United States contributed to which of the following social changes?
   a. increase in the commercialization of sex, which uses women in demeaning ways
   b. increase in the public's acceptance of sex as a normal part of social development
   c. increase in the percentage of women who have sexual intercourse before marriage
   d. All of the above statements about the sexual revolution are true.

4. The hierarchical ranking of different age groups in society that ensures people in different age groups will differ in their access to society's rewards and privileges is:
   a. life expectancy.
   b. age stratification.
   c. cohort experience.
   d. generational differentiation.

5. Which theory argues that an arrangement whereby older people gradually withdraw from participation in society, and are simultaneously relieved from some responsibilities, is efficient for the society?
   a. symbolic interaction theory
   b. social uselessness theory
   c. functionalist theory
   d. conflict theory

6. Research indicates that the *midlife crisis* is:
   a. a period when most men and women experience a pervasive emotional crisis.
   b. associated with women becoming fixated on what they have failed to achieve or the things they never attempted to do.
   c. largely a social myth, because mid-life is actually a happy, positive experience for most men and women.
   d. a period in which adults become especially vulnerable to being physically neglected and abused by their children.

7. Which of the following factors is **not** a central feature of the life course perspective?
   a. the roles individuals occupy during their lifetimes
   b. the sociohistorical context in which people grow up
   c. the personal events that individuals experience during their lifetimes
   d. the physical consequences of disease and disability for aging individuals

8. Individuals in which stage of the life course have the most rights, privileges, and social responsibilities relative to people in other stages of the life course?
   a. children
   b. adolescents
   c. adults
   d. old age

9. Young children learn what is appropriate sexual behavior for people of their gender from sexual:
   a. revolutions.
   b. activities.
   c. politics.
   d. scripts.

10. According to Laumann and colleagues' national survey of sexual practices in the United States:
   a. a large percentage of Americans have sexual intercourse before marriage.
   b. sex is fairly infrequent among people who are sexually active.
   c. relatively few Americans have extramarital affairs.
   d. All of the above statements are true.

11. Which stage of the life course is characterized by attempts to establish autonomy and independence from authority figures while developing a coherent identity?
   a. childhood
   b. adolescence
   c. middle adulthood
   d. old age

12. Which of the following is a common stereotype of elderly people in the United States?
   a. They are adorable, innocent, and charming.
   b. They are conservative and lonely.
   c. They are lazy and irresponsible.
   d. They are careless and selfish.

13. Which theory emphasizes the role of social meanings and social perceptions of age groups in explaining how the aging process varies cross-culturally?
   a. conflict theory
   b. eugenics theory
   c. functionalist theory
   d. symbolic interaction theory

14. Conflict theorists view sexuality and sexual relations as:
   a. linked to other forms of subordination that associate sex with power.
   b. contributing to the stability of social institutions such as the family.
   c. natural behavior that manifests itself similarly across societies.
   d. None of the above statements are consistent with conflict theory.

15. Rites of passage such as weddings, christenings, and Bar Mitzvahs:
   a. are rituals that celebrate or memorialize events in an individual's life.
   b. are public affirmations of a change in an individual's social status.
   c. provide transitions to different phases of the life cycle.
   d. All of the above statements about rites of passage are true.

16. Which of the following Supreme Court cases first defined the use of birth control as a right, rather than a crime, in the United States?
   a. Roe v. Wade (1973)
   b. Eisenstadt v. Baird (1972)
   c. Griswold v. Connecticut (1965)
   d. Roberts v. Food and Drug Administration (1960)

17. According to the social construction perspective, which of the following identities is learned through the socialization process?
   a. heterosexuality
   b. homosexuality
   c. bisexuality
   d. According to this perspective, all sexual identities are learned, rather than innate.

18. Adrienne Rich argues that social institutions define attraction to the opposite sex as the only legitimate form of sexual identity and enforce this definition through social norms and sanctions. She refers to this concept as:
    a.   compulsory heterosexuality.
    b.   double standard.
    c.   homophobia.
    d.   coming out.

19. Eugenics refers to the:
    a.   scientific study of human sexual response and behavior.
    b.   development of reproductive technology that allows previously infertile couples to have children.
    c.   application of scientific principles of genetic selection to efforts aimed at perfecting the human species.
    d.   development of medical technology that improves people's sensitivity to sexual stimulation and heightens their sexual pleasure.

20. Which concept refers to the public debate about whether one age group is being unfairly taxed in order to support the needs and interests of another age group in the United States?
    a.   graying of America
    b.   generational equity
    c.   age differentiation
    d.   generation gap

21. Which of the following statements about abortion in the United States is true?
    a.   Prior to 1973, only married women had a legal right to abortion in the United States, but after 1973, unmarried women were granted the same right.
    b.   The abortion rate has decreased steadily since 1973 when the United States Supreme Court issued a new decision placing more restrictions on the right to abortion.
    c.   The United States government has established different criteria for determining if abortion is allowed in the first, second, and third trimesters of pregnancy.
    d.   All of the above are true.

22. The birth control pill:
    a.   is one of the most widely used forms of contraception in the United States.
    b.   was approved by the federal Food and Drug Administration (FDA) in 1950.
    c.   has been legally available to women regardless of their marital status since 1960.
    d.   All of the above statements about the birth control pill are true.

23. Prior to the twentieth century, "death work," such as the preparation of a deceased person's body for viewing and burial, was primarily a:
    a.   profitable business handled by professional funeral directors.
    b.   medical process, handled by licensed physicians and nurses.
    c.   church matter, handled by ordained ministers and priests.
    d.   family matter, handled by women in the community

24. Which of the following statements about long-term institutional care in the United States is true?
   a. Approximately one fourth of all elderly men and women reside in nursing homes today.
   b. Nursing homes are increasingly likely to be operated by charitable organizations rather than private companies because operating a nursing home elicits little profit.
   c. Women are more likely than men to reside in nursing homes during old age.
   d. All of the above statements about institutional care for the elderly are true.

25. Which of the following sociological terms refers to the process whereby children in the United States were redefined as precious and emotionally priceless, but not economically useful?
   a. devaluation
   b. infantilization
   c. medicalization
   d. sentimentalization

True-False Questions

1. Conflict theory argues that systematically barring youths and the elderly from the labor market is a way of eliminating these groups from competition for jobs, which benefits middle-aged adults.

2. Depression is strongly associated with getting older because it is rooted in the inevitable deterioration of mental capacity that occurs during the aging process.

3. Financial exploitation is by far the most common form of elder abuse in the United States today.

4. White men have a longer life expectancy than any other group in the United States.

5. Most sociological research concerning sexuality in the United States relies on survey data.

6. A major factor contributing to the spread of AIDS worldwide is the international sex trade, which includes the sale of sex to promote tourism.

7. In recent years, discrimination cases based on sexual orientation have become one of the most frequently filed cases through the Equal Employment Opportunity Commission (EEOC).

8. According to national survey research, the proportion of young people who are sexually active has increased, particularly among young women.

9. Most states in the U.S. now grant homosexual couples the right to legally register their union and receive the same benefits as heterosexual married couples.

10. Among women and men whose first intercourse experience was wanted, a higher percentage of women cite "affection for partner" as a main reason they had sex, while a higher percentage of men cite "curiosity" as a main reason they had sex.

Fill in the Blank Questions

1. Sociologists refer to an aggregate of people born during the same period who share the same historical experiences as an age _____.

2. The _____ movement provided people who are ill with an alternative to hospital-based, technologically controlled death by providing more personalized care to dying individuals and their families within the home environment.

3. Sociologists refer to the institutionalized practice of age prejudice and discrimination as _____.

4. Despite social movement activity to secure equal rights for gay and lesbian people, the fear and hatred of homosexuals, or _____, is rampant in American culture.

5. Sexual _____ are reflected in personal relationships where one person is powerless or is defined as the property of someone else, and in the sexual exploitation of women in society through pornography and prostitution.

Essay Questions

1. Discuss the ways in which the cultural and social bases of sexuality are revealed, and provide an example for each feature that you identify.
2. Discuss how the Internet has contributed to greater sexual freedom at the same time it has increased the danger associated with sexual behavior.
3. Explain why the *international sex trade* flourishes in countries such as Thailand.
4. Discuss how the projected demographic changes for the United States are likely to influence care giving demands and social policies.
5. Identify the four stages of the life course and summarize the main features associated with each stage in the United States.

ANSWERS TO PRACTICE TEST

Answers to Multiple Choice Questions

1.	D	300	From a sociological perspective, little in human behavior is purely natural. Sexual identity is only one component of the self, and it continues to develop over one's life course, rather than being fixed at birth. Sexual identity develops within a particular cultural, social, and historical context.
2.	B	307	According to Vasquez, men and women who do not conform to strict social definitions of masculinity and femininity are perceived as engaging in gender betrayal, which increases the likelihood that they will be victims of hate crimes.
3.	D	315	The widespread changes in men's and women's roles, a greater public acceptance of sexuality as a normal part of social development, an increase in the use of birth control, and an increase in the incidence of premarital sex for men and women are all consequences of the sexual revolution.
4.	B	290	Age stratification results in the unequal distribution of society's resources and privileges based on the hierarchical ranking of age groups in society.
5.	C	291	Table 11.1 indicates that functionalist theory views the elderly as gradually withdrawing from social roles and being relieved of responsibilities, which provides for an orderly transition from one generation to the next.
6.	C	296	Despite considerable public attention to the midlife crisis, research indicates that most men and women experience midlife as happy and positive. Normative midlife events do not generally cause significant stress.
7.	D	294	The life course perspective connects people's personal attributes, the roles they occupy, the life events they experience, and their sociohistorical context. This perspective does not explain how illness and disability affect individuals

physically, although it could be used to understand how illness and disability are perceived and treated within particular social contexts and historical periods.

8. C 296 People have more roles, responsibilities, and privileges during adulthood than at any other stage of the life course. Children have the fewest rights.

9. D 301 Young children learn what is appropriate behavior for their gender through sexual scripts.

10. A 308 Laumann and colleagues conducted a comprehensive survey of the sexual practices of the American public in the early 1990's. The results indicate that young people are becoming sexually active earlier; the proportion of young people who are sexually active has increased, particularly among women; Americans are not very well informed about sex; a significant number of people have extramarital affairs; few people have just one sexual partner in their lifetimes; a considerable number of people are lesbian or gay; and sex is relatively frequent for those who are sexually active.

11. B 295 Establishing a coherent identity, personal autonomy, and independence from authority figures are key features of adolescence. Childhood is defined as a period of innocence and relative freedom from responsibility.

12. B 293 Age stereotypes are preconceived judgments about what different age groups are like. Adolescents are perceived as lazy, irresponsible, and sloppy. Elderly people are stereotyped as forgetful, set in their ways, conservative, meddlesome, inactive, unproductive, lonely, incompetent, and uninterested in sex.

13. D 292 Symbolic interactionists focus on the meanings and value attached to different age groups in society [Table 11.1].

14. A 304 Conflict theorists see sexuality as part of the system of power relations and economic inequality in society, thus, sexual relations are linked to other forms of subordination. For example, the international sex trade is related to women's high rates of poverty and low social status in many nations around the world.

15. D 294 Rites of passage (such as christenings, weddings, and the quinceanera ceremony) are cultural events that celebrate or memorialize events in an individual's life. These rituals publicly mark transitions from one phase in the life span to another.

16. C 309 The FDA first approved the birth control pill in 1960. The Supreme Court case, *Griswold v. Connecticut*, first defined contraception as a right, not a crime, in 1965, but restricted this right to married people. In 1972, the court extended this right to unmarried people in *Eisenstadt v. Baird*. In 1973, the court ruled that women have a legal right to abortion in *Roe v. Wade*.

17. D 305 The social construction perspective interprets sexual identity as learned, not inborn. All sexual identities develop through social experiences within particular social contexts.

18. A 305 Rich argues that institutions define heterosexuality as the only legitimate form of sexual identity and enforce it through social norms and sanctions, a concept she calls *compulsory heterosexuality*. Coming out is the process of publicly defining oneself as gay or lesbian, which involves a series of events and redefinitions in which a person comes to see himself or herself as having a gay identity.

19. C 309 Eugenics sought to apply scientific principles of genetic selection to "improve" the human race. This philosophy was criticized as being explicitly racist.

20. B 314 The public debate about whether one age group is being unfairly taxed in order to support the needs and interests of another age group in the United States is referred to as generational equity.

21. C 310 The right to abortion was first established in constitutional law by the Supreme Court case, *Roe v. Wade* (1973). The court ruled that at different trimesters during a pregnancy, separate but legitimate rights collide, including the right to

privacy, the right of the state to protect maternal health, and the right of the state to protect developing life. Thus, the government established different criteria for legal access to abortion depending on the stage of the pregnancy.

22. A 309 The FDA first approved the birth control pill in 1960, and today, it is one of the most widely used forms of contraception. The pill was not legally available to unmarried women until 1972.

23. D 300 Prior to the twentieth century and the emergence of undertaking as a profession, death was taken care of at home. Women in the family and from the community handled the preparation and display of the deceased's body.

24. C 298 The majority of elderly people are cared for by female family members at home. Approximately one-tenth of the elderly population resides in nursing homes in the United States. White women, who have the longest life expectancy of any group, are most likely to be institutionalized. With the expansion of Medicaid and Medicare funding for institutional care, nursing homes have become profitable businesses that are increasingly likely to be operated by private companies, rather than charitable organizations.

25. D 295 The *sentimentalization* of children occurred during the mid-nineteenth century in the United States, at least among the middle class. This process involved redefining children as emotionally priceless but not economically useful.

Answers to True-False Questions

1. T 292 Conflict theorists focus on the competition over scarce resources between age groups. Barring youth and the elderly from working provides employment advantages to middle-aged adults.

2. F 293 Aging may be an inevitable process, but how it is experienced varies by social class, race-ethnicity, gender, and other social factors. Depression is not an inevitable consequence of aging. For example, menopausal women are culturally depicted as cranky, overly emotional, and prone to irritability and depression, but a majority of menopausal women do not experience the physical symptoms presumed to be related to menopause.

3. F 299 Neglect is the most common form of elder abuse, followed by physical abuse. In some cases, elderly people are also subject to financial exploitation.

4. F 293 Life expectancy is the probable number of average years a particular group is likely to live. White women, who live an average of 79.9 years, have a longer life expectancy than any other group in the United States.

5. T 308 What we know about sexual behavior is typically drawn from surveys, such as the one conducted by Laumann and colleagues in the early 1990s. Most surveys ask about attitudes, not actual behavior.

6. T 304 The international sex trade is used to promote tourism and cater to business and military men in countries such as Thailand. It has been strongly implicated in the spread of AIDS worldwide.

7. F 291 Age discrimination cases are one of the most frequently filed complaints received by the EEOC. Legislation was passed in 1967 to protect people from age discrimination in employment, but federal law does not protect people from discrimination on the basis of sexual orientation.

8. T 308 Results of national surveys indicate that the proportion of young people who are sexually active has increased, especially among young women.

9. F 301 Heterosexual couples enjoy institutional privileges such as the right to marry and have mutual employee health benefits, options not usually available to gay and lesbian couples in the United States. Germany has recently legalized homosexual

relationships, yet these couples do not have the same tax advantages or child adoption rights as do heterosexual couples.

10. T   307   Figure 11.1 indicates that among men and women whose first intercourse was wanted, nearly 50 percent of women but only 25 percent of men cited "affection for partner" as a reason for having sex. Over 50 percent of men but only 25 percent of women cited "curiosity or readiness for sex" as a reason.

Answers to Fill in the Blank Questions

1.   cohort   290
2.   hospice   300
3.   ageism   291
4.   homophobia   306
5.   politics   301

CHAPTER 12
FAMILIES AND RELIGION

BRIEF CHAPTER OUTLINE

Defining the Family
> Comparing Kinship Systems
> Extended and Nuclear Families

Sociological Theory and Families
> Functionalist Theory and the Family
> Conflict Theory and the Family
> Feminist Theory and the Family
> Symbolic Interaction Theory and the Family

Diversity Among Contemporary American Families
> Female-Headed Households
> Married Couple Families
> Stepfamilies
> Gay and Lesbian Households
> Singles and Cohabitors

Marriage and Divorce
> Marriage
> Divorce

Families and Social Problems
> Family Violence
> Elder Care
> Teen Pregnancy

Changing Families/Changing Society
> Global Changes in Family Life
> Families and Social Policy

Defining Religion

The Significance of Religion in American Society
> The Dominance of Christianity
> Measuring Religious Faith
> Forms of Religion

Sociological Theories of Religion
> Emile Durkheim: The Functions of Religion
> Max Weber: The Protestant Ethic and the Spirit of Capitalism
> Karl Marx: Religion, Social Conflict, and Oppression
> Symbolic Interaction: Becoming Religious

Diversity and Religious Belief

Religious Organizations
> Churches
> Sects
> Cults

Religion and Social Change

CHAPTER FOCUS: This chapter identifies the features of family and religion as social institutions. It discusses how these institutions are related to each other, as well as to the economy and the state, in the United States. It also provides an overview of the diverse forms of family arrangements and kinship systems found around the world.

QUESTIONS TO GUIDE YOUR READING

1. Why do sociologists consider the family a social institution, and what are the main features of the family as an institution?
2. What features do sociologists use to classify kinship systems around the world?
3. What are the most pressing problems facing American families today, and why is the development of public policy concerning families so controversial?
4. Why are family and religion considered social institutions, and how do these institutions interact in the United States?
5. What influence has religion had on promoting social change in the United States?

SOCIOLOGY IN ACTION: AN INTERNET EXERCISE

Go to www.fatherhood.org and consider why there has been a proliferation of academic research about, government concern with, and media attention to, the importance of fathers in families and society. Then go to www.mothersandmore.org and find out why some mothers have interrupted their paid careers to care for their children full-time. What challenges do full-time mothers and mothers who work for pay experience in the United States? Does this organization recommend primarily individual or structural solutions to these problems?

KEY TERMS (defined at page number shown and in glossary)

bilateral kinship system 321
church 345
cult 346
exogamy 321
family 320
kinship system 320
matrilineal kinship system 321
monotheism 341
patriarchal religion 341
polygamy 321
profane 339
religion 338
ritual 342
sect 345
totem 339

charisma 346
collective consciousness 342
endogamy 321
extended families 322
Family and Medical Leave Act (FMLA) 337
matriarchal religion 341
monogamy 321
nuclear family 322
patrilineal kinship system 321
polytheism 341
Protestant Ethic 342
religiosity 340
sacred 339
secular 339
transnational family 336

KEY PEOPLE (identified at page number shown)

Emile Durkheim 342
Max Weber 342

Karl Marx 343

CHAPTER OUTLINE

The *family ideal*, represented by a father employed as the major breadwinner and a mother at home raising children, has long been defined within dominant American culture as the family to which we should all aspire, yet few families conform to this ideal today. Sociologists view the family as a social institution that is intertwined with other institutions, such as the law, economy, and religion. It is within the family that people first learn religious values, for example.

I. **DEFINING THE FAMILY**

    A.   Comparing Kinship Systems

          A **kinship system** is the pattern of relationships that define people's family relationships to one another. Kinship systems vary enormously across cultures and over time. Kinship systems are generally be categorized by five features:

- how many marital partners are permitted at one time
- who is permitted to marry whom
- how descent is determined and how property is passed on
- where the family resides
- how power is distributed.

1. **Polygamy** is the practice whereby men or women have multiple spouses. *Polyandry*, the practice of a woman having more than one husband, is extremely rare. The more common form of polygamy is *polygyny*, where a man has more than one wife, a practice found among a small group of Mormons in the U.S.

2. **Monogamy**, the practice of forming a sexually exclusive marriage with one spouse at a time, is the most common form of marriage in the United States.

3. **Exogamy** is the practice of selecting mates from outside one's group. The group may be based on religion, territory, or racial-ethnic identity.

4. **Endogamy** is the practice of selecting mates from within one's group.
   a. In the U.S., **antimiscegenation laws**, which prohibited marriage between people of different races, were not declared unconstitutional until 1967.
   b. Even if certain forms of marriage are not explicitly outlawed, societies establish norms about who is an appropriate marriage partner. Although interracial marriage has recently increased, it is still uncommon.

5. Kinship systems shape the distribution of property in society by proscribing how the lines of descent are determined. In **patrilineal kinship** systems, family lineage or ancestry is traced through the family of the father, whereas ancestry is traced through the mother in **matrilineal kinship** systems. In the U.S., there is a **bilateral kinship system**, where descent is traced through both parents.

B. Extended and Nuclear Families
   1. **Extended families** include the whole network of parents, children, and other relatives who form a family unit. For example, among African Americans, *othermothers* are kin who assist mothers with childrearing responsibilities; and among Chicanos, the system of *compadrazgo* includes help from godparents.
   2. The **nuclear family** is one where a married couple resides together with their children. The origin of this family form in Western society is linked to industrialization. With industrialization, paid labor was performed mostly in factories and public marketplaces, resulting in the separation of the family and the workplace and the development of the *family wage system*.
   3. For groups such as Chinese, Mexican, and Korean immigrants, as well as African Americans, the disruptions posed by slavery, migration, and urban poverty have affected how families are formed, their ability to stay together, and the resources they are able to secure to confront problems.

II. **SOCIOLOGICAL THEORY AND FAMILIES**
The complexity of family patterns makes it impossible to understand families from any single perspective. Sociologists have used four perspectives in their analysis of families [Table 12.1].

A. Functionalist Theory and The Family
   1. Functionalist theorists view the family as fulfilling particular societal needs, including socializing the young, regulating sexual activity and procreation, providing physical care for family members, and giving psychological support and emotional security to individuals. Over time, other institutions have begun to fulfill some of the functions originally performed by the family.
   2. Functionalists conceptualize marriage as a mutually beneficial exchange wherein women receive protection, economic support, and status in return for emotional support, sexual intimacy, household maintenance, and production of offspring.

3. When societies experience disruption and change, social institutions such as the family become disorganized, which weakens the social order.

B. Conflict Theory and the Family

Conflict theorists interpret the family as a system of power relations that both reinforces and reflects the inequalities in society at large. Families socialize children to obey authority and to become good consumers to fit the needs of capitalism.

C. Feminist Theory and the Family

Feminist theorists contributed new ways of conceptualizing the family by making gender a central concept in the analysis of the family as a social institution. Influenced by conflict theory, feminist scholars have asserted that the family does not serve the needs of all members equally, because the family is a system of gendered power relations.

D. Symbolic Interaction Theory and the Family

Symbolic interaction theory focuses how people define and understand their family experiences as well as how people negotiate family relationships. This perspective emphasizes the construction of meaning within families and notes that family roles continually evolve as participants actively create family life and relationships.

III. DIVERSITY AMONG CONTEMPORARY AMERICAN FAMILIES

Families are systems of social relationships that emerge in response to social conditions and that, in turn, shape the future direction of society. Compared to families in the past, families are smaller in size and devote fewer years to childbearing and childrearing. Divorced and never-married people make up a larger proportion of the population today.

A. Female-Headed Households

1. One of the most significant changes in family life has been an increase in single parent families, with one-fourth of all children now living with one parent.

2. The two main reasons for an increase in the number of women heading their own households are the high rates of divorce and unwed teen pregnancy.

3. Sociologists suggest that the economic pressures faced by women in female-headed households puts them under great strain due to poverty, a phenomenon known as the *feminization of poverty*.

4. The number of families headed by single fathers is also increasing. Male-headed households are less likely to experience severe economic problems, and single fathers generally get housework and childcare help from "mother substitutes."

B. Married Couple Families

Among married-couple families, one of the greatest changes in recent years has been the increased participation of women in the paid labor force. This has created other changes, such as an increase in the number of *commuter marriages*, an arrangement that typically arises when work requires one partner in a dual-earner couple to reside in a different city.

C. Stepfamilies

Stepfamilies have become more common in the United States, with about 40 percent of marriages involving stepchildren. Both parents and children must learn new roles when they become part of a stepfamily. Problems of jealousy and competition for time and attention can increase family tensions, which are exacerbated by a lack of clear norms.

D. Gay and Lesbian Households

1. Greater social acceptance of gay and lesbian identity has supported the development of family arrangements similar to marriage for homosexual couples, who share housing, expenses, decision making, and sometimes, childrearing.

2. Although only Hawaii and Vermont legally recognize gay marriage, 40 percent of the American public believes that gay partners who make a public commitment to each other should be entitled to the same rights and benefits as other married couples. However, there is still considerable public debate concerning gay and lesbian people raising children.

E.   Singles and Cohabitors

Single people, including those never married, widowed, and divorced, constitute 44 percent of the population today, an increase from 29 percent in 1970. Patterns of establishing intimate relationships have changed in the United States, with *cohabitation* becoming quite common. Additionally, a growing number of people are remaining in their parents' homes for longer periods of time, particularly for economic reasons.

IV.   MARRIAGE AND DIVORCE

The United States has the highest rate of marriage of any Western industrialized nation, but it also has a high divorce rate.

A.   Marriage

Often depicted as a consensual unit based on intimacy, economic cooperation, and mutual goals, marriage involves a complex set of social dynamics that also includes conflict, different patterns of resource allocation, and a gendered division of labor.

    1.   Research indicates that the amount of money a person earns establishes one's relative power within the marriage, including the ability to influence decisions.

    2.   The values of the partners and the roles they play also influence their experiences of marriage. For example, women do far more work in the home and have less leisure time than do men, a consequence of the *second shift* for working women.

B.   Divorce

    1.   The United States leads the world in the number of people who divorce, with divorce more likely for couples that marry young, for those in second marriages, for low-income couples, for African-Americans, and for those without a high school diploma.

    2.   Factors that contribute to the current high rate of divorce in the United States include longer life expectancy, the American cultural orientation toward individualism and personal happiness, and changes in women's roles that have resulted in women being less financially dependent on husbands than in the past.

    3.   Demi Kurz identified four main factors leading to women's marriages ending: dissatisfaction with gender roles, violence, alcohol or drug use, and infidelity.

    4.   Studies of the effects of divorce on children indicate that key factors in children's adjustment to divorce include the level of parental conflict before, during, and after the divorce, and the degree of father involvement after the divorce.

V.   FAMILIES AND SOCIAL PROBLEMS

For some people, families are centers of violence, disruption, and conflict rather than nurturance and protection.

A.   Family Violence

    1.   Partner violence occurs in both heterosexual and homosexual couples, with women significantly more likely than men to be victims of abuse and to suffer serious injury from their partners' assaults.

        b.   The American Medical Association estimates that one in three women will be physically assaulted by their husbands during their marriages.

        c.   Many victims of violence stay with their abusers because they believe their partners will change, and they perceive that the violence will escalate if they try to leave.

    2.   Child abuse includes neglect and physical violence. Women are as likely as men to be perpetrators of this type of family violence. Factors that increase the likelihood of child abuse include parental use of alcohol, unemployment, family isolation, and an absence of social supports.

    3.   Incest is a certain form of child abuse involving sexual relations between closely related persons, with fathers and uncles being the most likely perpetrators.

B.   Elder Care

As life expectancy increases, the need for elder care increases as well. The majority of caregivers for elderly people in the United States are female relatives. Caregivers often experience detrimental health consequences associated with the demands of care giving; however, caregiver stress can be reduced with appropriate social supports.

    C.   <u>Teen Pregnancy</u>
The United States has one of the highest rates of teen pregnancy in the world. Most babies born to teens will be raised by single mothers, who are twice as likely to be poor as older mothers. Teen pregnancy often occurs because sexually active teens use birth control inconsistently or not at all.

VI.   CHANGING FAMILIES/CHANGING SOCIETY

    A.   <u>Global Changes in Family Life</u>
The increasing global basis of the economy has facilitated new patterns of work and migration that have created a new family form, the **transnational family**. This is a family form where one or both parents live and work in one country, while their children remain in their countries of origin. Mothers in these families must develop new concepts of home and the maternal role.

    B.   <u>Families and Social Policy</u>
        1.   Social policies concerning families are the subject of intense national debate, particularly because some people claim that the family is breaking down, while others celebrate increasing diversity.

        2.   Among industrialized nations, the United States provides the least federal support for maternity and childcare policies. The 1993 **Family and Medical Leave Act (FMLA)** was the first law passed that recognized that family members need time off to care for children and other dependents, but several conditions limit its effectiveness, including the fact that the leave is unpaid.

        3.   There is a pressing need for affordable, quality childcare in the United States, a service that consumes a large portion of working parents' budgets.

VII.   DEFINING RELIGION

Sociologists study religion as both a belief system and a social institution. The belief systems of religion have a powerful hold on what people think and how they see the world. As a social institution, the patterns and practices of religion are among the most important influences on people's lives. Religious beliefs and practices are related to other social factors such as race, class, age, and gender. Sociologists define **religion** as an institutionalized system of symbols, beliefs, values, and practices through which a group of people interprets and responds to what they feel is sacred and that provides answers to questions of ultimate meaning.

- **Religion is institutionalized.**
- **Religion is a feature of groups.**
- **Religions are based on beliefs that are considered sacred.**
- **Religion establishes values and moral proscriptions for behavior.**
- **Religion establishes norms for behavior.**
- **Religion provides answers to questions of ultimate meaning.**

VIII.   THE SIGNIFICANCE OF RELIGION IN AMERICAN SOCIETY

    A.   <u>The Dominance of Christianity</u>
Despite the constitutional principle of the separation of church and state, Christian beliefs and practices dominate American culture. An example of this is that Christian traditions are publicly observed through the designation of national holidays in the United States.

    B.   <u>Measuring Religious Faith</u>
Religiosity refers to the intensity and consistency of a group's or person's faith, which is measured by asking people about their religious beliefs and tallying membership in

religious organizations and attendance at religious services. Over 50 percent of the population of the United States identify themselves as Protestant.

  C. Forms of Religion
      Religions are categorized according to the specific characteristics of the faiths and how religious groups are organized.
      1. **Monotheism** is the worship of a single god, as in Christianity, Judaism, and Islam, while **polytheism** is the worship of more than one deity, as in Hinduism.
      2. **Patriarchal religions** are those in which the beliefs and practices are based on male power and authority. **Matriarchal religions** are based on the centrality of female goddesses, who are often seen as the source of food, love, and nurturance, and may serve as emblems of the power of women.

IX. **SOCIOLOGICAL THEORIES OF RELIGION**
  A. Emile Durkheim: The Functions of Religion
      1. Durkheim argued that religion is functional for society because it reaffirms the social bonds that people have with each other, which creates social cohesion.
      2. Religious **rituals** are symbolic activities that express a group's spiritual conviction, such as a pilgrimage to Mecca.
      3. Durkheim believed that religion binds individuals to society by establishing what he called a **collective consciousness**, or the body of beliefs that are common to a community and that give people a sense of belonging.
  B. Max Weber: The Protestant Ethic and the Spirit of Capitalism
      Max Weber posited that the Protestant faith supported the development of capitalism in Western Europe and the United States by professing a belief in predestination, the idea that one's salvation is predetermined by god. Because material success was viewed as a gift from god, rather than something a person could earn, successful people appeared to be favored by god. Weber noted that the core features of the **Protestant Ethic**, hard work and self-denial, led not only to religious salvation, but also to the accumulation of capital.
  C. Karl Marx: Religion, Social Conflict, and Oppression
      1. Karl Marx viewed religion as a form of *false consciousness* and a tool for class oppression. He argued that oppressed people develop religion to soothe their distress, which prevents them from rising up to challenge the oppressive system.
      2. Marx defined religion as an *ideology*, or belief system that legitimates the existing social order. This is reflected in the historical situation of Christian principles being invoked by slave owners to justify slavery in the United States.
      3. It is important to note that religion can also be the basis for liberating social change, as was the case in the Civil Rights Movement in the United States.
  D. Symbolic Interaction: Becoming Religious
      People may become religious through a slow, gradual process or a more dramatic conversion. Sociologists view religious conversion, such as joining a cult, as linked to shifts in group consciousness as well as individual openness to changes in the social environment, rather than a process whereby individuals are "programmed."

X. **DIVERSITY AND RELIGIOUS BELIEF**
    Around the world, Christianity and Islam have the largest memberships [Figure 12.4]. In the United States, religious identification varies by race-ethnicity, gender, age, income and education level, and political affiliation. For example, young people are more likely than older people to express no religious preference, and considerably more women than men report that religion is very important to them [Figure 12.5]. For some racial-ethnic minority groups, religion can be a defense against racism, and churches have historically been among the most important institutions within African American and Latino communities.

XI. **RELIGIOUS ORGANIZATIONS**
     Sociologists define religious organizations using a classification system of three *ideal types*.

1. **Churches** are formal organizations that tend to define themselves, and be seen by society, as the primary and legitimate religious organizations. They are often organized as complex bureaucracies and membership is renewed as children of existing members are brought up in the church.

2. **Sects** are groups that have broken off from an established church, such as the Shakers' departure from the Society of Friends (also known as Quakers). Sects tend to focus less on the organization per se and more on the purity of members' faith, admitting only truly committed members to the group.

3. **Cults**, similar to sects in their intensity, are religious groups devoted to a specific cause or charismatic leader. Cult leaders tend to have great **charisma**, a quality attributed to individuals who are believed to have special powers. Cults are close-knit communities that attract people longing for personal attachments.

XII. RELIGION AND SOCIAL CHANGE

Religion remains an important social institution that, like other aspects of society, is becoming more commercialized. In the United States, the influence of conservative religious groups (such as evangelical Christians) on national politics has been increasing. Around the world, religion continues to play an important role in liberating social movements.

PRACTICE TEST

Multiple Choice Questions

1. From a sociological perspective, which of the following statements about religion is false?
   a. Religious faith provides a source of cohesion for members of society, but it also serves as a source of conflict in society.
   b. Religion cannot be studied as a social institution because it is based on faith rather than objective principles.
   c. A manifest function of religion is to provide a sense of ultimate meaning and purpose.
   d. Religion establishes values and norms that restrict people's behavior in society.

2. Religiosity refers to:
   a. the socialization mechanisms that teach people moral values and guidelines for ethical behavior.
   b. the degree of influence religious organizations have on a society's political system.
   c. whether one believes in a single, all powerful deity or multiple deities.
   d. the intensity and consistency of practice of a person's faith.

3. Which of the following religions is polytheistic?
   a. Protestantism
   b. Catholicism
   c. Judaism
   d. None of the above religions are polytheistic.

4. Religions based on the centrality of female goddesses are classified as which type of religion?
   a. Monotheistic
   b. Matriarchal
   c. Afrocentric
   d. Patriarchal

5.   The profane is anything that:
     a.   is supernatural.
     b.   excites awe and reverence.
     c.   is regarded as part of the ordinary world.
     d.   can be handled only by people who have been officially "blessed" or "ordained."

6.   Symbolic activities that express a group's spiritual conviction, such as a pilgrimage to Mecca, are religious:
     a.   orientations.
     b.   ideologies.
     c.   dctrines.
     d.   rituals.

7.   According to Emile Durkheim, religion is:
     a.   a system of socially constructed beliefs subject to individual interpretation.
     b.   no longer important in industrialized nations because it does not fulfill an essential purpose in modern society.
     c.   functional for society because it reaffirms the social bonds that people have with each other, which fosters cohesion.
     d.   an ideology that legitimates an oppressive social order and supports the status quo.

8.   Which theorist argued that the Protestant Ethic encouraged and supported the development of capitalism in the United States and Western Europe?
     a.   Karl Marx
     b.   Max Weber
     c.   Sigmund Freud
     d.   Emile Durkheim

9.   With which type of kinship system in the United States are fictive kin, "othermothers," and compadrazgo associated?
     a.   nuclear
     b.   bilateral
     c.   extended
     d.   patrilineal

10. When measured in terms of followers, the largest religion in the world is:
     a.   Islam.
     b.   Hinduism.
     c.   Buddhism.
     d.   Christianity.

11. The most common marriage pattern in the United States and other industrialized nations is:

     a.   exogamy.
     b.   polygamy.
     c.   monogamy.
     d.   patrilineality.

12. Research on decision making and household labor in married couple families reveals that:
   a. regardless of the amount of money that wives contribute to the household, they have more influence over household decisions than do their husbands.
   b. the men who are most likely to develop an egalitarian division of household labor when they get married are men whose own parents divided housework equitably.
   c. because women's paid labor force participation has increased so much in recent years, married men now do about half of all housework.
   d. All of the above statements about the household division of labor are true.

13. Which of the following is **not** a feature of the family *as a social institution*?
   a. Families are shaped by the personalities of each individual member.
   b. Families are affected by economic trends and political agendas.
   c. Families are defined and regulated by institutions of the state.
   d. Families are organized in a socially patterned way.

14. Functionalist theorists view families as:
   a. systems of power relationships that reinforce the inequalities in society at large.
   b. organized around a harmony of interests and beneficial to all of the members.
   c. gendered institutions that reflect the gender hierarchy in society at large.
   d. groups in which people interact and negotiate relationships with others.

15. Symbolic interaction theorists view families as:
   a. systems of power relationships that reinforce the inequalities in society at large.
   b. organized around a harmony of interests and beneficial to all of the members.
   c. gendered institutions that reflect the gender hierarchy in society at large.
   d. groups in which people interact and negotiate relationships with others.

16. Which perspective interprets people as moving into religious cults gradually, especially when they are open to changes in the social environment and seek meaningful personal attachments?
   a. symbolic interaction theory
   b. functionalist theory
   c. liberation theology
   d. conflict theory

17. Which of the following statements about single-parent households in the United States is (are) true?
   a. Fifty percent of all American children currently live with only one parent.
   b. Approximately one-fourth of all single parent households are headed by men.
   c. A primary cause for the increase in single-parent households is the high rate of divorce.
   d. All of the above statements about single-parent households are true.

18. The number of never-married mothers in the United States is higher today than in 1960 because:
   a. teenagers who become pregnant today are more likely to have the baby, whereas teenagers in the 1960s were more likely to have an abortion.
   b. teen mothers are easily able to complete school and be financially independent today, so they do not need any economic support from male partners.
   c. teenagers who become pregnant today are less likely to get married than they were in 1960.
   d. All of the above factors contributed to an increase in never-married mothers.

19. Karl Marx argued that religion is a form of false consciousness because:
    a. subordinate groups internalize religious ideology that justifies an oppressive social order.
    b. dominant religious ideology strongly encourages subordinate groups to seek justice and equality by challenging oppression.
    c. religion binds individuals to each other and to society, thereby enhancing cohesion and social harmony.
    d. religious worship no longer has strong meaning for people in modern societies because it takes place in large, formal organizations rather than small, intimate gatherings.

20. The majority of people in the United States identify their religious affiliation as:
    a. Jewish.
    b. Muslim.
    c. Protestant.
    d. Roman Catholic.

21. Cults tend to form around leaders with great _____, a quality attributed to individuals believed by their followers to have special powers.
    a. conservatism
    b. materialism
    c. liberalism
    d. charisma

22. Groups that have broken off from an established church, which are often characterized by emotionally charged worship services and concerns about the purity of members' faith, are:
    a. support groups.
    b. temples.
    c. totems.
    d. sects.

23. A(n) _____ is an object, such as a statue of Buddha, that a religious group regards with special awe and reverence.
    a. totem
    b. trinket
    c. ideology
    d. theology

24. Which industrialized nation provides the fewest federally supported maternity programs to its citizens?
    a. United States
    b. Canada
    c. Russia
    d. Japan

25. The Family and Medical Leave Act (FMLA) of 1993 provides twelve weeks of:
    a. free shelter to families who are homeless.
    b. free childcare to recipients of welfare who are engaged in a job search.
    c. paid leave to all full-time employees who experience a family emergency.
    d. unpaid leave to some employees to care for a newborn baby or a seriously ill parent.

True-False Questions

1.   Antimiscegenation laws, which prohibit marriage between people of different racial groups, were not declared unconstitutional until 1867.

2.   The influence of evangelical religious groups on the political system in the United States has decreased considerably in recent years.

3.   The United States leads the world not only in the number of people who marry, but also in the number of people who divorce.

4.   Religious organizations today reflect considerable gender equality, with all major denominations now allowing the ordination of women.

5.   Large numbers of African Americans have recently become Catholics because they are drawn to the church's emphasis on self-reliance, celebration of African identity, and prohibitions against gambling and using drugs or alcohol.

6.   Judaism has such enormous social significance because it is the second largest religion in the world.

7.   According to feminist theory, marriage is a mutually beneficial arrangement wherein women receive protection and financial support in exchange for providing emotional intimacy, child care, and housework.

8.   Research indicates that children who are raised by gay or lesbian parents experience significantly more psychological problems than do children raised by heterosexual parents.

9.   According to Khanna and colleagues' research on interracial dating and marriage in the United States, the families of White students react with hostility to the news that their relative is involved in an interracial relationship, but the families of Black students who date interracially are generally supportive of their relative's involvement in the relationship.

10.   The children who are most likely to have ongoing emotional difficulties as the result of their parents' divorce are those whose parents maintain joint custody.

Fill in the Blank Questions

1.   Science generates _____ beliefs based on logic and rational observations, rather than faith.

2.   Hinduism is a _____ religion because it is based on the belief that there are millions of gods and demons, rather than one powerful god.

3.   Christianity is categorized as a _____ religion because its doctrine and practices are based on male power and leadership.

4.   In a _____ family, one or both parents live in one country while their children remain in their countries of origin.

5.   In a _____ family, a married couple resides together with their children.

Essay Questions

1. Summarize the results of research on the consequences of divorce for children, noting which factors promote children's adjustment and which factors impede their development.
2. Discuss why social policies concerning family issues tend to generate intense national debate in the United States.
3. Define *social speedup* and discuss what consequences this phenomenon has for individuals and families in today's society.
4. Explain how African American people have historically drawn on religion as a defense against racism and discrimination.
5. Discuss how religion has contributed to, and has been affected by, large-scale social change in the United States and around the world.

ANSWERS TO PRACTICE TEST

Answers to Multiple Choice Questions

1.	B	338	From a sociological perspective, religion can be scientifically studied as a social institution. Religion establishes values, proscribes norms for moral behavior, and provides members of society with a sense of meaning. Religion can serve as a source of cohesion, conflict, and social change.
2.	D	340	Religiousity refers to the intensity and consistency of practice of an individual's or group's faith.
3.	B	341	Monotheistic religions such as Catholicism, Protestantism, Judaism, and Islam accept the idea that there is a single, all-powerful god. In Hinduism, a polytheistic religion, god is not a specific entity at all.
4.	B	341	Religions based on the centrality of female goddesses are classified as matriarchal, while patriarchal religions are based on male power and authority.
5.	C	339	The profane includes anything regarded as part of the ordinary world. The sacred refers to things of a supernatural nature that are regarded with awe and reverence. The handling of sacred objects is often restricted to religious authorities, or may be done by ordinary people if they undergo certain religious rituals.
6.	C	342	Symbolic activities that express a group's spiritual conviction are religious rituals. Totems are objects or living things that religious groups regard with awe.
7.	C	342	According to Durkheim, a functionalist theorist, religion is functional and necessary for all societies because it affirms and strengthens social bonds. Marx, who represents conflict theory, argued that religion is an ideology that legitimates the existing social order, supports the status quo, and benefits the ruling class. Symbolic interaction theory views religion as a system of socially constructed beliefs subject to various interpretations [Table 12.3].
8.	D	342	Max Weber noted that the Protestant Ethic encouraged hard work, self-denial, and personal accumulation of wealth, which was instrumental to the development of capitalism.
9.	C	322	Fictive kin, including *othermothers* and *compadrazgo*, provide childcare and other forms of assistance to families organized around extended kinship systems. The nuclear family, by contrast, consists of a married couple and their children.
10.	D	344	Figure 12.4 indicates that Christianity is the largest religion in the world.
11.	D	321	Monogamy, or being married to only one person, is the most common form of marriage in the United States and other Western, industrialized nations.

12.	B	330	Research indicates that most married couples do not share housework equally, although fathers' participation in child care has increased, especially when there are very young children in the household. Having parents who share housework equitably increases the likelihood that men and women will have an egalitarian division of labor in their own households when they grow up and get married.
13.	C	319	Sociologists emphasize that the family is a social institution because it interacts with other social institutions, including religion, the economy, and government. The personalities of each member within individual families do not contribute to family *as a social institution*.
14.	B	323	Functionalist theorists view families as cohesive groups organized around a harmony of interests and an efficient division of labor. Conflict and feminist theorists view families as systems of power relationships that reinforce social inequalities, and feminist theorists further emphasize that families are gendered institutions. Symbolic interaction theory focuses on families as groups in which members interact and negotiate relationships with each other [Table 12.1].
15.	D	325	Symbolic interaction theory focuses on families as groups in which members interact and negotiate relationships with each other [Table 12.1].
16.	A	344	Symbolic interaction theory views people as voluntarily moving into cults gradually as they seek a sense of meaning and attachment to other people.
17.	C	326	Although the number of single parent households headed by men has increased, the majority of single parent households are headed by women. The primary causes of single parent households in the United States are childbearing by single teens and the high rate of divorce in this country. Approximately one-fourth of American children live with only one parent.
18.	C	335	Teens who have babies are less likely to marry today than in the past, contributing to a higher percentage of never-married mothers in the United States. Abortion was not legally available or socially acceptable in 1960. Teen mothers have always experienced considerable economic disadvantages.
19.	A	343	Karl Marx, the founder of conflict theory, argued that religion is a form of false consciousness because subordinate groups internalize dominant ideology, which justifies an oppressive social order.
20.	C	340	A majority of people in the United States identify their religious affiliation as Protestant. Jewish people are least represented among these religious groups.
21.	D	346	Cults tend to form around leaders with charisma, a quality attributed to individuals believed by their followers to have special powers.
22.	D	346	Sects are groups that break off from established churches, such as the Shakers. Churches are formal organizations that are usually socially defined as the primary, legitimate religious organizations in American society. Cults, which are religious groups devoted to a specific cause or charismatic leader, are similar to sects in their intensity and concern with members' purity of faith.
23.	A	339	A totem is an object or living thing, such as a statue of Buddha, that religious groups regard with awe and reverence. An ideology is a belief system. Theology refers to the study of religious doctrine.
24.	A	337	As indicated by Table 12.2, the United States provides the fewest federally supported maternity program among all industrialized nations.
25.	D	337	The Family and Medical Leave Act, adopted by Congress in 1993, provides 12 weeks of unpaid leave to full-time employees in certain workplaces to care for a newborn, newly adopted child, or seriously ill child, spouse, or parent. The United States is the only industrialized nation that does not provide some period of paid leave for women who give birth.

Answers to True-False Questions

1.	F	321	Antimiscegenation laws were not declared unconstitutional until 1967.
2.	F	348	Conservative evangelical religious groups have had an increasing influence on American politics in recent years.
3.	T	329	The United States has the highest rates of both marriage and divorce among the industrialized nations.
4.	F	348	Although women's representation in the religious institution has increased, gender equality persists. Many denominations, including Catholicism, do not allow the ordination of women. Women earn one-fourth of theological degrees.
5.	F	345	Many African Americans have joined the Black Muslims, a religious group that celebrates Black people's African heritage and identity, has strict prohibitions against the use of alcohol and drugs, and proscribes dietary regulations.
6.	F	344	Around the world, Judaism has relatively few members compared to other major religious groups, such as Protestantism, Catholicism, and Islam [Figure 12.4].
7.	F	324	Functionalist theory views marriage as a mutually beneficial exchange for men and women. Feminist theory views the family as a gendered institution that reflects the pattern of gender inequality in the society at large, which tends to socially and economically disadvantage women [Table 12.1].
8.	F	329	There is no evidence that being raised by gay or lesbian parents increases the chance of a child developing psychological problems. Children of gay or lesbian parents may learn more flexible gender roles and learn to respect differences.
9.	F	322	Interracial marriage in the United States is still relatively uncommon. Khanna and colleagues' research indicates that both Blacks and Whites in interracial dating relationships report negative responses from their families, although the majority of these are not hostile reactions.
10.	F	332	Research indicates that those children who have the most difficulty adjusting to their parents' divorce are children who live in households where marital conflict was high before, during, and after the divorce.

Answers to Fill in the Blank Questions

1.	secular	339
2.	polytheistic	341
3.	patriarchal	341
4.	transnational	336
5.	nuclear	322

CHAPTER 13
EDUCATION AND WORK

BRIEF CHAPTER OUTLINE

Schooling and Society: Theories of Education
    The Functionalist View of Education
    The Conflict View of Education
    The Symbolic Interaction View of Education
Does Schooling Matter?
    Effects of Education on Occupation and Income
    Effects of Social Class Background on Education and Social Mobility
    Education, Social Class, and Mobility Seen Globally
Education and Inequality
    Cognitive Ability and Its Measurement
    Ability and Diversity
    The Bell Curve Debate
    Tracking and Labeling Effects
    Teacher Expectancy Effect
    Schooling and Gender
    Stereotype Threat
Economy and Society
    The Industrial Revolution
    Comparing Economic Systems
The Changing Global Economy
    Deindustrialization
    Technological Change
Theoretical Perspectives on Work
    Defining Work
    The Division of Labor
    Functionalism, Conflict Theory, and Symbolic Interaction
Characteristics of the Labor Force
    Who Works?
    Unemployment and Joblessness
    Diversity in the American Occupational System
Power in the Workplace
    Sexual Harassment
    Gays and Lesbians in the Workplace
    Disability and Work

CHAPTER FOCUS: This chapter examines the structure of education and the economy in the United States. It provides an in-depth look at how social characteristics influence people's access to schooling and employment, and reviews the key factors that contribute to people's different experiences in these social institutions.

QUESTIONS TO GUIDE YOUR READING

1.   Why has education become increasingly important in the United States over the last century?
2.   How do race, ethnicity, social class, and gender influence the likelihood of achieving success in school and employment?

3. What are the three main types of economic systems found around the world, and how is each system organized?

4. Why is the concept of the global economy so important for understanding recent changes in the structure of employment in the United States?

5. What efforts have been made to improve both the employment opportunities and the quality of workplace experiences for women and people with disabilities in the United States?

SOCIOLOGY IN ACTION: AN INTERNET EXERCISE

Go to http://eric-web.tc.columbia.edu to explore the resources available from the Urban Education Web, a site devoted to providing information to urban students, their families, and educators. Why do you think a site about urban education places special emphasis on issues facing minority students and their parents? What does this suggest about the structure of schools and communities in the United States?

Go to http://wdsc.doleta.gov/ms/fw to learn about the National Farmworker Jobs Program, which is organized by the United States Department of Labor. Where are farm workers located in the labor market? Why are seasonal and migrant farm workers and their families at risk for social and economic problems? How does the government attempt to address the particular needs of this group?

KEY TERMS (defined at page number shown and in glossary)

alienation 370	automation 368
capitalism 365	communism 366
contingent worker 368	credentialism 354
dual labor market theory 373	economic restructuring 366
economy 365	glass ceiling 375
global economy 366	labeling effect 361
predictive validity 358	self-fulfilling prophecy 362
sexual harassment 376	socialism 365
teacher expectancy effect 361	tracking 360
unemployment rate 371	work 368
xenophobia 366	

KEY PEOPLE (identified at page number shown)

Robert Blauner 530	Arlie Hochschild 368
Samuel Lucas 363	Claude M. Steele 364
Irving Zola 377	

CHAPTER OUTLINE
I.   SCHOOLING AND SOCIETY

Education in society is concerned with the systematic transmission of society's knowledge. *Schooling* refers to the formal, institutionalized aspects of education. By 1900, compulsory education was established by law in all states except for a few in the South, where Black Americans were still largely denied formal education of any kind. Today, high school completion for Blacks and Hispanics lags behind that of Whites.

A.   The Functionalist View of Education

All known societies have some sort of educational institution, which is generally large and highly formalized in industrialized societies such as the United States. Functionalist theory argues that education accomplishes certain functions for society.

1.   *Socialization* occurs as the cultural heritage is transmitted from one generation to another. In addition to teaching a variety of skills and knowledge, schools also inculcate values such as loyalty and punctuality.

2. *Occupational training* is provided by schools. Modern industrialized societies especially need a system to train people for jobs. Most jobs today require at least a high school education, and many professions require a graduate degree.

3. *Social control* is also provided by the educational institution. This indirect, non-obvious consequence of schools is called a *latent function*. One perceived benefit of compulsory education in the late 19th century was to keep kids off the streets and out of trouble as crime, overcrowding, and other problems intensified with urbanization and immigration.

C. The Conflict View of Education

Conflict theory emphasizes the disintegrative and disruptive aspects of education by focusing on competition between groups for power, income, and social status. The unequal distribution of education can allow educational level to be used as a tool for discrimination through the process of **credentialism**, or the insistence upon educational credentials for their own sake, even if the credentials bear little relationship to the intended job.

C. The Symbolic Interactionist View of Education

Symbolic interaction theory focuses on what emerges from the process of interaction between school staff and students during the schooling experience. For example, the expectations a teacher has for a student can create the very behavior that is expected, such as high or low test performance, through the *expectancy effect*.

II. DOES SCHOOLING MATTER?

A. Effects of Education on Occupation and Income

1. One way that sociologists measure a person's social class or socioeconomic status (SES) is to determine the person's amount of schooling, income, and type of occupation, which are *indicators* of SES.

2. In the general population, there is a strong correlation between level of formal education and *occupational prestige*, or the social value attributed to jobs.

3. Gender also influences the relationship between education and income, with women's average income being less than men's at each education level.

B. Effects of Social Class Background on Education and Social Mobility

Education has traditionally been viewed as the principal route to upward social mobility in the United States. However, research demonstrates that the effect of education upon a person's eventual job and income depends to a great extent upon the social class into which the person was born.

C. Education, Social Class, and Mobility Seen Globally

Some people have argued that there is more occupational and income mobility in the U.S. than in other countries because of the American educational system, but the degree of mobility is relatively limited. For example, there is a dramatic increase in average SAT (Scholastic Aptitude Test) scores as family income increases [Table 13.3]. This increases the likelihood that students from higher-income families will get into the best colleges.

III. EDUCATION AND INEQUALITY

To some extent, education reduced social inequalities during the twentieth century. For example, the percentage of high school graduates has risen among Whites and minorities, both male and female, and there has been an overall increase in minorities' and women's college attendance.

A. Cognitive Ability and Its Measurement

1. The American educational system relies heavily on *standardized ability tests* (such as the SAT) to measure "intelligence."

2. There are three major criticisms of the use of standardized tests as measures of cognitive ability.

a. They tend to measure only limited ranges of ability, such as quantitative or verbal aptitude, while ignoring other cognitive endowments, such as creativity.

b. These tests possess a degree of cultural bias and gender bias that may perpetuate social, economic, and educational inequality.

c. The **predictive validity** of these tests, or the extent to which the tests accurately predict later college grades, is compromised for minorities and women. In fact, SAT scores are only moderately accurate predictors of college grades, even for White students.

B. Ability and Diversity

1. Average scores on cognitive ability tests such as the SAT differ by racial-ethnic group, social class, and gender. Overall, Whites score higher on average than minorities; men score higher than women, especially on the math portion; and the higher a person's social class, the higher the test score.

2. There is no evidence that *between-group* differences are genetically inherited. Certain *within-group* differences may reflect genetic differences among individuals within the same racial or ethnic group, but even in this category, the effects of social environment are greater than the effects of genes.

C. *The Bell Curve* Debate

1. *The Bell Curve*, published in 1994, created an intense debate about the nature of intelligence. Authors Herrnstein and Murray argued that not only does the distribution of intelligence in the general population closely approximate a bell-shaped curve, or *normal distribution*, but that there is one basic, fundamental kind of intelligence.

2. Drawing on studies of identical twins, the authors concluded that intelligence has 70 percent *heritability*, while only 30 percent of the difference in intelligence throughout the population is determined by environment.

3. The authors argued that the lower classes are on average less endowed with genes for high intelligence, while the upper classes are relatively more endowed with high-intelligence genes, thereby creating a *cognitive elite*.

4. The authors have been strongly criticized for their methodology and for largely ignoring the abundant research indicating that intelligence tests and standardized ability tests do not measure intelligence and ability as accurately for some groups as for others.

D. Tracking and Labeling Effects

1. Over one-half of elementary and secondary schools in the U.S. currently use some kind of **tracking**, or ability grouping, to separate students according to some measure of cognitive ability.

2. The basic idea behind tracking is that students will get a better education and be better prepared after high school if they are grouped according to ability.

3. Proponents of *detracking* argue that including students of varying cognitive abilities is more beneficial because students will learn from each other. They also believe that students in lower tracks get less teacher attention, thus, they learn less than when they are included in mixed groups.

4. One of the most consistent findings from research on tracking is that students in the higher tracks receive more positive effects, but lower track students suffer more negative effects, including being taught less.

5. Both high- and low- track students are subject to the **labeling effect**, whereby students are assigned to particular tracks and thereby labeled, whether or not the label accurately reflects the student's ability.

E. Teacher Expectancy Effect

The **teacher expectancy effect** refers to the influence of teacher expectations on a student's actual performance, independent of his or her actual ability. The expectations a teacher has for a student can dramatically influence how much the student will learn, as illustrated by Rosenthal and Jacobson's study of elementary schools. Through the **self-fulfilling prophecy,** merely applying a label has the effect of justifying that label.

F. Schooling and Gender

Teachers hold different expectations about boys and girls in school, which affects students' actual performance. A comprehensive report prepared by the American Association of University Women (AAUW) summarized the findings of over 1,000 studies of gender and schooling.

1. Teachers pay less attention to girls and women than boys and men, particularly in math and science classes.

2. Women lag behind men in math and science achievement scores.

3. Some standardized math and science tests still retain gender bias, despite the efforts of education specialists and testing organizations to weed out such bias, which results in a tendency to under-predict women's actual grades in math.

4. Teachers are more likely to rebuff Black girls and interact more with White girls.

5. As girls and boys approach adolescence, their self-esteem tends to drop, with the erosion of self-esteem occurring more quickly among girls than boys.

G. Stereotype Vulnerability, Race, and Gender

1. A negative stereotype about one's self can affect one's own behavior. Research by Steel and associates indicates that Black students internalize the stereotype that Blacks have some inherent "deficiency" in math and verbal ability.

2. Internalization of such stereotypes leads to the *stereotype threat effect*. Consequently, when Black students and female students are told in advance that a test they will take is a "genuine" test of ability, they receive lower scores than do similar groups who are given the identical test minus the misinformation about the test being a "genuine" test of ability.

IV. **ECONOMY AND SOCIETY**

The economy is the system by which goods and services are produced, distributed, and consumed in a society. Sociologists understand work in the context of this social institution.

A. The Industrial Revolution

1. The Industrial Revolution is giving way to the growth of post-industrial societies, which reflects a development in the economic system that has far-reaching consequences for how society is organized.

2. The development of agricultural societies followed the introduction and use of technologies that enabled people to increase the production of food from simple hunting and gathering techniques to more large-scale production.

3. Industrialization was probably the most significant historical development to affect the social organization of work.

4. Although the United States is largely industrial, it is being quickly transformed into a post-industrial society, which is mainly organized around the provision of services such as banking, retail sales, and health care.

B. Comparing Economic Systems

The three major kinds of economic systems found in the world today are capitalism, socialism, and communism. These are ideal types, because many societies have a mix of economic systems.

1. **Capitalism** is an economic system based on private ownership of the means of production and the principles of private property, market competition, and the pursuit of profit. The United States is a capitalist society.

2. **Socialism** is an economic institution characterized by state ownership and management of basic industries, where the means of production are the property of the state. The People's Republic of China was formerly a socialist society, but is now developing a mix of socialist and capitalist principles.

3. **Communism** is sometimes described as socialism in its purest form. In pure communism, the state is the sole owner of the systems of production. Nineteenth century communist theorists believed class divisions and private property would be eliminated when capitalism was overthrown during a workers revolution, but history has not borne out this prediction.

V.   **THE CHANGING GLOBAL ECONOMY**

The concept of a **global economy** acknowledges that all dimensions of the economy now cross national borders, including investment, production, management, markets, labor, information, and technology. The global economy now links the lives of millions of Americans to the experiences of other people throughout the world. In the global economy, the most developed countries control research and management, while assembly line work is performed in nations with less privileged positions in the global economy. The relocation of manufacturing to places where labor is cheap and management is strong has led to the emergence of the *global assembly line*, a new international division of labor. Women and children in poor, underdeveloped nations now assemble most toys and other goods that are sold in the rich nations. In the United States, the development of a global economy has created anxieties about foreign workers, particularly among the working class, who are developing **xenophobia**, or the fear and hatred of foreigners. The development of a global economy is part of a broad process known as **economic restructuring**, which refers to transformations in the basic structure of work that are permanently altering the workplace. This process also includes the changing composition of the workplace, deindustrialization, and the use of enhanced technology. For example, women and racial-ethnic minorities are expected to comprise an even larger proportion of the labor force in the coming years. Furthermore, there will be an increase in the number of people over age 55 in the labor market as the Baby Boomer cohort ages.

A.   Deindustrialization

1.   *Deindustrialization* refers to the transition from a predominantly goods-producing economy to one based on the provision of services.

2.   This process is most easily observed by looking at the number of jobs in the manufacturing sector of the United States economy since World War II, when the majority of workers were employed in manufacturing-based jobs. Today, at least 70 percent of workers are employed in the service sector, including childcare, food preparation, banking, and clerical work.

3.   Among the areas that have been hardest hit by deindustrialization are communities that were heavily dependent on a single industry, including steel towns and automobile-manufacturing cities, where there are high rates of joblessness and few prospects for economic recovery.

B.   Technological Change

1.   Rapidly changing and developing technologies, such as the invention of the semiconductor, are bringing major changes in work, including how it is organized, who does it, and how much it pays.

2.   Increasing reliance on the rapid transmission of electronic data has produced *electronic sweatshops*, a term referring to the back offices found in many industries where workers at computer terminals process hundreds of transactions per day.

3. **Automation**, the process by which human labor is replaced by machines, eliminates many repetitive tasks and facilitates rapid communication; however, it may also make workers subservient to machines.

4. *Deskilling*, a side effect of automation and technological progress in which the level of skill required to perform certain jobs declines over time, has several consequences.

   a. Employees are paid less and have less control over the tasks they do.

   b. Jobs require less mental labor and become routine and boring.

   c. There is greater polarization of the work force.

5. Along with deskilling, there has been an increasing reliance on temporary or **contingent workers**, those whose employment is contracted as needed. Although these jobs offer workers flexibility and autonomy, contingent workers are paid less and are less likely to receive benefits than those who hold regular jobs.

VI. THEORETICAL PERSPECTIVES ON WORK

A. Defining Work

1. Sociologists define **work** as productive human activity that creates something of value, either goods or services, whether or not a person gets paid for their labor.

2. Housework is not included in the official measure of productivity that economists use to indicate the work output of the United States.

3. Some sociologists argue that referring to only physical and mental labor as work is too narrow a definition. Arlie Hochschild introduced the concept of *emotional labor* to refer to another form of work that is common in a service-based economy, in which workers try to produce a certain feeling or desired state of mind in a consumer.

4. Some forms of work, such as mental labor, are more highly valued than other forms, such as manual labor, both in how the work is perceived by society and in how it is rewarded.

5. Stereotypes about the "undeserving poor" are common in the United States, and reflect the widespread belief that people are poor because of their own failures and refusal to internalize the values of diligence and hard work, despite the fact that 43 percent of the poor in this country are working.

B. The Division of Labor

The division of labor is the systematic interrelatedness of different tasks that develops in complex societies. In the United States, the division of labor is most affected by gender, race-ethnicity, social class, and age.

1. The *class division of labor* can be observed by examining the work done by those with different educational backgrounds, because education is a fairly reliable indicator of class.

2. The *gender division of labor* refers to the different work that women and men do in society. There is a cultural tendency toward placing more value on men's than women's work.

3. The *racial division of labor* is seen in the pattern of people from racial and ethnic minority groups disproportionately working in the lowest paid, least prestigious, and most arduous jobs.

C. Functionalism, Conflict Theory, and Symbolic Interaction

1. Conflict theorists view the transformations taking place in the workplace as resulting from tensions inherent in the social system. These tensions develop because groups with unequal power are competing for economic resources.

2. Functionalist theorists interpret work and the economy as functional for society. When the society changes too rapidly, due to technological developments and globalization, for example, institutions may experience social disorganization,

and individuals may experience **alienation**, or feelings of powerlessness and separation from society.

      3.   Symbolic interaction theory is less focused on the workings of the whole society; but this theory would be useful for studying the meaning of work to those who do it, as well as how interaction in the workplace supports or undermines social bonds between people.

VII.   CHARACTERISTICS OF THE LABOR FORCE

Data on the characteristics of the American labor force are typically drawn from the official statistics reported by the United States Department of Labor. In 1999, 139 million people, or 67 percent of the working-age population, were in the labor force.

A.   <u>Who Works?</u>

      1.   Employment patterns vary considerably for different groups in the population. For example, Hispanic men are most likely, and Hispanic women are least likely, to be employed [Figure 13.4].

      3.   One of the most dramatic changes in the labor force since World War II has been the number of women employed, which increased from 35 to 60 percent from 1948 to 1999. This has resulted in greater demands on workplaces and society to provided childcare facilities and more progressive family leave policies.

B.   <u>Unemployment and Joblessness</u>

      1.   The U.S. Department of Labor regularly reports data on the **unemployment rate**, or the percentage of people not working but officially defined as actively looking for work, so unemployment statistics are most likely to undercount the people for whom unemployment runs the highest, including the youngest and oldest workers, women, and members of racial minority groups.

      2.   With 38 to 48 percent unemployment, Native Americans currently experience the highest unemployment rate in the United States. As a group, Native Americans seriously lack adequate education and appropriate job training.

      3.   Unemployment among African Americans, Puerto Ricans, and Mexican Americans is currently at a level associated with a major economic depression, because these groups have been hardest hit by the processes of globalization and economic restructuring.

      4.   While popular explanations often attribute unemployment to the failings of individual workers, sociologists explain unemployment by examining structural problems in the economy, such as deindustrialization and discriminatory employment practices.

      5.   Contrary to popular belief, the employment of women and minorities does not cause White male unemployment, because women are not usually employed in the same jobs as men, and racial minorities are heavily concentrated in certain segments of the labor force where few White men work.

      6.   The contemporary labor force is also being shaped by the employment of recent immigrants, where the proportion of professionals and technicians among legal immigrants exceeds the proportion of professionals in the labor force as a whole.

      7.   Even illegal immigrants tend to have higher levels of education and occupational skill than typical workers in their homeland, because the poorest members of the population are seldom able to migrate.

C.   <u>Diversity in the American Occupational System</u>

      1.   **Dual labor market theory**, a branch of conflict theory, views the labor market as composed of two major segments: the *primary labor market* and the *secondary labor market* [Table 13.6].

           a.   The *primary labor market* offers jobs with relatively high wages, benefits, stability, good working conditions, opportunities for promotion, job protection, and due process for workers, meaning that workers are treated according to established rules and procedures that are allegedly fairly administered.

b. The *secondary labor market* is characterized by low wages, few benefits, high turnover, poor working conditions, little job protection or opportunity for advancement, and the arbitrary treatment of workers. Women and racial-ethnic minorities are the groups most likely to be employed in the secondary labor market.

c. In addition to these two major segments, there is the *underground economy*, which includes both legal and illegal, unreported work.

2. **Occupational distribution** describes the pattern by which workers are located in the labor force. Workers are dispersed throughout the occupational system in patterns that vary greatly by race-ethnicity, class, and gender, revealing a pattern of *occupational segregation.*

a. Work in the United States is classified into six broad categories: managerial and professional; technical, sales, and administrative support; service; precision production, craft, and repair; operators, fabricators, and laborers; and farming, forestry, and fishing.

b. Several changes in occupational distribution have occurred, including: a decline in the number of Black women in private domestic work, an increase in the number of racial minorities in professional-managerial work (such as business, law, and municipal management), and an increase in the number of women employed in working-class jobs traditionally held only by men (such as precision, craft, and repair work).

3. **Occupational prestige** is the perceived social value of an occupation according to the general public. There is a strong correlation between occupational prestige and the race and gender composition of workers in given jobs.

4. Sociologists have documented that earnings from work are highly dependent on the race-ethnicity, gender, and class of the workers, with White men earning the most. Functionalist and conflict theorists explain this disparity differently.

a. To functionalists, differential wages are a source of motivation for workers, and higher wages reflect the most valued characteristics that workers bring to jobs.

b. From a conflict perspective, wage inequality is one way that the systems of race, class, and gender inequality are maintained, because some of the most essential jobs are the most devalued and poorly rewarded.

VIII. **POWER IN THE WORKPLACE**
Obvious, tangible factors such as level of pay and benefits influence workers' degree of satisfaction with their jobs. Other factors include the value accorded to one's job and opportunity for advancement. The **glass ceiling** refers to the limits that women and racial-ethnic minorities experience in job mobility.

A. Sexual Harassment

1. **Sexual harassment** is defined as unwanted physical or verbal sexual behavior that occurs in the context of a relationship of unequal power and that is experienced as a threat to the victim's job or educational activities.

2. The law recognizes two forms of sexual harassment.

a. *Quid pro quo sexual harassment* forces sexual compliance in exchange for an employment or educational benefit.

b. The other form of sexual harassment is the creation of a *hostile working environment*, in which unwanted sexual behaviors are a continuing condition of work, including touching, teasing, and/or sexual comments.

3.	Sexual harassment was first made illegal by Title VII of the 1964 Civil Rights Act, which identifies it as a form of employment discrimination. The Supreme Court upheld this principle in *Meritor Savings Bank vs. Vinson* in 1986.

4.	Sexual harassment tends to be underreported, but surveys indicate that half of all employed women experience this form of discrimination at some time.

B.	Gays and Lesbians in the Workplace

As gays and lesbians are more open about their sexuality, more attention has been given to sexual identity and workplace experiences. Public opinion polls indicate that the majority of people are now accepting of gays and lesbians in the workplace, except as teachers and clergy. Any negative experience in the workplace can affect self-esteem, productivity, and economic well being. Many gays and lesbians fear that they will suffer adverse career consequences if their coworkers know that they are homosexual.

C.	Disability and Work

Sociologist Irving Zola was one of the first to suggest that people with disabilities face issues similar to minority groups. This approach emphasizes the group rights of people with disabilities, who are protected from discrimination in education, employment, and public facilities (such as transportation) under the Americans with Disabilities Act, adopted by Congress in 1990.

PRACTICE TEST

MULTIPLE CHOICE QUESTIONS

1.	According to conflict theory:
    a.	schools equally prepare all children for participation in society by teaching them essential skills and knowledge.
    b.	schools are tools for discrimination because tracking perpetuates social inequalities.
    c.	the most important determinant of a child's success in school is how well the child gets along with his or her teachers.
    d.	schools today fulfill functions that were historically provided by other social institutions, such as the family.

2.	Which of the following is a latent function of the educational institution in the United States?
    a.	pass on cultural heritage, including ethics and norms of the society.
    b.	train adolescents for jobs as adults by transmitting knowledge and skills.
    c.	inculcate values that are important to the workplace, such as punctuality.
    d.	reduce juvenile delinquency by keeping youth off the streets during the day.

3.	The extent to which a test provides an accurate monitor of future college grades or some other criterion, such as likelihood of graduation, is:
    a.	general accuracy.
    b.	predictive validity.
    c.	cognitive reliability.
    d.	achievement potential.

4.	According to Herrnstein and Murray, the authors of *The Bell Curve*, differences in test performance between Black and White students result mainly from differences in:
    a.	home environments, including the availability of books and educational toys.
    b.	nutritional deficiencies in infancy and early childhood.
    c.	the form of the test given to each group.
    d.	heredity or genetic makeup.

5. Which of the following is (are) a main criticism of the results reported in *The Bell Curve*?
    a. The authors overemphasize environmental factors and dismiss the influence of heredity, or genetic makeup, on intelligence.
    b. The authors draw too many conclusions about between-group differences from within-group results.
    c. The authors place heavily rely on the assertion that standardized tests are not accurate measures of intelligence for racial minority groups.
    d. All of the above are criticisms of the study.

6. Jamie was labeled "bright" and placed in the college preparatory track in high school, where she was encouraged and praised. She therefore enjoyed school and developed high educational and occupational aspirations. This reflects the:
    a. hidden curriculum.
    b. detracking process.
    c. self-fulfilling prophecy.
    d. stereotype vulnerability.

7. Based on a study commissioned by the American Association of University Women (AAUW), researchers have found that:
    a. in general, teachers pay less attention to male students than female students.
    b. standardized math tests tend to over-predict women's actual grades in mathematics.
    c. self-esteem erodes more quickly for girls than boys as they approach adolescence.
    d. All of the above outcomes were reported in the AAUW study.

8. According to symbolic interaction theory:
    a. in terms of securing a high-paying job, the dollar value of a college degree has declined so much that getting a degree is no longer cost-effective.
    b. standardized tests are an important mechanism for eliminating certain groups from competition for coveted spaces in universities..
    c. one of the most important determinants of a child's success in school is what kind of perceptions and expectations his/her teachers have of and for him/her.
    d. contemporary schools provide many functions for children and youth that used to be the responsibility of families and religious organizations.

9. Feagin, Vera, and Nikitah's study of Black college students indicates that:
    a. racism on most college campuses has been eliminated due to the introduction of multicultural programs and diversity education.
    b. Black parents are not very supportive of their children who want to go to college because they do not recognize the importance of higher education.
    c. Black students rarely attend predominantly White colleges because they are unable to meet the stringent admission requirements at those schools.
    d. Black students often face the agonizing dilemma of trying to succeed academically while being treated as intruders at predominantly White colleges.

10. Joe failed ninth grade. When his brother Frank entered ninth grade, he was assigned the same teacher as Joe. The teacher anticipated that Frank would be a poor student and invested little effort in helping Frank learn. At the end of the year, Frank nearly failed. This is an example of:
    a. student interaction effect.
    b. teacher expectancy effect.
    c. stereotype vulnerability.
    d. educational deflation.

11. Which of the following statements is true concerning the labeling effect?
    a. Once a student has been labeled as having a low ability level, that label can easily be altered if the student performs better on subsequent measures of his/her ability.
    b. Assigning labels to students is a fair, objective, and efficient mechanism for separating children into groups where they will be assigned material that is consistent with their ability levels.
    c. Once a label concerning ability is assigned to a student, it tends to stick, whether or not it is accurate.
    d. None of the above statements are true, because schools stopped assigning such labels to students after ending the practice of tracking.

12. Which of the following economic systems is characterized by private ownership of the means of production, profit generated by the workers' production of the goods and services, and owners' disproportionate consumption of goods and profits?
    a. Communism
    b. Democracy
    c. Capitalism
    d. Socialism

13. American workers who feel anxious about unemployment in the rapidly changing global economy are particularly prone to _____, or the fear and hatred of foreigners.
    a. alienation
    b. xenophobia
    c. homophobia
    d. technophobia

14. The United States has experienced a transition from a predominately goods-producing economy to an economy based on the provision of information and services, a process known as:
    a. deindustrialization.
    b. underemployment.
    c. downsizing.
    d. inflation.

15. Which of the following is a consequence of *deskilling*?
    a. Employees gain greater control over their tasks.
    b. Jobs become more complex and challenging.
    c. Employees are paid less for their work.
    d. All of the above are consequences of deskilling.

16. Conflict theorists:
    a. view recent transformations in the workplace as the result of societal tension caused by power imbalances between social groups.
    b. define work as a functional necessity for society because it integrates people and supports social order.
    c. are primarily interested in how the workplace encourages the formation of social bonds.
    d. explain wage inequality as an incentive system that makes people work harder.

17. Which of the following racial-ethnic groups in the United States experiences the greatest unemployment today?
    a. Mexican Americans
    b. African Americans
    c. Native Americans
    d. Asian Americans

18. Occupational prestige ratings are based on the:
    a. U.S. Department of Commerce's ranking of the relative contribution of particular jobs to economic growth.
    b. U.S. Bureau of the Census' ranking of the average wages paid for particular jobs.
    c. U.S. Department of Labor's ranking of the objective value of particular jobs to society.
    d. general American public's ranking of the value of particular jobs to society.

19. Jane works in an auto parts store where her male coworkers hang *Playboy* magazine centerfolds in the lunchroom and tell jokes about the female body that make her very uncomfortable. Under federal law, this is an example of:
    a. *quid pro quo* harassment.
    b. *hostile environment* harassment.
    c. *emotionally abusive* harassment.
    d. This is not an example of sexual harassment under the law because Jane's coworkers never physically touched her.

20. Which sector of the economy includes illegal and unreported work, such as drug dealing, prostitution, and undocumented domestic work?
    a. feudal
    b. primary
    c. secondary
    d. underground

21. It would cost a day's wages for an Indonesian woman to buy the Barbie doll that she helps make for distribution in the United States. This international division of labor is a component of the:
    a. military industrial complex.
    b. global assembly line.
    c. industrial revolution.
    d. glass ceiling.

22. Research on pregnancy and employment in the United States indicates that:
    a. most women take relatively short maternity leaves because they need to return to work out of economic necessity.
    b. women who work in higher-status jobs are the most likely to leave a job following the birth of a child.
    c. single mothers return to work more quickly than do married mothers.
    d. All of the above statements are true.

23. Amott and Matthei argue that in addition to employment discrimination, which factor is primarily responsible for Native American women's low occupational status?
    a. cultural restrictions on women working for pay outside the home
    b. personal reluctance to work for White-owned businesses
    c. inaccessible education and inadequate job training
    d. inability to find babysitters for their children

24. Which of the following conditions is covered as a disability under the Americans with Disabilities Act of 1990?
    a. blindness
    b. pregnancy
    c. drug addiction
    d. All of the above are designated as disabilities because they impair a person's ability to work.

25. One of the most dramatic changes in the United States labor force since World War II has been an increase in the percentage of _____ who work full-time.
    a. White men
    b. Black adolescents
    c. White women with children
    d. All of the above groups have experienced dramatic increases in full-time employment over the last fifty years

True-False Questions

1. Sexual harassment was first declared illegal by the 1986 Glass Ceiling Act, which identified harassment as a form of employment discrimination.

2. Although the average income for women without a high school diploma is less than the average income for men with the same education level, women and men with college degrees earn about the same average income.

3. Among White people of the upper classes, education is more important than social class origin in determining occupation and income.

4. As family income increases, students' Scholastic Aptitude Test (SAT) scores dramatically increase.

5. The United States is the only industrialized nation that filters out potential university students by requiring success on standardized tests prior to college admission.

6. A smaller percentage of American workers are located in the farming, fishing, and forestry category than in any other occupational category.

7. White students are more likely than Black or Hispanic students to be placed in high ability tracks in school, even when the students receive the same test scores.

8. Federal employment legislation does not cover same-sex harassment in the workplace, because by definition, sexual harassment is restricted to men's exploitation of women.

9. Under the Americans with Disabilities Act (ADA), a reasonable accommodation for a student with a disability would be to excuse him from taking exams if he feels that test-taking is too emotionally or physically stressful.

10. Both legal and illegal immigrants to the United States tend to have higher levels of education and occupational skills than the typical worker in their homelands.

Fill in the Blank Questions

1.   Exams that are given to large populations and scored with respect to population averages are _____ tests.

2.   Those who do not hold regular jobs, but whose employment is dependent on demand, such as independent consultants, are _____ workers.

3.   The ____ rate reflects the percentage of people who are not working and are officially defined as looking for work.

4.   The concept of the _____ economy acknowledges that all dimensions of the economy now cross national borders, from research and development to assembly and distribution.

5.   Jobs in the _____ labor market are characterized by relatively high wages, good benefits, greater stability, and opportunities for promotion.

Essay Questions

1.   Compare and contrast the functionalist, conflict, and symbolic interaction perspectives on the relative importance of individual merit on school performance.
2.   Identify the functions of the educational system in industrialized nations such as the United States and discuss why formal education is so important in today's society.
3.   Discuss why Herrnstein and Murray's book, *The Bell Curve*, has generated so much controversy in the United States.
4.   Identify an occupation for which emotional labor is required, and explain why this type of labor is not highly valued or rewarded in the American economy.
5.   Identify the primary causes of economic restructuring in the United States and discuss the consequences of these workplace alterations for American workers.

ANSWERS TO PRACTICE TEST

Answers to Multiple Choice Questions

1.   C   354   Conflict theory views education as reinforcing and perpetuating inequalities in the society at large through processes such as tracking. Functionalist theory focuses on the functions provided by social institutions, noting that schools prepare all children equally for participation in society. Symbolic interaction focuses on interactions between teachers and students [Table 13.1].

2.   D   353   Social control is a latent function of education. A perceived benefit of compulsory education is that it keeps young people out of trouble.

3.   B   358   The extent to which a test accurately predicts future college grades, likelihood of graduation, or some other criterion is predictive validity.

4.   D   359   In *The Bell Curve*, Herrnstein and Murray argue that heredity, or genetic makeup, determines 70 percent of intelligence. They assert that the upper class constitutes a genetically-based cognitive elite in America, consisting of those with high IQs and high incomes.

5.   B   360   The authors have been criticized for drawing too many conclusions about between-group differences from within-group results. The authors dismissed previous research that indicated environment significantly contributes to

differences in test performance, and that standardized tests do not accurately measure intelligence for all racial-ethnic or social class groups.

6.	C	362	The self-fulfilling prophecy is a powerful mechanism whereby labeling a student has the effect of justifying the label and producing the expected behavior.
7.	C	363	Both girls and boys experience a drop in self-esteem as they approach adolescence, but the erosion of self-esteem occurs more quickly for girls. In schools, teachers generally pay more attention to male students. Math tests tend to under-predict girls' actual grades in mathematics.
8.	C	354	Symbolic interaction theory focuses on the nature and quality of interaction between people in social settings, such as students and teachers in schools. This theory recognizes that how a teacher perceives and treats, which varies by gender, race, and class, affects the student's school performance.
9.	D	362	In their book, *The Agony of Education*, Feagin and colleagues argue that while the importance of education is recognized in Black communities, Black students continue to face stereotyping and discrimination on predominantly White university campuses. The authors note that some positive changes have occurred, but many White students continue to deny that racism exists
10.	B	361	The teacher expectancy effect refers to the process whereby the teacher's expectations affect the student's actual performance, independent of the student's actual ability.
11.	C	361	Both high- and low-track students are subject to the labeling effect. Once a label has been assigned, it tends to stick, whether or not it is accurate. These labels are not necessarily based on fair, objective, or relevant criteria for determining a student's ability.
12.	C	365	Under capitalism, property and the means of production are privately owned, whereas industry is owned and managed by the state under communism. Democracy and monarchy are political, not economic, systems.
13.	B	366	Americans, particularly those in the working class who feel anxious about loss of employment due to economic restructuring, are prone to xenophobia, the fear and hatred of foreigners.
14.	A	367	Deindustrialization is the process whereby the United States has moved from a predominately goods-producing economy to a primarily post-industrial economy, which is based on the provision of information and services.
15.	C	368	The process of *deskilling* usually simplifies the work process, reduces workers' control over tasks, and decreases pay.
16.	A	370	Conflict theorists view transformations in the workplace as the result of inherent tensions in the social system caused by power differences between groups vying for economic and social resources. Symbolic interactionists focus on the formation of social bonds at work. Functionalists assert that work integrates people into society, and wage inequality acts as an incentive for people to work harder [Table 13.5].
17.	C	372	Native Americans have the highest unemployment in the United States due to inadequate training, inaccessible education, and considerably higher rates of disability than people from other racial-ethnic groups.
18.	D	374	Occupational prestige ratings are based on the general public's ranking of the value of particular jobs to the United States.
19.	B	376	Sexual harassment is the repeated, unwanted physical or verbal behavior of a sexual nature that occurs in the workplace. The law defines two forms of harassment: 1) *quid pro quo* harassment involves the exchange of sexual favors as a condition of employment, and 2) *hostile environment* harassment occurs

when the conditions of work are made uncomfortable for the worker due to verbal comments of a sexual nature and the display of sexualized objects.

20.   D   373   As indicated in Table 13.6, the underground economy includes illegal and unreported work. The primary labor market includes professional jobs that provide relatively good salaries, benefits, and opportunities for advancement. The secondary labor market includes jobs that are less stable, pay less, and provide workers with less autonomy and opportunities for growth.

21.   B   366   The global assembly line refers to the new international division of labor where research, development, and management are controlled by the most developed countries (such as the U.S., Japan, and Germany) and assembly line work is performed in the less developed countries (such as Indonesia), where materials and labor costs are low.

22.   A   378   Most women in the United States take relatively short maternity leaves because they must work out of economic necessity. Women with higher status jobs are least likely to leave their jobs after giving birth. Women with another adult in the household return to work after giving birth sooner than women living alone.

23.   C   379   Amott and Matthei note that Native American women's occupational status is so low due to seriously inadequate job training and inaccessible education.

24.   A   378   The Americans with Disabilities Act (ADA), adopted by Congress in 1990, states that employers with fifteen or more employees are prohibited from discriminating against job applicants who are physically disabled or current employees who become physically disabled. A disability is defined as a condition or history of a condition that impairs a major life activity, such as work. Drug addiction and pregnancy are excluded from this federal law, but people who are blind or deaf are entitled to protection under this law.

25.   C   371   Since World War II, there has been a dramatic increase in full-time employment for women with young children.

Answers to True-False Questions

1.   F   376   Sexual harassment is considered a form of employment discrimination under the rules of the Civil Rights Act of 1964. The glass ceiling refers to the invisible barriers that prevent women and racial-ethnic minorities from being promoted to the highest levels of management in the workplace.

2.   F   355   Table 13.2 indicates that at all education levels, women's average income is lower than men's average income in the United States.

3.   F   356   Among White people of the upper classes, social class origin is more important than education in determining occupation and income.

4.   T   357   Table 13.3 indicates that there is a dramatic increase in students' SAT scores as family income increases.

5.   F   365   England, Germany, and Japan also require students to perform at a certain level on standardized tests to be admitted to college.

6.   T   374   Figure 13.5 indicates that there are fewer workers in the farming, fishing, and forestry occupational category than in all other categories.

7.   T   361   Race and ethnicity continue to influence tracking decisions in schools.

8.   F   376   Sexual harassment is an abuse of power in the workplace regardless of the sex of the perpetrator and the victim. The law no longer distinguishes between same-sex and opposite sex parties in defining certain behaviors as harassment.

9.   F   377   Under the ADA, a reasonable accommodation could include altering the format of the test that the student must take, but it does not excuse students (or workers) from performing the essential tasks required of all students (or employees).

10.   T   372   Both legal and illegal immigrants tend to be better educated and more skilled than their poorest counterparts in their homeland.

Answers to Fill in the Blank Questions

1.   standardized   358
2.   contingent   368
3.   unemployment   371
4.   global   366
5.   primary   373

CHAPTER 14
GOVERNMENT AND HEALTHCARE

BRIEF CHAPTER OUTLINE

Defining the State
>The Institutions of the State
>The State and Social Order
>Global Interdependence and the State

Power and Authority
>Types of Authority
>The Growth of Bureaucratic Government

Theories of Power
>The Pluralist Model
>The Power Elite Model
>The Autonomous State Model
>Feminist Theories of the State

Government: Power and Politics in a Diverse Society
>Diverse Patterns of Political Representation
>Political Power: Who's in Charge?
>Women and Minorities in Government
>The Military

Health Care in the United States
>Health and Sickness in America: A Picture of Diversity
>Race and Health Care
>Social Class and Health Care
>Gender and Health Care
>AIDS: Illness and Stigma

Theoretical Perspectives on Health Care
>The Functionalist View of Health Care
>The Conflict Theory View
>Symbolic Interaction and the Role of Perceptions

The Health Care Crisis in America
>The Fee-for-Service System
>Malpractice
>A Response to the Problem: HMOs

CHAPTER FOCUS: This chapter examines two important social institutions in the United States. The state, which includes the government, military, courts, and police, maintains social order. The health care institution is responsible for promoting the population's well being by preventing and treating illness.

QUESTIONS TO GUIDE YOUR READING
1.   What is the purpose of the state as an institution, and what systems make up the state?
2.   What are the three types of authority identified by Weber, and which type is most prevalent in modernized societies such as the United States?
3.   How do each of the four main theories of power and the state view the political system of the United States?
4.   How do social characteristics such as race, ethnicity, gender, and social class structure people's access to health care in the United States, and what consequences does differential access have for the well being of various social groups?

5.   Why do sociologists consider the health care system in the United States to be "in crisis," and what attempts have been made to resolve these problems?

SOCIOLOGY IN ACTION: AN INTERNET EXERCISE

Go to www.wufpac.org to learn more about a political action committee (PAC) that provides information and assistance to women under forty who are interested in running for political offices. Why are women, particularly in this age group, underrepresented in the United States government? Which theory of power and the state is reflected in the philosophy of this organization?

Go to www.WebMD.com and learn more about a health issue that interests you. Which groups of people in the United States are most likely to have access to this kind of information? How might having this information readily available to patients influence the relationship between patients and their health care providers? How can the Internet be used as an effective tool for promoting health in American society?

KEY TERMS (defined at page number shown and in glossary)

anorexia nervosa 397
autonomous state model 389
charismatic authority 386
democracy 390
government 390
interlocking directorates 389
Health Maintenance Organizations 406
Medicare 397
political action committees 388
power elite model 389
rational-legal authority 386
social epidemiology 398
stigma 401
Tuskegee Syphilis Study 399

authority 385
bureaucracy 386
defensive medicine 406
epidemiology 398
interest group 388
law 384
Medicaid 397
pluralist model 388
power 384
propaganda 384
sick role 403
state 383
traditional authority 385

KEY PEOPLE (identified at page number shown)

Karl Marx 389
Max Weber 385

C. Wright Mills 389

CHAPTER OUTLINE
I.   DEFINING THE STATE

The **state** is an abstract concept that includes the institutions that represent official power in society, such as the government and its legal system, the police, and the military. The state exists to regulate social order and has a central role in determining the rights and privileges of different groups. Sociological analyses of the state focus on several important issues such as the relationship between the state and inequality in society, and the connections between the state and other social institutions, including religion and the family.

A.   The Institutions of the State
   1.   The government creates laws and procedures that govern society.
   2.   The court system punishes wrongdoers and adjudicates disputes, and the prison system punishes those who have violated the law.
   3.   The **law** is a type of formal social control that outlines what is permissible and forbidden in a society.
   4.   The police are responsible for enforcing the law and maintaining public order at the local level.

B.   The State and Social Order
1.   Through its power to regulate the media, the state influences public opinion. The state can also direct public opinion through censorship or by circulating **propaganda**, which is information disseminated by a group or organization that is intended to justify its power.
2.   The state's role in maintaining public order is apparent in how it manages dissent. For example, states may use options such as surveillance, imprisonment, and military force to respond to protests, as seen in the Civil Rights Movement.
3.   Even in a democratic state like the United States, the state typically protects the interests of the groups with the most power, leaving the least powerful groups in society more vulnerable to oppressive state action.
C.   Global Interdependence and the State
On an international level, there are increasingly strong ties between the state and the global economy. Globalization has profound effects on the relationships of states to each other. For example, the World Trade Organization was created in 1984 to monitor and resolve disputes between nations.

II.   POWER AND AUTHORITY

Power is the ability of one person or group to exercise influence and control over others. Sociologists are most interested in how power is structured at the societal level, who has it, how it is used, and how it is built into institutionalized structures. **Authority** is power that is perceived by others to be legitimate. Authority emerges not only from the exercise of power, but also from the constituents' belief that the power is legitimate. Those who accept the status quo as a legitimate system of authority perceive the guardians of the law to be exercising *legitimate power. Coercive power* is achieved through force, often against the will of the targeted people.

A.   Types of Authority
Max Weber identified three types of authority in society.
1.   **Traditional authority** stems from the long-established patterns that give certain people or groups legitimate power in society, such as a monarchy.
2.   **Charismatic authority** is derived from the personal appeal of a leader, who is often believed to have special gifts, even magical powers, which inspire devotion and obedience.
3.   **Rational-legal authority**, the most common form of authority in the contemporary United States, stems from rules and regulations, typically written down as laws, procedures, or codes of conduct. Under rational-legal authority, authority is gained through having been elected or appointed in accordance with society's rules.

B.   The Growth of Bureaucratic Government
1.   According to Weber, rational-legal authority inevitably leads to the formation of **bureaucracy**, a type of formal organization characterized by an authority hierarchy, a clear division of labor, explicit rules, and impersonality.
2.   Bureaucracy, the modern system of administration, is supposed to be a highly efficient mode of organization, although the reality is often much different.
a.   Bureaucracies tend to proliferate rules, often to the point that the organization becomes ensnared in its own bureaucratic requirements, and the actual work of the system bogs down.
b.   Within bureaucracies, personal temperament and individual discretion are not supposed to influence the application of rules; however, bureaucratic workers frequently exercise discretion in applying rules and procedures, and people may receive widely different treatment based on their race, gender, age, or other characteristics.

III.   THEORIES OF POWER

Table 14.1 summarizes the four different models sociologists have developed to explain how power is exercised in society.

A.   The Pluralist Model

1.   The **pluralist model** interprets power in society as coming from the representation of diverse interests of different groups in society.

   a.   This model assumes that in democratic societies, the system of government works to balance the different interests of groups in society.

   b.   An **interest group** can be any constituency in society organized to promote its own agenda, including large, nationally-based groups such as the American Association of Retired Persons (AARP); groups organized around professional interests, such as the American Medical Association (AMA); or groups that concentrate on a single political or social goal, such as Greenpeace.

   c.   According to the pluralist model, interest groups achieve power and influence through their organized mobilization of concerned people.

2.   The pluralist model, which views the state as representative of the whole society, has its origins in functionalist theory.

   a.   Power is broadly diffused across the public, and any group that wants to effect a change or express their opinion need only mobilize to do so.

   b.   Because the state is benign and representative of the whole society, different interest groups compete for government attention with equality of political opportunity.

   c.   This model helps explain the importance of **political action committees** (PACs), groups of people who organize to support candidates they feel will represent their views.

B.   The Power Elite Model

1.   The **power elite model** originated in the work of Karl Marx, who argued that the dominant group controls the main institutions in society. The state is simply an instrument by which the ruling class exercises its power, rather than a representative, rational institution.

2.   C. Wright Mills elaborated on Marx's work in his analysis of the power elite, arguing that the true power structure consists of people well-positioned in three areas: the economy, the government, and the military.

   a.   The power elite model posits a strong link between government and business, a view that is supported by the role of military spending as a principal component of economic affairs in the United States.

   b.   This model emphasizes how power overlaps between influential groups. **Interlocking directorates** are organizational linkages created when the same people sit on the boards of directors of several corporations.

C.   The Autonomous State Model

1.   The **autonomous state model** interprets the state as its own major constituent; thus, the state seeks to promote its own interests, independent of other interests and the public that it allegedly serves.

2.   This theory emphasizes that states tend to grow over time, possibly including expansion of their territory beyond their original boundaries, as illustrated by the development of NAFTA, the North American Free Trade Agreement.

D.   Feminist Theories of the State

1.   Feminist theory begins with the premise that an understanding of power cannot be achieved without a strong analysis of gender.

2. The feminist model concludes that the state is devoted primarily to men's interests, and the actions of the state tend to support gender inequality.

3. Groups that exercise state power, such as Congress and the military, are predominantly male, and these organizations are structured by values that are culturally masculine.

IV. **GOVERNMENT: POWER AND POLITICS IN A DIVERSE SOCIETY**

The **government**, one of several institutions that make up the state, includes those state institutions that represent the population and make rules that govern the society. Although the United States is a **democracy**, or a system of government based on the principle of representing all people through the right to vote, the actual composition of the government is not representative of the nation's population.

A. Diverse Patterns of Political Participation

1. Among democratic nations, the United States has one of the lowest voter turnouts, with 50 percent or less of the eligible voters typically participating in national elections [Figure 14.1].

2. In sociological terms, age, income, and education are the strongest predictors of whether someone will vote. The group most likely to vote is older, better educated, and financially better off than the average American citizen.

3. There is significant variation in voting patterns by race, with African Americans being less likely to vote than Whites, which reflects the disproportionate numbers of African Americans in the poor and working classes.

4. Race, ethnicity, and gender also influence for whom people vote; for example, female, African American, and Latino voters are more likely than male and White voters to vote as Democrats.

B. Political Power: Who's in Charge?

Most of the 535 members of Congress are well-educated White men from upper middle class or upper class backgrounds who have an Anglo-Saxon Protestant heritage. Simply getting into politics requires a substantial investment of money, and many of the members of Congress are millionaires. Surveys indicate that most American citizens have little confidence in the political process, and few trust government officials.

C. Women and Minorities in Government

Whereas 51 percent of the population of the United States is female, only 9 percent of United States Senators are women. African Americans, Hispanics, Asian Americans, and Native Americans are vastly underrepresented at both the state and the federal levels of government [Figure 14.2].

D. The Military

The military is among the most powerful and influential social institutions in all societies. In the United States, it is the single largest employer, and a majority of Americans report having a lot of confidence in the military. *Militarism*, or the pervasive influence of military goals and values throughout the culture, is evident in the toys, movies, and fashions of the nation.

1. Institutions are stable systems of norms and values that fill certain functions in society. The military's function is to defend the nation against external, and sometimes internal, threats.

   a. The military hierarchy is extremely formalized, which is reflected in the practice of explicitly labeling its members with rank, and conformity is highly valued, as seen in solders' identical uniforms and haircuts.

   b. A striking feature of the military as a social institution is the diverse representation of racial minority groups and women within the armed forces, particularly since the elimination of the all-male draft in 1973 and the initiation of an all-volunteer force in the U.S. armed services.

2. African Americans have served in the military for almost as long as the armed services have been in existence, although the armed forces were officially segregated by race until 1948.

    a. Black Americans are the most over-represented group relative to their proportion in the civilian population, although there are still few people of color at the highest ranks.

    b. For groups with limited opportunities in civilian society, joining the military seems to promise an educational and economic boost. In fact, for both Blacks and Whites, serving in the military leads to higher earnings relative to one's non-military peers.

3. There have been profound changes in the military since military academies began accepting women in 1976; however, there is still resistance to the full inclusion of women in the military, particularly in combat.

    a. In 1996, the Supreme Court ruled that women can not be excluded from state-supported military academies such as the Citadel and VMI.

    b. Gender relations in the military extend beyond the women who serve. For example, the experience of military wives is greatly affected by the frequent relocation associated with their husbands' employment.

4. According to the 1992 *"don't ask, don't tell"* policy, recruiting officers cannot ask recruits about sexual preference, and individuals who keep their sexual preference a private matter shall not be discriminated against. This controversial policy reveals continuing prejudice and discrimination against lesbian women and gay men. The longstanding policy against gays and lesbians in the military has kept homosexuality in the military hidden, but not nonexistent, while disparaging comments and harassment toward gay service personnel persists.

V. HEALTH CARE IN THE UNITED STATES

Overall, citizens of the United States are quite healthy in relation to the rest of the world; however, there are great discrepancies among Americans in terms of longevity, general health, and access to health care. By the start of the nineteenth century, advances in biology and chemistry ignited a century of explosive growth in medical knowledge. The American Medical Association (AMA) was founded in 1847, and the social prestige of medicine greatly increased. In an attempt to have some form of widespread guaranteed health services, at least for groups of people defined as vulnerable, the United States government established the **Medicare** and **Medicaid** programs. Medicare, begun in 1965, provides medical care in the form of insurance that covers hospital costs for all individuals who are age 65 or older. Medicaid provides medical care in the form of health insurance for poor people and people with disabilities.

A. Health and Sickness in America: A Picture of Diversity

The definitions of *sick* and *well* have varied greatly over time. For example, since the1950s, the United States has assigned positive value to being thin. The prevalence of eating disorders has increased in the American population, where **anorexia nervosa** particularly affects young, White women from upper and middle class families where parents place great pressure on their daughters to be high achievers. Men are not exempt from social pressure to achieve a particular body type, as evidenced by their increased use of *anabolic steroids*, which can have devastating consequences for men's health.

B. Race and Health Care

1. **Epidemiology** is the study of all the factors – biological, social, economic, and cultural – that are associated with disease. **Social epidemiology** is the study of the effects of social, cultural, temporal, and regional factors on health.

2. Race-ethnicity, class, gender, and age are among the more important factors affecting health in the United States. Although differences in culture, diet, and

lifestyle account for some differences in health across racial groups, racial minorities do not receive equivalent medical treatment compared to Whites.

    a.   African American women are more likely than Whites to suffer from cancer, heart disease, stroke, diabetes, and death during childbirth.

    b.   Mortality rates are one and one-half times greater for Native Americans than for the general population.

    c.   Hispanics have infant mortality rates similar to African Americans and Native Americans, and are even less likely than those groups to use available health services due to language barriers.

    3.   One of the most infamous studies to demonstrate the connection between race and the treatment of illness in the United States is the **Tuskegee Syphilis Study**, one of the most serious examples of ethical violations in medical and behavioral scientific research in the country. Although penicillin was discovered as an effective treatment for syphilis during the forty years that the study ran, scientists chose not to give penicillin to the hundreds of African American male subjects.

C.   <u>Social Class and Health Care</u>

    1.   Social class has a pronounced effect on health and the availability of health services in the United States. The effects of social class are evident in the infant mortality and stillbirth rates as well as the distribution of diseases such as diabetes, tuberculosis, heart disease, cancer, and arthritis.

    2.   Although personal habits, such as smoking, are partly responsible for disparities in health, social circumstances are also influential. For example, stress due to financial difficulties, poor living conditions, elevated levels of pollution in low-income neighborhoods, and lack of access to health care facilities also contribute to the high rate of disease among lower-income people.

    3.   Sociologists have found that during interactions between health care providers and poor patients, especially those who are Black or Hispanic, the patients are more likely to be *infantilized* and to receive health counseling that is incorrect, incomplete, or delivered in language not likely to be understood by the patient.

D.   <u>Gender and Health Care</u>

    1.   Even though women live longer on average than men, older women are more likely than older men to suffer from stress, hypertension, and chronic illness.

    2.   Some of the differences in health between men and women are due to variations in personal habits (such as smoking) and social behaviors (such as travel).

    3.   The effects of employment on women's health can be positive or negative. For example, women are more likely to be "tokens" in the workplace, an experience that contributes to a greater incidence of depression and anxiety. However, housewives have higher rates of illness than women who work outside the home.

E.   <u>AIDS: Illness and Stigma</u>

AIDS (Acquired Immune Deficiency Syndrome) is the term for a category of disorders that result from a breakdown of the body's immune system. Attitudes toward people suffering from sexually transmitted diseases, particularly AIDS, represent one of the strongest examples of how stigma operates in our society. **Stigma** occurs when an individual is socially devalued because of having some malady, illness or similar misfortune. A stigma is viewed as a relatively permanent characteristic of the individual.

VI.   THEORETICAL PERSPECTIVES ON HEALTH CARE

A.   <u>The Functionalist View of Health Care</u>

    1.   Functionalist theory developed the notion of the *sick role*, defined as a pattern of expectations that society applies to someone who is ill. Functionalism asserts that any institution, group, or organization can be examined by looking at its positive and negative functions in society.

2.   Positive functions, such as the prevention and treatment of disease, contribute to the harmony and stability of society, while negative functions contribute to social instability. Prominent problem areas in the U.S. health care system include:

    a.   **Unequal distribution of health care by race-ethnicity, social class, or gender**, a problem that is especially serious for Native Americans.

    b.   **Unequal distribution of health care by region**, with people in isolated rural areas such as Appalachia sometimes living over one hundred miles from a doctor or hospital.

    c.   **Inadequate health education of inner-city and rural parents**, who are particularly suspicious of immunization programs.

B.   The Conflict Theory View

Conflict theory stresses that structural inequality is inherent in capitalist society, and this inequality is responsible for different groups' unequal access to medical care. Restricted access to health care is further exacerbated by the high costs of medical care; excessive bureaucratization, which leads to the alienation of patients; and prolonged waits in the emergency rooms of many urban hospitals in the United States.

C.   Symbolic Interactionism and the Role of Perceptions

Symbolic interactionists assert that illness is partly socially constructed, resulting in the definitions of illness and wellness being culturally relative and time-dependent. The health care system itself has a socially constructed aspect. For example, one socially constructed problem is the tendency of medical practitioners to subject patients to *infantilization*, which refers to the treatment of adults as if they were children. Some medical schools now train their students to be more sensitive to their patients' feelings.

VII.   THE HEALTH CARE CRISIS IN AMERICA

The cost of medical care in the United States is currently more than 11 percent of the gross national product, making health care the nation's third leading industry. The United States tops the list of all countries in per-person expenditures for health care, yet serious problems have placed the nation's health care system in crisis.

A.   The Fee-For-Service System

The central element in the payment system is the fee-for-service principle, whereby the patient is responsible for paying the fees charged by the physician or hospital. The greatest contributors to skyrocketing health care costs are the soaring costs of hospital care and the rise in fees for physician services. Another culprit is the third-party payment system, whereby patients pass on the escalating health care costs to insurance providers.

B.   Malpractice

1.   There has been an increase in the number of patients who sue their physicians. The American public has traditionally accorded high social status and incomes to physicians, but the recent popularity of malpractice suits suggests that the public is beginning to question the privileged status of doctors.

2.   Several specific reasons have been suggested for client revolts against the medical profession, including:

    a.   declining standards of care and a higher incidence of medical negligence;

    b.   the failure of doctors to establish rapport with patients, making patients less attached to their physicians and more likely to turn hostile; and

    c.   the increasing animosity of patients who resent the high cost of medical care and the generous incomes of physicians.

3.   Doctors are increasingly practicing **defensive medicine**, which entails ordering expensive, excessively thorough tests at the least indication that something is wrong in order to protect themselves against potential malpractice suits.

C.   <u>A Response to the Problem: HMOs</u>
1.   **Health Maintenance Organizations** (HMOs) are private clinical care organizations that provide medical services in exchange for a set membership fee; thus, they have direct responsibility and control over the costs incurred.
2.   Doctors in an HMO earn salaries rather than fees, and services are ultimately paid for by the membership fee that subscribers give to the HMO, thereby eliminating both the fee-for-service system and third-party insurers.
3.   Critics of HMOs argue that the system decreases the physician's right to determine treatments and limits the patient's right to choose a doctor.

PRACTICE TEST

Multiple Choice Questions

1.   Which of the following state institutions is responsible for maintaining public order and enforcing laws at the local level?
    a.   government
    b.   military
    c.   prisons
    d.   police

2.   The state institution that creates laws and procedures to establish order in society is the:
    a.   government.
    b.   military.
    c.   prisons.
    d.   police.

3.   According to Max Weber, which type of authority inevitably leads to the formation of bureaucracies?
    a.   global
    b.   traditional
    c.   charismatic
    d.   rational-legal

4.   A monarchy derives its legitimate right to rule from which type of authority?
    a.   global
    b.   traditional
    c.   charismatic
    d.   rational-legal

5.   Which sociological model of power interprets power in society as derived from the representation of the diverse interests of different groups in society?
    a.   pluralist
    b.   feminist
    c.   power elite
    d.   autonomous state

6. Feminist theories of the state assert that:
   a. power is derived from the organized activities of multiple public interest groups, all of which have equal opportunities to influence the political system.
   b. the state is fundamentally feminine in its values because decisions are based on the principle of caring for the nation's citizens.
   c. social conflict derives from the domination of the upper class elites over other groups with fewer economic resources.
   d. the state is fundamentally masculine in its values, and its actions tend to support gender inequality in society.

7. The landmark U.S. Supreme Court case, *United States versus Virginia* (1996), declared that:
   a. gay and lesbian soldiers cannot be discharged from the military if they openly declare their sexual orientation.
   b. women cannot be excluded from participating in combat during state-declared military invasions
   c. male and female soldiers cannot be assigned to separate living quarters on military bases.
   d. women cannot be denied admission to state-supported military academies.

8. The organizational linkages created when a small number of people from elite groups sit on the Board of Directors of several companies, universities, and foundations are called:
   a. political action committees.
   b. interlocking directorates.
   c. marginalized groups.
   d. national alliances.

9. Which model of power interprets the state as its own major constituency that develops and perpetuates its own interests?
   a. pluralist
   b. power elite
   c. congressional
   d. autonomous state

10. One way that the state directs public opinion is through _____, or the restriction of people's access to certain information, such as sexually explicit materials on the Internet.
    a. coercion
    b. revolution
    c. censorship
    d. propaganda

11. According to Max Weber, which of the following is characteristic of bureaucracy?
    a. shared decision-making between managers and workers
    b. clear and specific division of labor
    c. vague policies and procedures
    d. close personal relationships

12. Under rational-legal authority, authority is gained through the:
    a. long-standing personal relationship the leader and his/her family has with the citizens of the state.
    b. personal appeal of the leader, who is believed to have special gifts that inspire devotion.
    c. process of being elected or appointed in accordance with a formal set of procedures.
    d. use of physical force and other forms of coercion.

13. Which of the following statements about the United States military is true?
    a. The representation of women in the military has increased considerably since the elimination of the draft.
    b. Although Black men have a long history of military service, the armed services were segregated by race until 1973.
    c. The admission of women into military academies has led to a reduced emphasis on competition and hierarchy in the military.
    d. All of the above statements about the United States military are true.

14. In sociological terms, the best predictors of whether someone in the United State will vote in an election are:
    a. age, gender, and marital status
    b. sex, occupation, and income
    c. age, income, and education
    d. race, ethnicity, and gender

15. Of these democratic nations, which country has the lowest rate of voter participation?
    a. United States
    b. South Africa
    c. Australia
    d. Japan

16. Which government program provides medical insurance to citizens who are 65 years of age and older to subsidize the cost when they are hospitalized?
    a. Social Security
    b. Eldercare
    c. Medicaid
    d. Medicare

17. Which theory argues that the inequality inherent in capitalist society is responsible for the unequal access various social groups have to medical care?
    a. symbolic interaction
    b. functionalist
    c. defensive
    d. conflict

18. In the United States, health care for most citizens is paid for through the fee-for-service system, which places primary responsibility for payment on:
    a. pharmaceutical companies.
    b. government programs.
    c. medical practioners.
    d. private citizens.

19. Which of the following statements about medical malpractice in the United States is true?
    a. The number of patients who sue their physicians is steadily increasing.
    b. The number of tests that doctors order for their patients is declining due to high costs.
    c. Lawyers are reluctant to accept most malpractice cases because they do not believe that medical errors occur that often.
    d. All of the above statements are true.

20. Which of the following ethical violations was committed in the Tuskegee Syphilis Study?
   a. After discovering that penicillin was an effective treatment for syphilis, medical researchers failed to prescribe penicillin to hundreds of Black men who had the disease.
   b. Researchers purposely infected hundreds of Black men with syphilis without their knowledge or consent to determine how long it takes for infected people to become ill.
   c. Clinic doctors who tested Black male patients for syphilis did not tell the patients who tested positive that they had the disease because there was no known cure at the time.
   d. None of the above ethical violations occurred during the study, because medical researchers in the U.S. are bound by a strict code of ethics that prevents such behavior.

True-False Questions

1. For people of all races, serving in the military leads to higher earnings relative to their non-military peers.

2. The United States has one of the highest voter turnout rates among democratic nations.

3. One example of the gender gap in politics is that men are more likely than women to vote as Democrat.

4. Medicare is a form of medical insurance provided by the government to poor people and people with disabilities.

5. Black Americans are the most over-represented racial group in the military relative to their proportion in the civilian population.

6. Full-time housewives have lower rates of illness than do women who work outside the home.

7. The occurrence of breast cancer is lower for Black women than White women, but the mortality rate from breast cancer is considerably higher for Black women than White women.

8. Functionalist theory argues that the health care system contributes to the stability of society by preventing and treating disease in the population.

9. Native Americans have a higher mortality rate than every other racial-ethnic group in the United States.

10. According to Weber, leaders that inspire devotion and obedience through personal appeal have traditional authority.

Fill in the Blank Questions

1. The American Association of Retired Persons (AARP), a constituency organized to promote its own agenda, is an example of a(n) ___ group.

2. One way that the state influences public opinion is by distributing _____, or information disseminated by an organization that is intended to justify its own power.

3. The United States is a ___, meaning that it is based on the principle of representing all people through the right to vote.

4. People are especially likely to assign a _____ to people who are ill from sexually transmitted diseases such as AIDS.

5. Medical practitioners who treat adult patients like children by speaking to them in a condescending or patronizing manner are subjecting their patients to ___.

Essay Questions

1. Explain why there was considerable controversy over voting methods in the 2000 Presidential election and discuss what consequences that controversy might have for future elections.
2. Explain why there are dramatic differences in life expectancy among different racial-ethnic and social class groups in the United States.
3. Identify three of the most pressing problems in the United States health care system today, and suggest at least one solution for addressing each of those problems.

ANSWERS TO PRACTICE TEST

Answers to Multiple Choice Questions

1.	D	384	The police are responsible for local law enforcement. The military defends the nation against domestic and foreign conflicts. Prisons punish people who violate the law, which is created by the government.
2.	A	384	The government creates laws and procedures that help maintain order in society.
3.	C	387	Rational-legal authority, which is based on the election or appointment of leaders according to formal procedures, leads to the formation of bureaucracies.
4.	A	386	Monarchies derive their power from traditional authority, or long-established patterns of leadership.
5.	A	388	The pluralist model interprets power in society as coming from group representation of the diverse interests in society. The autonomous state model asserts that social order is maintained by an administrative system that supports the status quo. The power elite model views the state as representing the interests of a small ruling class [Table 14.1].
6.	D	390	Feminist theories of the state view state institutions as reflecting masculine values and protecting men's interests [Table 14.1].
7.	D	395	The Supreme Court case, United States versus Virginia, declared that state-supported military academies such as the Citadel can not exclude women.
8.	B	387	Interlocking directorates are created when people drawn from the same elite group serve on several boards of directors.
9.	D	389	The autonomous state model of power views the state as its own major constituency that works to maintain the status quo [Table 14.1].
10.	C	384	Censorship occurs when the state restricts the public's access to information.
11.	B	387	Bureaucracy is characterized by a hierarchy of authority, clear division of labor, explicit rules and procedures, and impersonality.
12.	C	386	Rational-legal authority is based on the election or appointment of leaders according to formal procedures. Traditional authority is derived from long-established patterns of leadership. Charismatic authority is derived from the personal appeal of a leader assumed to have special gifts.
13.	A	394	The United States armed forces were segregated by race until 1948. Women's participation in the military increased after the all-male draft was eliminated in 1973, but their participation has not altered the competitive nature or hierarchical structure of the institution.

14.	C	390	The social factors that best predict voting patterns in the United States are age, education, and income. People who are older, well educated, and in the middle or upper class are most likely to vote.
15.	D	391	Japan and the United States have very low voter participation rates. Australia has a higher voter turnout for elections than all other democratic nations, and South Africa has the third highest turnout.
16.	D	397	Started in 1965, the Medicare program is a form of health insurance provided by the government to people age 65 and older to subsidize hospitalization costs. Medicaid is a government program that provides medical insurance to poor people and people with disabilities.
17.	D	404	Conflict theory views differential access to health care as the result of the economic inequality inherent in capitalist society [Table 14.3].
18.	D	405	The fee-for-service system of medical care places responsibility for payment on private citizens. The government provides medical insurance to some vulnerable groups, such as the elderly, veterans, poor people, and people with disabilities.
19.	A	406	The number of patients who sue their physicians is increasing, and the trend toward filing malpractice suits is supported by lawyers who argue that medical errors and negligence have increased. In response, physicians are practicing defensive medicine, whereby they order more tests for patients, despite the cost.
20.	A	399	Hundreds of Black men already known to be infected with syphilis participated in the Tuskegee Syphilis Study, which lasted 40 years. When researchers became aware that penicillin was an effective treatment for the disease, they did not give it to the participants.

Answers to True-False Questions

1.	T	394	People of all racial-ethnic groups who serve in the military have higher earnings relative to their non-military peers.
2.	F	391	As indicated in Figure 14.2, the U.S. has a very low rate of voter turnout compared to other industrialized countries.
3.	F	392	Women, Blacks, and Latinos are more likely than men and Whites to vote Democrat.
4.	F	397	Medicaid is a government program that provides medical insurance to poor people and people with disabilities. Medicare is a government program that provides insurance to elderly people to pay for hospitalization.
5.	T	394	Black Americans are the most over-represented racial group in the military today.
6.	F	401	Full time housewives have higher rates of illness than do employed women.
7.	T	398	White women are more likely than Black women to develop breast cancer, but once developed, Black women are more likely to die of the disease.
8.	T	403	Functionalist theory views the health care system as contributing to the stability of society by preventing and treating illness.
9.	T	399	The mortality rate for Native Americans is one and one-half times that of the general population. The limited delivery of health care services to Native American people is a particularly serious problem in the United States.
10.	F	386	According to Weber, charismatic authority is derived from the strong personal appeal of a leader who is believed to have special gifts, which inspires obedience.

Answers to Fill in the Blank Questions

1.	interest	388
2.	propaganda	384
3.	democracy	390
4.	stigma	401
5.	infantilization	404

CHAPTER 15
POPULATION, URBANISM, AND THE ENVIRONMENT

BRIEF CHAPTER OUTLINE

Demography and the U.S. Census
Diversity and the Three Basic Demographic Processes
      Birth Rate
      Death Rate
      Migration
Population Characteristics
      Sex Ratio and the Population Pyramid
      Cohorts
Theories of Population Growth Locally and Globally
      Malthusian Theory
      Demographic Transition Theory
      The "Population Bomb" and Zero Population Growth
Checking Population Growth
      Family Planning and Diversity
      Population Policy and Diversity
Urbanism
      Urbanism as a Lifestyle
      Race, Class, and the Suburbs
      The New Suburbanites
Ecology and the Environment
      Vanishing Resources
      Environmental Pollution
      Environmental Racism and Classism
      Feminism and the Environment
      Environmental Policy
Globalization: Population and Environment in the Twenty-First Century

CHAPTER FOCUS: This chapter examines the size, characteristics, and location of the human population, with particular emphasis on how the population of the United States interacts with the physical environment and how social factors affect demographic processes.

QUESTIONS TO GUIDE YOUR READING

1.   What are the main sources of data that demographers use to study the population?
2.   What are the three most important variables in the study of the population and how are they measured?
3.   What is an age-sex pyramid and what implications do different pyramid structures have for societies?
4.   What efforts have been made to manage population growth around the world, and how effective are these policies?
5.   What are the primary concerns among environmental policy makers today?

SOCIOLOGY IN ACTION: AN INTERNET EXERCISE

Go to www.plannedparenthood.org and click on "international" to see what programs this organization supports to manage population growth worldwide. In what ways do the activities of this organization reflect the assumptions made by the demographic theories that you read about in this chapter?

KEY TERMS (defined at page number shown and in glossary)

age-sex pyramid 416   census 411
cohort 416   crude birth rate 412
crude death rate 413   demographic transition theory 419
demography 411   ecological demography 432
ecological globalization 432   emigration 412
environmental racism 428   greenhouse effect 427
human ecology 425   human ecosystem 425
immigration 412   infant mortality rate 413
life expectancy 414   Malthusian theory 418
population density 425   population replacement level 420
sex ratio 415   thermal pollution 427
urbanism 422   vital statistics 412

KEY PEOPLE (identified at page number shown)

Ansley Coale 419   Ann Erlich 420
Paul Erlich 420   William Frey 424
Herbert Gans 423   Thomas Malthus 418
George Simmel 422   Louis Wirth 423

CHAPTER OUTLINE

Population growth and density are largely responsible for many current policy issues. For example, people's childbearing decisions greatly affect the educational and occupational structure of the entire country. The population of the United States, presently over 250 million people, will reach almost 300 million people by year 2025 at the current rate of growth.

I.   **DEMOGRAPHY AND THE U.S. CENSUS**

        Demography is the scientific study of the population. This field of sociology draws on bodies of data generated by a variety of sources, including the United States Census Bureau. A **census** is a head count of the entire population of a country. In the U.S., the census is conducted every ten years as required by the Constitution. Although it attempts to count every individual, some groups are missed or undercounted. In the 2000 Census, the Census Bureau added the category "multiracial" (or "mixed race") along with the other racial-ethnic categories that already appear on the census questionnaire, and added. The Supreme Court recently ruled that the Census Bureau may not use probability sampling to estimate the total count of the population. Another body of data used in demography is **vital statistics**, which include information about births, marriages, deaths, and migrations in and out of the country.

II.   **DIVERSITY AND THE THREE BASIC DEMOGRAPHIC PROCESSES**

        The total number of people in society is determined by three variables: births, deaths, and migrations. These variables show different patterns by race, ethnicity, social class, and gender. **Immigration**, or migration into a society from outside, adds to the population, while **emigration**, the departure of people from a society, reduces the population. Population grows exponentially, with an upward accelerating curve.

        A.   Birth Rate

                1.   The **crude birth rate** of a population is the number of babies born for every thousand members of the population each year.

2. The crude birth rate reflects the *fertility* of a population, which is the number of live births per number of women in the population.

3. Different countries and subgroups within a country can have dramatically different birth rates. For example, Kenya has the highest birth rate in the world, while the San Marino has the lowest.

4. Fertility is different from *fecundity*, which is the potential number of children in a population that could be born per thousand women if every woman reproduced at her maximum biological capability during the childbearing years.

5. The overall birth rate for the U.S. is about 16 per thousand people. The rate varies according social factors such as racial-ethnic group membership, region, socioeconomic status, and religious affiliation.

   a. Racial-ethnic minority groups and lower-income groups tend to have somewhat higher birthrates than do White non-minority groups and middle- and upper-income groups.

   b. Religious and cultural differences are apparent in the birth rate; for example, Catholics have a higher birth rate than do non-Catholics of the same socioeconomic status.

B. Death Rate

   1. The **crude death rate** of a population is the number of deaths each year per thousand people. Lower death rates are found in countries, and regions within nations, that have higher standards of living and better quality health care.

   2. The **infant mortality rate**, or the number of deaths per year of infants less than one year old for every thousand live births, also reflects the standard of living in a country. For example, the overall infant mortality rate in the U.S. is about 11 deaths for every thousand live births, compared to about 35 deaths per thousand live births in developing countries such as Kenya. Factors that contribute to high infant mortality rates include: lack of adequate health care, little or no access to health care facilities, the presence of toxic wastes, and inadequate food supply.

   3. The **life expectancy** of a population or group is defined as the average number of years that members of the group can expect to live. Life expectancy varies by gender, race-ethnicity, and social class. In the U.S., life expectancy has gone from 40 years of age in 1900 to 77 years of age today, which is lower than the average life expectancy in most other industrialized nations.

C. Migration

   Migration can occur between nations as well as within the boundaries of a country. In the 1980s, for example, extensive internal migration by African Americans, Hispanics, Asian Americans, and Pacific Islanders occurred within the U.S. Migration patterns are often linked to employment availability in particular industries.

III. **POPULATION CHARACTERISTICS**

The composition of a society's population can reveal a tremendous amount about the society's past, present, and future. The demographic data of a society are a record of its national history. The important data that sociologists investigate include a population's sex ratio, age composition, age-sex population pyramid, and age cohorts.

A. Sex Ratio and the Population Pyramid

   1. The **sex ratio** is the number of males per one hundred females. A sex ratio above 100 means that there are more males than females in the population, while a ratio below 100 indicates that there are more females than males in the population.

   2. In almost all societies, there are more boys born than girls, but because males have a higher infant mortality rate and a higher death rate after infancy, there are usually more females than males in the overall population.

213

3.   The *age composition* of the U.S. population is currently undergoing major changes as more people are entering the 65-and-over age bracket. As the population ages, its older members will have more influence on national policy and a greater impact on health care, housing, and other areas where the elderly have traditionally experienced age discrimination.

4.   Sex and age data can be combined in a graphical format called an **age-sex pyramid**, which reflects the birth rate of a society [See Figure 15.2].

B.   Cohorts

A birth cohort, or more simply, a **cohort**, consists of all the people born within a given period. The baby boom cohort, born between 1946 and 1964, now comprises about one third of the entire United States population. This cohort has had a major impact on the practices, policies, habits, preferences, and culture of American society.

IV.   THEORIES OF POPULATION GROWTH LOCALLY AND GLOBALLY

There is no scientific consensus on the planet's *carrying capacity*, or the number of people the planet can support on a sustained basis.

A.   Malthusian Theory

1.   Like other animals, humans can survive and reproduce only when they have access to the means of *subsistence*, or necessities of life, such as food and water.

2.   **Malthusian** theory represents Thomas Malthus' idea that populations tend to grow faster than the subsistence needed to sustain them. Rather than adding the same number of individuals each year, populations tend to grow by *exponential increase*, in which the number of individuals added each year grows.

3.   Malthus asserted that there were three major *positive checks* on population growth: famine, disease, and war. These checks inevitably come into play when populations rise to the level of subsistence and slightly beyond.

4.   Malthusian theory actually predicted rather well the population fluctuations of many agrarian societies such as Egypt from about 500 AD through Malthus' own lifetime. However, Malthus failed to foresee three revolutionary developments that derailed his predicted cycle of growth and catastrophe.

     a.   In agriculture, technological advances have permitted farmers to work larger plots of land and grow more food per acre, resulting in higher subsistence levels than Malthus predicted.

     b.   In medicine, scientific developments have treated diseases that Malthus expected to wipe out entire nations, such as the bubonic plague.

     c.   The development and widespread use of contraceptives in many places has kept the birth rate lower than Malthus would have thought possible.

B.   Demographic Transition Theory

An alternative to Malthusian theory is **demographic transition theory**, which proposes that countries pass through a consistent sequence of population patterns linked to the degree of development in the society [See Figure 15.3]. The three main stages of population change according to this theory are:

1.   Stage 1: characterized by a high birth rate and high death rate.

2.   Stage 2: characterized by a high birth rate but a low death rate, resulting in an overall population increase.

3.   Stage 3: characterized by a low birth rate and low death rate, resulting in stabilization of the overall level of the population as medical advances continue and general cultural changes occur, such as a smaller ideal family size.

C.   The "Population Bomb" and Zero Population Growth

1.   In 1968, Paul Erlich noted that worldwide population growth has outgrown food production, and that massive starvation must inevitably follow.

2. Erlich was among the earliest thinkers in modern times to argue that the quality of the environment, especially the availability of clean air and water, was a critical factor in the growth and health of populations.

3. Many of the dire predictions Erlich made have come true, including mass starvation in parts of Africa and starvation among some Black and Hispanic populations in the U.S.; increased homelessness in American cities, especially among minorities; acid rain; and extinctions of plant and animal species.

4. Organizations such as Zero Population Growth (ZPG) are dedicated to reaching the **population replacement level**, a condition in which the combined birth and death rate of a population sustains the population at a steady level. By 1980, the U.S. had reached this level of reproduction, partly due to the use of birth control.

V. CHECKING POPULATION GROWTH

By the 1980s, countries representing 95 percent of the world's population had formulated policies aimed at stemming population growth, although there is no consensus on how population growth should be controlled. Efforts to encourage the use of contraceptives, for example, have had mixed support, because some political and religious groups are opposed to the use of birth control.

A. Family Planning and Diversity

1. Many governments make contraceptives available to individuals, but this is not always consistent with the beliefs and cultural practices of all groups in the society. Governmental programs that advocate contraception can only be successful if couples themselves choose smaller families over larger ones.

2. Birth rate and family size are correlated with the overall level of economic development of a country, as well as the economic status of certain ethnic groups within a country, as reflected in the lower birth rates and smaller average family size in more economically developed nations.

3. The assumed relationship between economic development and family size in demographic transition theory has been challenged. In Bangladesh, for example, the population has become receptive to birth control programs, thereby lowering the birth rate in the absence of Western-style economic development.

B. Population Policy and Diversity

Family planning programs offer great potential for achieving significant declines in birth rates. In overpopulated countries where such programs can have the most effect, the demand for family planning resources surpasses the supply. In the U.S., there is some cultural resistance on the part of some racial and ethnic groups to government-sponsored contraceptive programs due to fears that widespread use of contraception threatens the very survival of these groups. Such governmental programs may be perceived as racist.

VI. URBANISM

The growth and development of cities, or centers of human activity with a high degree of population density, is a relatively recent occurrence in the course of human history. The extent to which a community has the characteristics of city life is referred to as **urbanism**.

A. Urbanism as a Lifestyle

1. Georg Simmel argued urban living has profound social psychological effects on the individual, including insensitivity to the people and events around him or her due to the intensity of city life, and discouragement of close, personal interaction.

2. Louis Wirth agreed that the city was a center of distant, cold impersonal interaction, resulting in the urban dweller experiencing alienation, loneliness, and powerlessness. However, both Simmel and Wirth believed that city life, with its relative absence of close, restrictive ties, offered individuals a feeling of freedom.

3. Herbert Gans provided a contrasting view of urban life, concluding that many city residents have strong loyalties to others and develop a sense of community. Gans classified the *urban village* as having several "modes of adaptation."

        a.   *Cosmopolites* are typically students, artists, writers, and musicians who choose urban living to be near the city's cultural facilities, and together, form a tightly knit community.

        b.   *Ethnic villagers* live in ethnically and racially segregated neighborhoods.

        c.   The *trapped* are individuals who, similar to today's *urban underclass*, are unable to escape from the city because of extreme poverty, homelessness, unemployment, and other familiar urban problems.

B.   Race, Class, and the Suburbs

    1.   The impact of race and class is clear in the distinction between city and suburb, as only about one-fourth of African Americans live in suburban areas today.

    2.   In the suburbs, one chooses one's neighbors and friends on the basis of race and educational and occupational similarity. Segregation in interpersonal interaction is encouraged by practices that support residential segregation.

    3.   People of color, particularly African Americans, often become as segregated in suburbs as in cities due to the practices of White landlords, homeowners, and realtors, who may selectively show particular properties only to people of a certain racial group.

    4.   Banks that practice *redlining* make it virtually impossible for persons of color to get a mortgage loan for a specific property, further intensifying residential segregation.

C.   The New Suburbanites

    1.   One consequence of the 1924 National Origins Quota Law was that it encouraged immigration from Northern and Western Europe, while discouraging additional immigration from Eastern and Southern Europe.

    2.   Today, the most prominent immigrants in suburban neighborhoods are Hispanics and Asian Americans. Suburban Whites may perceive themselves to be in competition for jobs and housing with these new immigrant groups.

    3.   Current immigration has led to the *new demographic divide*, which refers to settlement that is concentrated in small cities and suburbs on the East and West coasts, with little effect on the other parts of the country.

VII. ECOLOGY AND THE ENVIRONMENT

It should be apparent that population size has an important social dimension. Social forces can cause changes in the size of a population, and population changes can transform society. **Population density** is the number of people per unit of area, usually per square mile. As population density rises to high levels, the familiar problems of urban living appear, including high rates of crime and homelessness. Interacting with these problems are crises of the physical environment, such as air and water pollution, acid rain, and a growth in hazardous waste output. **Human ecology** is the scientific study of the interdependencies between humans and their physical environment. A **human ecosystem** is any system of interdependent parts that involves human beings interacting with each other and the physical environment. Two fundamental, closely related problems confront our present ecosystems -- overpopulation and exhaustion of natural resources.

A.   Vanishing Resources

In all ecosystems, organisms depend upon each other and the physical environment for survival. The supply of many natural resources is finite, and if one element in an ecosystem is disturbed, the entire system is affected. This was exemplified by the problems that emerged in the 1940s and 1950s with the use of DDT in the United States. Whereas growing population is a problem of the developing world, shrinking resources are problematic in the industrialized world, where real estate development takes over millions of acres of farmland each year in the United States alone.

B.   Environmental Pollution
1.   The most threatening forms of pollution are the poisoning of the planet's air and water, with the U.S., Japan, and Russia acting as leading air and water polluters.
2.   On the industrial side, the Environmental Protection Agency (EPA) estimates that the hazardous and cancer-causing pollutants released into the air by industry are responsible for about 2,000 deaths a year.
3.   A daunting international issue has grown around a group of chemicals called chlorofluorocarbons (CFCs), which are used in the manufacture of plastics, as a coolant in refrigerators, and as an aerosol propellant.
4.   Related to the problem of ozone depletion is the **greenhouse effect**, which results in small changes in the average temperature of the earth that can have dramatic consequences. For example, it can cause melting in the arctic regions, which raises the level of the sea, affecting water, land, and weather systems worldwide.
5.   Only a very small portion of the earth's water is usable by humans. The nation's rivers and lakes have been dumping grounds for heavy industry, yet these same industries (paper, steel, automobile and chemical) depend upon clean water for their production processes, during which they take water from the rivers and lakes and return it heated and polluted. The difference in temperature can alter aquatic habitats and kill aquatic life, earning it the name **thermal pollution**.
6.   The EPA estimates that 63 percent of rural Americans may be drinking water that is contaminated as a result of agricultural runoff and improper disposal of toxic substances in landfills. Polluting continues despite legislative prohibitions.
C.   Environmental Racism and Classism
Toxic wastes are stored and dumped with disproportionate frequency in areas that have high concentrations of racial-ethnic minorities, a phenomenon known as **environmental racism**. [See Map 15.2] For example, the largest commercial hazardous waste landfill in the U.S. is in Emelle, Alabama, an area where 80 percent of the population is Black.
D.   Feminism and the Environment
Women generally feel more vulnerable than men to risks posed by environmental problems. Consequently, they show greater concern with issues of environmental risk. Lack of attention on the part of local and federal governments to environmental issues can be interpreted as lack of attention to policy that differentially affects women.
E.   Environmental Policy
Environmental policy in the U.S. has been affected by an organized environmental movement, which brought increasing attention to environmental hazards and threats. In the past three decades, federal and local agencies have made better managed the problems of environmental pollution through stiffer antipollution laws and the encouragement of alternative technologies. However, industry has resisted antipollution laws because they require expensive adaptations of manufacturing processes, and unions have resisted such laws for fear that the added expense to industry would reduce jobs.

VIII.   **POPULATION AND ENVIRONMENT IN THE TWENTY-FIRST CENTURY**
Sociologists predict that the United States will continue to experience increasing suburban development, with accompanying increases in heavy industry and therefore additional pollution. Today's sociologists are concerned with both the effect that a changing planet will have upon our lifestyle, as well as the effects our lifestyle will have on the planet. Ecological concern helped stimulate the development of **ecological demography**, a field of study that combines the studies of demography and ecology to explore alternative technologies. **Ecological globalization** has resulted in increasing attention to environmental problems on the international political agenda.

PRACTICE TEST

Multiple Choice Questions

1.   Which of the following statements about the census is (are) true?
      a.   The U.S. constitution requires that the census be conducted every ten years.
      b.   The U.S. census uses probability sampling to estimate the population because counting every individual is too expensive and time-consuming.
      c.   The U.S. census collects information about people's opinions on key social issues.
      d.   All of the above statements about the U.S. census are true.

2.   The scientific study of the size, composition, and distribution of the population is:
      a.   epidemiology.
      b.   demography.
      c.   urbanism.
      d.   ecology.

3.   The measure of the potential number of children in a population that could be born per thousand women, if every woman reproduced at her maximum biological capacity during the childbearing years, is the _____ rate.
      a.   fertility
      b.   fecundity
      c.   mortality
      d.   maternalism

4.   The major restructuring of the age-sex pyramid that will occur in the U.S. over the next twenty-five years is due to the:
      a.   considerable increase in infant mortality among minority populations.
      b.   significant increase in the immigration of Hispanics to the country.
      c.   recent explosion in the birth rate for Whites.
      d.   aging of the Baby Boom cohort.

5.   Who was one of the first modern theorists to argue that the quality of the environment, such as the availability of clean air and water, is a critical factor in the health of the population?
      a.   Paul Erlich
      b.   Herbert Gans
      c.   Kingsley Davis
      d.   Thomas Malthus

6.   Which of the following industrialized nations has the lowest infant mortality rate?
      a.   China
      b.   Japan
      c.   Russia
      d.   United States

7.   Which of the following factors did Malthus surmise were positive checks on population growth?
      a.   immunizations
      b.   abortion
      c.   disease
      d.   All of the above.

8.   The state in which the combined birth and death rate of a population simply sustains the population at a steady level is the _____ level.
   a.   positive check
   b.   limited growth
   c.   population explosion
   d.   population replacement

9.   Which of the following statements about life expectancy in the U.S. is (are) true?
   a.   Average life expectancy in the U.S. increased from 40 years old to 77 years old in the period between 1900 and 2000.
   b.   Average life expectancy in the U.S. is higher for men than for women and higher for White people than for Black people.
   c.   Average life expectancy is higher in the U.S. than in all other industrialized nations.
   d.   All of the above statements about life expectancy are true.

10. The age-sex pyramid of Mexico in 1990 visually resembles which shape?
   a.   horizontal rectangle
   b.   vertical rectangle
   c.   triangle
   d.   square

11. Simmel and Wirth have both argued that urban life has what social-psychological effect(s) on individuals?
   a.   feeling of liberation or freedom from restrictions
   b.   heightened sensitivity to events surrounding them
   c.   increased opportunity for close, personal interaction
   d.   All of the above are consequences of urban living.

12. In Gans' vision of the urban village, which of the following groups choose urban living to be near the city's cultural facilities?
   a.   urban underclass
   b.   ethnic villagers
   c.   cosmopolites
   d.   the trapped

13. The examination of ecosystems has demonstrated that:
   a.   the supply of natural resources is finite.
   b.   humans and the physical environment are interdependent.
   c.   a disturbance in one element of an ecosystem has an effect on the entire system.
   d.   All of the above statements are true.

14. According to population bomb theory, the **most** significant factor in reaching population equilibrium in the U.S., especially among the middle-class, has been:
   a.   better crop yields, leading to increased food production.
   b.   official government policies restricting family size.
   c.   increased use of birth control.
   d.   sexual abstinence.

15. Which demographic theory is fundamentally pessimistic, predicting that the population will ultimately outstrip the food supply, resulting in worldwide starvation and rampant disease?
    a.   Malthusian theory
    b.   Doomsday theory
    c.   Rational Choice theory
    d.   Demographic Transition theory

16. Stage two of the demographic transition is characterized by a:
    a.   low birth rate and low death rate.
    b.   declining birth rate and high death rate.
    c.   high birth rate and declining death rate.
    d.   high birth rate and high death rate.

17. The internal migration patterns of Hispanics in the U.S. have been strongly linked to what factor?
    a.   desire to live in sparsely populated, rural areas
    b.   availability of bilingual educational facilities
    c.   presence of Catholic Churches
    d.   availability of employment

18. To reach zero population growth, the average number of children per family in a society would have to be:

    a.   one.
    b.   two.
    c.   three.
    d.   zero.

19. Vital statistics include which of the following types of information?
    a.   births and deaths
    b.   marriages and divorces
    c.   immigration and emigration
    d.   All of the above information is included in the vital statistics of a nation.

20. In the United States, babies of which racial-ethnic group are *most* likely to contract Acquired Immune Deficiency Syndrome (AIDS)?
    a.   African American
    b.   Chinese American
    c.   Mexican American
    d.   European American

True-False Questions

1.   In almost all societies, there are more girls than boys born, resulting in a greater number of females than males in all age groups.

2.   Israel has experienced considerable population growth since 1948 due to the migration of Jews from Europe and the United States.

3.   The United States was in the first stage of the demographic transition during the industrialization period of the late 1800s.

4.   The U.S. Census Bureau resolved the controversial issue of whether to use probability sampling instead of counting the entire population by allowing probability sampling in the 2000 Census.

5.   The practice of *redlining* by banks contributes to racial integration in the suburbs by allocating a certain percentage of mortgages to African Americans who want to purchase housing in predominantly White neighborhoods.

6.   Because stricter environmental laws were passed in the last two decades, the United States is no longer a large contributor to air and water pollution around the world today.

7.   According to Herbert Gans, *cosmopolites* are city residents who are trapped in urban areas due to extreme poverty and unemployment.

Fill in the Blank Questions

1.   A human _____ consists of the interdependent forces of human population, natural resources, and the condition of the physical environment.

2.   The departure of people from a society, or _____, results in a decrease in population.

3.   The group of approximately 75 million babies born in the U.S. between 1946 and 1964, which now represents nearly one-third of the population, is known as the _____.

4.   Population _____, which usually refers to the number of people per square mile, is higher in urban areas than in rural areas.

5.   The crude birth rate reflects the _____ of a population, which is the number of live births per number of women in that population.

Essay Questions

1.   Discuss how the level of industrialization and economic development of a society influences its birth and infant mortality rates.
2.   Discuss how and why life expectancy in the U.S. varies by sex, race, and social class.
3.   Explain how racism and classism intersect with environmental pollution in the United States, citing a specific example of environmental racism that has been documented by researchers.
4.   Explain why there might be cultural resistance to government-sponsored family planning programs among certain racial-ethnic minority groups in the United States.
5.   Who are the "new suburbanites" and what issues does their immigration present for social institutions in the United States?

ANSWERS TO PRACTICE TEST

Answers to Multiple Choice Questions

1.   A   411   The U.S. census, conducted every ten years, attempts to count every individual and collect basic demographic information such as race, marital status, and income. The Census does not ask people for their opinions on social issues.

2.   B   411   Demography is the scientific study of the population. Epidemiology is

			the study of all factors associated with disease. Ecology is the study of the physical environment. Urbanism is the extent to which a community has the characteristics of city life.
3.	B	413	Fecundity refers to the potential number of children that could be born if every woman reproduced at her maximum capacity, while fertility is the number of live births per number of women in the population. The crude death rate is the number of deaths each year per thousand people, while the infant mortality rate refers to the number of deaths per year of infants under one year old for every thousand births.
4.	D	416	The aging of the Baby Boom cohort, a trend called the "graying of America," has resulted in major restructuring of the age-sex pyramid in the United States.
5.	A	419	In the 1960s, Paul Erlich noted that the quality of the environment is related to the health of the population. Erlich advocates reducing population growth until the population replacement level is attained.
6.	B	414	Table 15.1 shows that Japan has the lowest infant mortality rate, while the U.S. and Russia have the highest infant mortality rates of all industrialized nations.
7.	C	418	Malthus argued that war, disease, and famine were positive checks on population growth. Immunizations increase population by lowering the death rate. Writing in the 1700s, he could not foresee the contributions of abortion and artificial birth control to reducing population growth.
8.	D	420	The state in which the combined birth and death rate of a population sustains the population at a steady level is the population replacement level.
9.	A	414	Average life expectancy in the U.S. has increased to 77 years old, which is considerably longer than in 1900, but lower than the average life expectancy in nearly every other industrialized nation. Within the U.S., life expectancy is lower for men, members of racial-ethnic minority groups, and lower-income people.
10.	C	417	Figure 15.2 depicts the age-sex pyramid of Mexico as a triangular shape. The pyramid of the U.S. resembles a vertical rectangle with a bulge in the middle.
11.	A	422	Both Simmel and Wirth recognized that city life could be personally liberating, but it is also characterized by cold, impersonal relationships, decreased sensitivity to one's surroundings, and feelings of alienation and powerlessness.
12.	C	424	In Gans' vision of the urban village, cosmopolites consist of students, artists, and musicians who live in the city to be near cultural facilities. Ethnic villagers live in segregated neighborhoods, or ethnic enclaves. The trapped are similar to today's urban underclass, consisting of those people who are unable to escape from the city due to poverty.
13.	D	425	The examination of ecosystems reveals that the supply of many natural resources is finite, humans and the physical environment are interdependent, and a disturbance in one part of the ecosystem has an effect on the whole system.
14.	C	420	By 1980, the U.S. had reached the population replacement level of reproduction, partly due to the effective, widespread use of birth control.
15.	A	418	As summarized in Table 15.2, Malthusian theory suggests that the population will eventually surpass the food supply despite positive checks on growth.
16.	C	419	As depicted in Figure 15.3, stage two of the demographic transition is characterized by a high birth rate and declining death rate. Stage one is characterizes by high birth and death rates, while low birth and death rates are characteristic of stage three.
17.	D	415	Internal migration patterns of Hispanics have traditionally been linked to the agricultural industry, and more recently, to the meatpacking and textile industries located near urban centers; thus, migration is strongly influenced by the availability of employment.

18.	B	420	To reach population replacement level, which would result in zero population growth, each family has to have an average of two children.
19.	D	412	The vital statistics for a nation include the number of births, deaths, marriages, divorces, and migration into (immigration) and out of (emigration) the country.
20.	A	414	African American babies are almost thirty times more likely than White babies to contract AIDS, and Hispanic babies are twenty-five times more likely to contract the disease, contributing to lower infant survival rates for these groups compared to White European Americans.

Answers to True-False Questions

1.	F	415	In almost all societies, more boys than girls are born, but boys and men have higher mortality rates, resulting in more women than men in adulthood.
2.	T	419	Israel has experienced population growth due to the migration of Jews from Europe and the U.S. Those who migrate are more likely to be younger adults.
3.	F	419	The U.S. was in stage one of the demographic transition during the Colonial period and stage two during Industrialization. It is currently in stage three.
4.	F	412	The Supreme Court ruled that the U.S. Census Bureau may not use probability sampling to count the population every ten years due to concerns about undercounting particular groups.
5.	F	424	The practice of *redlining* is a form of discrimination whereby banks deny mortgages to prospective homeowners who are members of racial or ethnic minority groups, which supports continued residential segregation, particularly in the suburbs.
6.	F	426	Despite stricter legislative prohibitions on pollution, the United States continues to be one of the largest contributors in the world to air and water pollution.
7.	F	424	According to Gans, cosmopolites tend to be students and artists who choose urban living to be close to cultural facilities. Ethnic villagers live in segregated neighborhoods, or ethnic enclaves. The trapped are similar to today's urban underclass, consisting of those people who are unable to escape from the city because of unemployment and extreme poverty.

Answers to Fill in the Blank Questions

1.	ecosystem	425
2.	emigration	412
3.	Baby Boomers	417
4.	density	425
5.	fertility	412

CHAPTER 16
SOCIAL CHANGE AND SOCIAL MOVEMENTS

BRIEF CHAPTER OUTLINE

What is Social Change?
Theories of Social Change
      Functionalist and Evolutionary Theories
      Conflict Theories
      Cyclical Theories
Global Theories of Social Change
      Modernization Theory
      World Systems Theory
      Dependency Theory
Modernization
      From Community and Society
      Mass Society and Bureaucracy
      Social Inequality, Powerlessness, and the Individual
The Causes of Social Change
      Collective Behavior
      Social Movements
      Cultural Diffusion
      Inequality and Change
      Technological Innovation and the Cyberspace Revolution
      War and Social Change
Collective Behavior and Social Movements
      Characteristics of Collective Behavior
      The Organization of Social Movements
      Origins of Social Movements
      Theories of Social Movements
Diversity, Globalization, and Social Change

CHAPTER FOCUS: This chapter examines the causes of social change, offers explanations for why change occurs, and discusses how the processes of modernization and globalization have altered social relationships and social institutions.

QUESTIONS TO GUIDE YOUR READING

1.   What are the four common characteristics of social change?
2.   What is the difference between a unidimensional and a multidimensional theory of social change, and with which major sociological theory are evolutionary theories of social change associated?
3.   What are the differences between a gemeinschaft and a gessellschaft, and which type of community becomes prevalent with modernization?
4.   What are the basic assumptions of the three global theories of social change, and what evidence exists to support each of these theories?
5.   What is a social movement and what are the necessary conditions for a social movement to develop?

SOCIOLOGY IN ACTION: AN INTERNET EXERCISE

Go to www.nraila.org and identify the philosophy and goals of the National Rifle Association (NRA) Institute for Legislative Action. Then go to http://www.paxusa.org and compare this organization's philosophy and goals to the NRA. Why do you think gun control has emerged as a social problem in the contemporary United States? How would you classify these competing movements using the categories presented in the text? How do competing interest groups define the problem differently, and what solution does each group pose to the problem?

KEY TERMS (defined at page number shown and in glossary)

collective behavior 451

frames 457

gesellschaft 445

inner-directedness 446

modernization 444

multidimensional evolutionary theory 440

other-directedness 446

political process theory 456

reactionary movements 453

resource mobilization theory 455

social change movements 453

tradition-directedness 655

world systems theory 443

dependency theory 444

gemeinschaft 444

globalization 443

mobilization 455

modernization theory 443

new social movement theory 457

personal transformation movement 453

radical movements 453

reform movements 453

social change 436

social movements 451

unidimensional evolutionary theory 440

KEY PEOPLE (identified at page number shown)

Peter Berger 446

Rolf Dahrendorf 446

Abby Ferber 454

Gerhard Lenski 440

Karl Marx 441

Marshall McLuhan 443

William Ogburn 437

Robert Reich 444

Theda Skocpol 442

Pitrim Sorokin 443

Patrick Tierney 448

Ferdinand Tonnies 444

Sherry Turkle 451

Theodore Caplow 443

Emile Durkheim 440

Jurgen Habermas 446

Ralph Linton 447

Herbert Marcuse 447

Lewis Morgan 440

Talcott Parsons 440

David Reisman 446

Herbert Spencer 440

Robert Farris Thompson 447

Charles Tilly 456

Arnold Toynbee 442

Immanuel Wallerstein 443

CHAPTER OUTLINE

Technological innovations can transform a society, but not all of these changes represent "progress." For example, technological disasters such as the Love Canal incident in New York led to political and social changes directed at eliminating toxic wastes in the environment.

I.   **WHAT IS SOCIAL CHANGE?**

Social change is the alteration of social interactions, institutions, stratification systems, and elements of culture over time. Societies are always in a state of flux. Some changes are rapid, while others are more gradual. With increased urbanization, more rapid social change becomes possible, and new technologies circulate quickly. *Microchanges* are subtle alterations in the day-to-day interactions between people, such as fads. *Macrochanges* are gradual transformations that occur on a broad scale and affect many aspects of society. In the process of *modernization*, societies absorb the changes that develop. One trend that accompanies modernization is the increasing social differentiation of society. Whether large or small, fast or slow, social change typically has a number of shared characteristics. Social change is uneven because some parts of a society lag behind others in the rate of change, a principle William Ogburn referred to as *cultural lag*. The onset and consequences of social change are often unforeseen, and social change often creates conflict. Finally, the direction of social change is not random and social changes cannot erase the past. Change has "direction" relative to a society's history, and as a society moves toward the future, it carries along its history, its traditions, and its institutions.

II. THEORIES OF SOCIAL CHANGE

A. Functionalist and Evolutionary Theories

1. Functionalist theory builds upon the belief that all societies, past and present, possess basic elements and institutions that perform certain *functions* that permit a society to survive and persist.

2. Functionalist theorist Emile Durkheim identified two types of societies.

   a. Foraging and pastoral societies are structurally simple, homogeneous societies based on *mechanical solidarity*, where members engage in largely similar tasks.

   b. Agricultural, industrial, and post-industrial societies are structurally more complex, heterogeneous societies based on *organic* or *contractual solidarity*, where great social differentiation exists and there is extensive division of labor among people who perform many specialized tasks.

3. **Evolutionary theories** of social change are a branch of functionalist theory.

   a. **Unidimensional evolutionary theory**, now out of favor, argued that societies follow a single evolutionary path from "simple," relatively undifferentiated societies to more complex societies, which were perceived as more "civilized."

   b. **Multidimensional evolutionary theory** argues that the structural, institutional, and cultural development of a society can follow many evolutionary paths simultaneously, with the different paths emerging from the circumstances of the society.

      1) The nature of social evolution in the society depends upon the interplay between the society's technology, population characteristics, extent of social differentiation, and other structural and cultural elements.

      2) Gerhard Lenski and colleagues posit that technology has a central role in development because technological advances are significantly, although not wholly, responsible for other changes, including the nature of law, alterations in religious preference, form of government, and relations between diverse groups.

4. Although earlier functionalist theories made the implicit assumption that European and American societies, which are predominantly White, were more evolved or advanced than other societies around the world, the new functionalism rejects the "primitive" versus "civilized" dichotomy and acknowledges the importance of racial, ethnic, social class, and gender differences in the process of social change.

B. Conflict Theories

1. The central notion of conflict theory is that conflict is built into social relations. For Karl Marx, social conflict, particularly between the two major social classes in any society (proletariat and bourgeoisie) was the driving force behind all social change.

2. Sociologists now think that conflict between Whites and racial-ethnic minorities is at least partly rooted in class conflict, because there are important cultural differences *within* broadly defined racial-ethnic categories, and minorities are disproportionately represented among the lower-income classes.

3. A central feature of Marx's work is that revolution and dramatic social change will come about when class conflict inevitably leads to a decisive social rupture.

Although the worldwide revolution predicted by Marx never developed, his analysis of class-related conflict has advanced understandings of social change.

    4.   Marx seems to have overemphasized the role of economics and ignored the importance of other relevant social factors in the social tensions he observed. For example, Theda Skocpol has noted that in France, Russia, and China, countries where major revolutions have occurred, serious internal conflicts between classes were combined with major international crises that the elite classes proved unable to resolve before they were overthrown.

    5.   Ethnic, racial, and religious differences join social class differences as major causes of conflict within and between countries. Examples of this include recent bouts of so-called "ethnic cleansing," in which one ethnic group attempts to annihilate another, as in Bosnia in the 1990's.

  C. Cyclical Theories

    1.   **Cyclical theories** of social change invoke patterns of social structure and culture that are believed to recur at more or less regular intervals.

    2.   Arnold Toynbee, social historian and a principal theorist of cyclical social change, argues that societies are born, mature, decay, and sometimes die.

    3.   Sociological theorists Pitrim Sorokin and Theodore Caplow have argued that societies proceed through three different phases or cycles.

        a.   In the first phase, called *idealistic culture*, the society wrestles with the tension between the ideal and the practical.

        b.   The second phase, *ideational culture*, emphasizes faith and new forms of spirituality.

        c.   The third phase is *sensate culture*, which stresses practical approaches to reality and involves the hedonistic and sensual elements of culture.

III. GLOBAL THEORIES OF SOCIAL CHANGE

Globalization refers to the increased interconnectedness and interdependence of different societies around the world. In Europe, this trend has proceeded as far as a common currency for all nations participating in the newly constructed, common economy. As societies become more interconnected, cultural diffusion between them creates common ground; however, cultural differences may become more important as relationships among nations become more intimate.

  A. Modernization Theory

    1.   Strongly influenced by functionalist theories of social change, **modernization theory** states that global development is a worldwide process affecting nearly all societies that have been touched by social change.

    2.   Recent proponents of modernization theory assert that in addition to the U.S. and western European countries, Japan, Taiwan, and South Korea have also led the process of technological globalization and its resultant homogenization.

    3.   As a result of their involvement, Japan, with its cultural emphasis on the importance of small friendship groups in the workplace and a traditional work ethic, has profoundly influenced the organization of work in other countries.

  B. World Systems Theory

    1.   **World systems theory**, formulated by Immanuel Wallerstein, argues that all nations are members of a worldwide system of unequal political and economic relationships that benefit the more developed, technologically advanced countries at the expense of the less developed, less technologically advanced countries.

    2.   Wallerstein noted that the world system consists of *core nations* (such as the U.S. and Japan) that produce goods by importing raw materials and cheap labor from *noncore nations* (situated in Africa, Latin and South America, and parts of Asia), which suffer exploitation in the global economy.

C.   <u>Dependency Theory</u>
Closely allied with Wallerstein's world systems theory is **dependency theory**, which maintains that highly industrialized nations tend to imprison developing nations in dependent relationships, rather than spurring the upward mobility of developing nations with transfers of technology and business acumen.

    1.   Dependency theory views industrialized core nations as transferring only those narrow capabilities that it serves them to deliver.

    2.   Once these unequal relationships are forged, core nations seek to preserve the status quo because they derive benefits in the form of cheap raw materials and labor from noncore nations.

    3.   The developing nations remain dependent upon the core nations for markets and support to keep what industry they have acquired in working order, while at home they experience minimal social development, limited economic growth, and increased income stratification among their own population.

    4.   Robert Reich noted that *borrowing dependency* develops when core nations impose terms on loans to noncore nations that put the noncore nations under severe economic strain.

IV.   MODERNIZATION

Modernization is a process of social and cultural change that is initiated by industrialization and followed by increased social differentiation and division of labor. The process of modernization is characterized by the decline of small, traditional communities as a society becomes more bureaucratized and interactions come to be shaped by formal organizations. There is generally a decline in the importance of the religious institution, and with the mechanization of daily life, people often feel that they have lost control of their lives.

A.   <u>From Community (Gemeinschaft) to Society (Gesellschaft)</u>

    1.   The German sociologist Ferdinand Tonnies viewed the process of modernization as a progressive loss of **gemeinschaft**, which is German for "community." A gemeinschaft is characterized by a sense of fellowship, strong personal ties and primary group memberships, and a sense of personal loyalty to one another.

    2.   Tonnies argued that urbanization and the industrial revolution, with its emphasis on efficiency and task-oriented behavior, destroyed the sense of community and personal ties associated with an earlier rural life, substituting instead feelings of rootlessness and impersonality.

    3.   These changes resulted in the condition of **gesellschaft**, which is German for "society." This kind of social organization is characterized by a high division of labor, less prominence of personal ties, the lack of a sense of community among the members of society, and the absence of a feeling of belonging.

    4.   One measurement of the impersonality associated with the gesellschaft is the effect an urban setting has on the likelihood that someone will come to the aid of a person in distress. For example, a person in trouble on the street is more likely to receive assistance by a bystander if the event takes place in a small town than if it takes place in a large city, because people in a large city are more likely to merge with the crowd, or *deindividuate*, when there are more people around.

B.   <u>Mass Society and Bureaucracy</u>

    1.   Modernization has produced what is called a **mass society**, or one in which industrialization and bureaucracy reach exceedingly high levels and the change from gemeinschaft to gesellschaft is accelerated.

    2.   The breakup of primary ties is particularly pronounced in a mass society, where the government expands to include tasks that were previously done by the family, and it becomes more common to identify people by personal attributes (such as job or gender) than by kinship or their hometown.

3. Mass society theorists Dahrendorf and Berger argue that bureaucracies have obtained virtually complete control of the individual's life, and the overall bureaucratization of social life has supported the rise of large government.

C. Social Inequality, Powerlessness, and the Individual
1. Another product of modernization is pronounced social stratification, which results in greater personal feelings of powerlessness because building a stable personal identity is difficult in a highly modernized society that presents the individual with complex, conflicting choices about how to live.
2. According to Habermas, individuals in highly modernized environments are more likely to experiment with new religions, social movements, and lifestyles in search of a fit with their conception of their own "true self."
3. Social theorist David Reisman argued that there are three main orientations of personality that can be traced to social structural conditions.
   a. Modernization tends to produce **other-directedness**, which occurs when the behavior of the individual is guided by the observed behavior of others. It is characterized by rigid conformity and openness to the influences of group pressures, changing styles, and shifting interests.
   b. **Inner-directedness,** more common in less modernized societies, occurs when the individual is guided by internal principles and morals rather than the superficialities of the external environment.
   c. **Tradition-directedness** is characterized by a strong conformity to long-standing and time-honored norms, practices, and styles of life.
4. The inner-directed are less likely to sway with the presence or absence of modernization. Because modernization tends to produce other-directedness, anyone who happens to be inner-directed or tradition-directed in a modernized society such as the United States is likely to be seen as a deviant person.
5. Social theorist Herbert Marcuse argued that modernized society fails to meet people's basic needs, including the need for a fulfilling identity and a feeling of control over one's own life, resulting in *alienation* of the individual from society. Those groups who have traditionally been denied access to power, such as racial minorities, women, and the working class, particularly experience this alienation.

V. **THE CAUSES OF SOCIAL CHANGE**
A. Cultural Diffusion
Cultural diffusion is the transmission of cultural elements from one society or cultural group to another. Diffusion of cultural elements can occur by means of trade, migration, mass communications media, and social interaction. For example, many contemporary practices among Black Americans, such as step shows, are traceable to Africa.

B. Inequality and Change
Inequalities between groups of people on the basis of sex, class, race, ethnicity, or other social structural characteristics can be a powerful spur toward social change. Culture itself can sometimes contribute to the persistence of social inequality, therefore, it may become a source of discontent for certain groups in society.

C. Population and Change
1. Limitations placed on the population by the natural environment can greatly influence the nature of social relationships. For example, crowding affects how people interact with each other.
2. Major social change can also result from shifts in the age composition of a population. For example, as the average age in the United States increases, the society must respond to the needs and desires of the aging population.
3. Immigration is having profound effects on the ethnic and racial composition of the United States. By the year 2050, it is expected that Hispanics will comprise

25 percent and Asians will comprise 9 percent of the U.S. population, which will influence the structure of the economy, the ethnic mix in education and employment, and styles of dance, music, and language.

D. War and Social Change

War and serious political conflict result in significant changes for both conquering and conquered groups. For example, World War II transformed the United States into a mass-production economy.

E. Technological Innovation and Cyberspace Revolution

Technological innovations can be strong catalysts of social change. The historical movement of societies from agrarian to industrialized has been tightly linked to the emergence of technological innovations. For example, the advent of the electronic computer and the development of the Internet has transformed our entire society.

F. Collective Behavior and Social Movements

Collective behavior occurs when people establish new patterns of interaction and social structure, and it is often associated with efforts to promote change. *Social movements* are highly organized and persistent forms of collective behavior.

VI. **COLLECTIVE BEHAVIOR AND SOCIAL MOVEMENTS**

Collective behavior occurs when the usual conventions of behavior are suspended and people establish new norms in response to an emerging situation. Types of collective behavior include crowds, panics, disasters, riots, fads, and fashion. **Social movements** are groups that act with some continuity over time to promote or resist change in society.

A. Characteristics of Collective Behavior

1. Collective behavior always represents the actions of groups of people, not of individuals. It is rooted in the relationships between people and the norms governing group behavior.

2. Collective behavior involves new or emergent relationships that arise in unusual or unexpected circumstances. It arises when uncertainty in the environment creates the need for new forms of social action.

3. Because of its emergent nature, collective behavior captures the more novel, dynamic, and changing elements of society to a greater degree than other forms of action.

4. Collective behavior may mark the beginnings of more organized social behavior. It often precedes the establishment of formal social organizations.

5. Collective behavior is patterned behavior, not the irrational behavior of crazed individuals. It is relatively coordinated among the participants.

6. Most forms of collective behavior appear to be highly emotional; however, what defines a crowd is its spontaneity, rather than its emotionality.

7. During collective behavior, people communicate extensively through *rumors*, which develop when people try to define ambiguous situations because they lack adequate information to interpret a problematic event.

B. The Organization of Social Movements

1. There is typically tension between spontaneity and structure in social movements, which contain routine elements of organization, yet may have to continually develop new strategies and tactics to accomplish change.

2. **Personal transformation movements** focus on the development of new meaning within individual lives, rather than pursuing social change. An example is the New Age movement, which promotes relaxation and spiritualism as an emotional release from highly stressful, overly rational mainstream life.

3. **Social change movements** aim to change some aspect of society using a variety of tactics, strategies, and organizational forms to achieve their goals.

      a.   **Reform movements** seek change through mainstream political or legal means, such as lobbying for legislation that protects the environment.

      b.   **Radical movements** seek fundamental change in the structure of society, often by using more dramatic, disruptive tactics, such as sit-ins.

    4.   **Reactionary movements** organize to resist change or reinstate an earlier social order. For example, the militia movement in the U.S. resists government authority and seeks to reinstate the perceived lost power of White people.

    5.   The organizational structure of the movement may be formal and bureaucratic or more decentralized and interpersonal, with many movements combining both.

C.   Origins of Social Movements

    1.   For a social movement to begin, there must be a *pre-existing communication network* that facilitates communication among the people who will participate in the new movement. For example, Rosa Parks, who refused to give up her seat on a Montgomery, Alabama bus in 1955, was the secretary of the local NAACP. When she was arrested, the news spread quickly via an already established network of friends, kin, church members, and school organizations.

    2.   There must also be *a perceived sense of injustice among the potential participants*. For example, the environmental justice movement developed from grassroots organizations in communities where toxic waste sites and polluting industries posed a perceived threat to residents' health and safety.

    3.   The *ability of groups to mobilize* is the third factor needed to initiate a social movement. **Mobilization** is the process by which social movements and their leaders secure and coordinate people and resources for the movement.

D.   Theories of Social Movements

    1.   **Resource mobilization theory** is an explanation of how social movements develop that focuses on how movements gain momentum by successfully garnering and mobilizing resources while competing with other movements for money, communication technology, interpersonal contacts, special technical or legal knowledge, and members with organizational and leadership skills.

    2.   **Political process theory** posits that movements achieve success by exploiting a combination of internal factors, such as the ability of organizations to mobilize resources, and external factors, such as changes occurring in society. This theory stresses that the political system may become structurally vulnerable to social protest during situations such as war, demographic shifts, or economic crisis.

    3.   Resource mobilization theory and political process theory are social structural explanations that focus on forces external to individuals, while other theories are more cultural in their focus [Table 16.2].

    4.   Sociologists use the concept of *framing* to explain the process whereby people in social movements develop a shared definition of the situation. **Frames** are specific schemes of interpretation that allow people to identify, perceive, and label events within their lives that can become the basis for collective action.

    5.   **New social movement theory** conceptually links culture, ideology, and identity to explain how members socially construct new identities through their participation in a social movement. This theory explains the demise of the American Indian Movement as a result of the failure to build a pantribal sense of identity *and* the inability to mobilize resources due to government repression.

VII. DIVERSITY. GLOBALIZATION, AND SOCIAL CHANGE

As nations become increasingly economically interdependent and technology facilitates better worldwide communication, social movements that have transformed American society have inspired similar movements around the world. In the United States, some of the most significant social movements are associated with the nation's diverse population, making much of the population more conscious of the harmful effects of racism, sexism, and homophobia.

PRACTICE TEST

Multiple Choice Questions

1.   Which of the following is a common characteristic of collective behavior?
      a.   It reflects the consistent, well-established elements of society.
      b.   It involves people acting as a group to establish new norms of behavior.
      c.   It is completely unpredictable because it emerges in response to new situations.
      d.   It usually results from the actions of a group of overly emotional, irrational individuals.

2.   Gradual transformations that occur on a broad scale and affect many aspects of society, such as the rise of the computer and emergence of digital culture, are:
      a.   microchanges.
      b.   macrochanges.
      c.   cultural diffusions.
      d.   demographic shifts.

3.   Which one of the following statements about social change is true?
      a.   Social change often creates conflict in society.
      b.   Sociologists can accurately predict all of the consequences of social change.
      c.   Social change is a process that affects all segments of society equally and similarly.
      d.   All of the above statements about social change are true.

4.   According to _____ theory, social change is the result of inevitable conflict between social classes in capitalist societies.
      a.   symbolic interaction.
      b.   functionalist
      c.   conflict
      d.   cyclical

5.   Toynbee's assertion that all societies are born, mature, decay, and sometimes die reflects the principles of the _____ theory of social change.
      a.   modernization
      b.   functionalist
      c.   conflict
      d.   cyclical

6.   Lenski argues that although other elements contribute to social change, _____ are especially important in facilitating social changes such as alterations in religious preferences, the nature of law, and the form of government in modern societies.
      a.   immigration patterns
      b.   technological advances
      c.   changes in family structure
      d.   changes in the age composition of the population

7. Sherry Turkel argues that the United States has moved to a culture of _____, in which widespread Internet use allows individuals to easily develop a new self.
    a. irresponsibility
    b. calculation
    c. simulation
    d. anonymity

8. White youth from the suburbs regularly listen to rap music, a cultural form that began in urban African American communities. This is an example of cultural:
    a. lag
    b. conflict
    c. diffusion
    d. inequality

9. Patrick Tierney argues that the introduction of steel into the Yanomami Indian communities of Brazil and Venezuela has led to:
    a. increase in deadly warfare.
    b. tribes' inability to continue farming efficiently.
    c. emergence of environmental pollution due to automobile emissions.
    d. All of the above have occurred since steel was introduced in these communities.

10. Because crowding is a pervasive feature of Japanese culture,
    a. close bodily contact in public places such as subway stations has strong sexual overtones.
    b. subway stations hire workers whose job is to push as many passengers as possible into each train.
    c. it is considered a violation of other people's personal space to have one's entire body pressed against a stranger.
    d. All of the above are true.

11. Which of the following is **not** a feature of modernization?
    a. decline in importance of secondary groups to social interaction
    b. decrease in the number of small, close-knit communities
    c. increase in feelings of uncertainty and powerlessness
    d. increase in the mechanization of daily life

12. According to Toennies, the kind of social organization characterized by a high division of labor, less prominence of personal ties, the lack of a sense of community among the members of society and the absence of a feeling of belonging is typically found in a(n) _____ society.
    a. agrarian
    b. gesellschaft
    c. gemeinschaft
    d. homogeneous

13. Rumors are especially likely to develop when people:
    a. are uncomfortable in large group situations.
    b. have low levels of education.
    c. lack adequate information.
    d. do not question authority.

14. The movement against drunk driving in the U.S., led by groups such as M.A.D.D. and S.A.D.D., has introduced social change by working within the existing political and legal structures. This is an example of what type of social movement?
    a.   reactionary
    b.   rational
    c.   radical
    d.   reform

15. According to Sorokin's cyclical model of social change, the contemporary New Age movement represents _____ culture.
    a.   utopian
    b.   sensate
    c.   ideational
    d.   technological

16. According to David Reisman, _____ is the personality orientation whereby individuals are relatively impervious to the superficialities around them and are guided by strong internal moral principles.
    a.   inner-directedness
    b.   other-directedness
    c.   value-directedness
    d.   tradition-directedness

17. According to Marcuse, _____, or a feeling of individual powerlessness, is more likely to affect those who have traditionally been denied access to power, such as women and racial minorities.
    a.   isolation
    b.   alienation
    c.   deindividuation
    d.   identity disruption

18. Which theory asserts that all nations are members of a worldwide system of unequal political and economic relationships that benefit the highly developed, technologically advanced countries at the expense of the less technologically advanced, less developed countries of the world?
    a.   Exploitation theory
    b.   Modernization theory
    c.   World Systems theory
    d.   Global Network theory

19. Nations such as the U.S. and England import raw materials and cheap labor from _____ nations, which are commonly located in Africa, Latin and South America, and parts of Asia.
    a.   mass
    b.   core
    c.   noncore
    d.   evolutionary

20. Which theory views social movements as starting when structural weaknesses, such as war or economic crisis, present opportunities for collective behavior to occur?
    a.   new social movement theory
    b.   resource mobilization theory
    c.   political process theory
    d.   competition theory

True-False Questions

1. Tonnes observed that both patriarchy and the role of the family are considerably less prominent in a gessellschaft than in a gemeinshaft.

2. Demographers predict that by 2050, Asians will comprise 25 percent of the American population.

3. According to dependency theory, industrialized nations loan developing nations money at unusually low interest rates to promote economic and social development in the developing nations.

4. According to cyclical theory, the first phase of societal development is characterized by tension between the ideal and the practical.

5. Tradition-directedness, or strong conformity to long-standing norms, practices, and lifestyles, is the most common personality orientation found in horticultural and agricultural societies.

6. Skocpol's research on Russia provides strong support for Marx's argument that class conflict is the single most important variable in explaining why some nations collapse.

7. People in cities are more likely than people in small towns to help individuals in need because they interact with many people and recognize the importance of group affiliation.

8. It is more common to identify people by kinship and hometown than by personal attributes, such as gender and occupation, in a gemeinschaft society.

9. The spread of bungie jumping as a form of recreation represents a macrochange in society.

10. With increasing modernization, there is generally a decrease in the social importance of formal religious institutions.

Fill in the Blank Questions

1. According to _____ theory, societies change from simple to complex and from an undifferentiated to a highly differentiated division of labor.

2. Sociologists refer to the specific schemes of interpretation that allow people to perceive, identify, and label events in their lives as _____.

3. The Right to Life Movement in the U.S., which is organized around the goal of overturning the Supreme Court decision, *Roe v. Wade*, is an example of a _____ social movement.

4. According to Sorokin, the third phase societies pass through is _____ culture, which involves the hedonistic and sensual elements of culture.

5. According to Reisman, the personality orientation guided by rigid conformity and attempts to "keep up with the Joneses" in modern society is _____.

Essay Questions

1. Identify the main characteristics of social change and give an example of each characteristic as it relates to the cyberspace revolution.
2. Explain why the unidimensional evolutionary theory of social change has been strongly criticized, and discuss how functionalist theorists now view social diversity.
3. Identify a significant change in the population and discuss how it affects social relationships and social institutions in the United States.
4. Use dependency theory to explain why developing nations have not been able to achieve mobility within the global economic system.
5. Identify the elements necessary for a social movement to begin, and give specific examples of these elements as they relate to the civil rights movement in the United States.

ANSWERS TO PRACTICE TEST

Answers to Multiple Choice Questions

1.	B	451	Collective behavior occurs when the usual norms are suspended and people collectively establish new norms in response to an emerging situation. Collective behavior captures the novel, dynamic, and changing elements of society. Although it may appear irrational, it is patterned and coordinated.
2.	B	437	Gradual transformations that occur on a broad scale and affect many aspects of society, such as the rise of the personal computer, are macrochanges. Microchanges are subtle alternations in the daily interaction between people, such as fads. Cultural diffusion is the process of transmission of cultural elements, such as fashion, from one society or cultural group to another. Demographic shifts represent changes in the population.
3.	A	437	Social change often creates conflict in society. Social change is uneven, affecting different parts of society to varying degrees and at different rates. The onset and consequences of social change are often unforeseen. The direction of social change is not random; rather, it occurs relative to a society's history.
4.	C	440	As summarized in Table 16.1, functionalist theorists view societies as moving from structurally simple and homogeneous to more complex and heterogeneous. They view technology as the primary cause of social change. Conflict theorists view social change as the result of the inevitable economic conflict between social classes in capitalist societies. Cyclical theorists view social change as necessary for growth as the society moves through the phases of its life cycle.
5.	D	442	Toynbee's ideas are associated with the cyclical theory of social change, which views societies as moving through a life cycle.
6.	B.	440	Lenski's ideas are associated with multidimensional evolutionary theory. He asserts that technological advances are primarily responsible for other changes in modern societies.
7.	C	451	According to Turkle, the Internet allows people to develop new identities and interact in a virtual world, resulting in a culture of simulation.
8.	C	447	The popularity of rap music with White suburban youth in the United States is an example of cultural diffusion, in which cultural elements from one society or group are transmitted to another.
9.	A	448	The Yanomami tribes do not use electricity or automobiles, and the introduction of steel tools generally makes farming more efficient. Tierney argues that warlike

behavior in these groups has increased as a result of contact with outsiders, or at least that warfare has become more deadly with the use of steel weapons.

10.   B   449   Because crowding is a pervasive feature of Japanese culture, strangers are often in close contact with each other in public places. Workers are actually hired to push as many people as possible into subway trains. This kind of close bodily contact is not considered an invasion of privacy, nor does it have sexual overtones, in Japan.

11.   A   441   Modernization is a process of social and cultural change that is initiated by industrialization and followed by increased social differentiation and a more complex division of labor. The importance of small, traditional communities declines, as does the centrality of the religious institution to society. Feelings of uncertainty and powerlessness increase, as does the importance of secondary groups to social interaction.

12.   B   445   According to Tonnies, the kind of social organization characterized by a high division of labor, less prominence of personal ties, the lack of a sense of community among the members of society, and the absence of a feeling of belonging is typically found in a gesellschaft society. In a gemeinschaft society, there is more homogeneity, members feel a greater sense of belonging, and personal ties are more important to social interaction.

13.   C   453   When they lack adequate information, people communicate through rumors in an attempt to define an ambiguous situation.

14.   D   453   M.A.D.D. has facilitated change in laws concerning drunk driving by placing pressure on existing social and political institutions, making it a reform movement. Radical movements often rely on more disruptive tactics to transform the social structure.

15.   C   443   According to cyclical theories of social change, the first phase is characterized by idealistic culture, in which there is tension between the ideal and practical aspects of society. In the second phase, ideational culture emerges, which emphasizes new forms of spirituality. The third phase, sensate culture, stresses practical approaches to reality and involves the hedonistic and the sensual.

16.   A   446   According to Reisman, other-directedness occurs when the individual's behavior is guided by the observed behavior of others. Inner-directedness occurs when the individual is guided by strong internal principles. Tradition-directedness is characterized by strong conformity to long-standing norms and practices.

17.   B   447   Marcuse argues that alienation, or a feeling of powerlessness, is more likely to affect women, racial-ethnic minorities, and the working class, groups traditionally denied access to power in society.

18.   C   443   World systems theory argues that all nations are members of a worldwide system of unequal political and economic relationships that benefit the developed and technologically advanced countries at the expense of the less technologically advanced and less developed countries. Modernization theory states that global development is a worldwide process that affects nearly all societies. Functionalist theory views societies as evolving from structurally simple, homogeneous societies to more complex, highly differentiated societies.

19.   C   443   World systems theory asserts that core nations such as the U.S. import raw materials and cheap labor from noncore nations located in less developed areas of the world. Dependency theory asserts that this arrangement exploits noncore nations by imposing dependency to benefit core nations economically.

20.   C   456   Table 16.2 indicates that political process theory argues that movements exploit structural opportunities, such as war, which make political systems vulnerable to social protest.

Answers to True-False Questions

1.	T	445	Tonnes observed that both patriarchy and the role of the family are less prominent in a gesselschaft than in a gemeinshaft.
2.	F	450	Demographers predict that Hispanics will be 25 percent and Asians will comprise 8 percent of the U.S. population by 2050.
3.	T	444	Dependency theory asserts that industrialized nations keep developing nations dependent through trade and borrowing practices.
4.	F	443	The society wrestles with the tension between the ideal and the practical in the idealistic culture, which represents the first phase of societal development according to cyclical theory.
5.	T	446	Tradition-directedness is common in less modernized gemeinschafts.
6.	F	442	Skocpol's research indicates that the relationship *between* societies is a critical factor in explaining why some nations collapse.
7.	F	446	People in cities are less likely to help someone in distress than people in small towns. Furthermore, the larger the number of people observing an emergency, the less likely any of them will offer assistance, because individuals tend to merge with the crowd in large cities, a process called deindividuation.
8.	T	654	In gesellschaft societies, people are more likely to be identified by occupation, while in gemeinschaft societies, people are more likely to be identified by kinship group.
9.	F	437	Because the spread of bungie jumping represents a subtle alteration in the daily interaction between people, rather than a broad social transformation, it is an example of a microchange.
10.	T	444	Modernization results in the decline in the importance of the religious institution and the prevalence of small, close-knit communities. The role of the government in people's lives increases, as does the importance of the mass media.

Answers to Fill in the Blank Questions

1.	functionalist	440
2.	frames	457
3.	reactionary	453
4.	sensate	443
5.	other-directed	446